SINGING
With Understanding

Other Publications by Kenneth Osbeck

The Ministry of Music
Pocket Guide for the Church Choir Member
A Junior's Praise
My Choir Workbook
Teen Age Praise
Choral Praises
Choir Responses

SINGING
With Understanding

including
101 FAVORITE HYMN BACKGROUNDS
by
Kenneth W. Osbeck

KREGEL PUBLICATIONS
Grand Rapids, Michigan 49501

Library of Congress Cataloging in Publication Data

Osbeck, Kenneth W.
  Singing With Understanding.

  Bibliography: p.
  Includes index.
  1. Hymnal—Development, Content and Usage
  2. Hymns, English—History and application.
I. Title.
ML3186.086   783.9′09   78-19960
ISBN 0-8254-3414-9

Printed in the United States of America

CONTENTS

Contents

Contents

PREFACE

Evangelical Christians have rightly been called the "people of the Book." It could also be stated, however, that they are really the people of two books, the Bible and the hymnal. It is a generally accepted fact throughout Protestant history that, apart from the Bible, the hymnal has been the most important book used in the worship of God. Like the Scriptures, however, the hymnal is understood and deeply appreciated by too few of God's people. How different our response to it would be if we would heed the words of the Apostle Paul in I Corinthians 14:15, when he instructed the Corinthian believers in the two important spiritual activities of worship–*prayer* and *praise:*

> What is it then? I will pray with the spirit, and I will pray with the understanding also: I will sing with the spirit, and I will sing with the understanding also.

This verse clearly teaches that both of these activities of worship must be brought under the influence of the Holy Spirit and exercised with a conscious awareness of their true meaning.

As responsible church leaders we should be cognizant of the fact that our convictions about church music do make a difference in the spiritual atmosphere of our congregations. From time to time it is needful for each leader to re-evaluate and re-appraise his own thinking in this matter. Periodically it is good to ask oneself questions such as these:

1. Do I have a Biblical basis for my music program? What are my spiritual standards for music used in the church?
2. Could I defend intelligently the type of music used in the church as well as the way in which it is performed?
3. Is the music program really accomplishing anything of spiritual worth in the lives of the people?
4. How much time do I actually spend in trying to improve this phase of church life?

Conviction of this type and deeper perception of the importance of congregational singing are not easily attained. Although a leader's personality, enthusiasm and public relations are extremely important, these qualities alone are not enough for an effective ministry. Genuine spiritual leadership demands a developed sensitivity to such areas as the doctrinal integrity, spiritual worth, literary significance and musical merit of each song chosen to be sung. Moreover, a leader should realize the objectives of congregational singing. He should keenly desire to accomplish these spiritual ideals each time he is entrusted with this important leadership. If a leader lacks such an awareness and desire, singing can easily degenerate into sheer entertainment or merely a time-consuming activity. The following suggestions are offered as basic objectives for congregational singing:

1. Singing should provide the means of unifying a group by providing a common channel through which individuals may join together in worship, prayer and praise.
2. Singing should teach and reinforce spiritual truths and should create a unique awareness of God–His greatness, His majesty, and His other attributes.
3. Singing should provide individuals with an outlet for expression of personal attitudes and experiences which often are difficult to verbalize.
4. Singing should create the proper mood for the message and the other activities of the service.

This type of leadership implies that a leader must be thoroughly familiar with his hymnal and be truly Biblically oriented. Moreover, an appreciative study of the subject of hymnology is strongly recommended as a foundational basis for this ministry.

A church which forgoes the use of hymns in her office of teaching neglects one of the most efficacious instruments for correcting error and for disseminating truth, as well as for ministering comfort and edification.

Christopher Wordsworth, 1807–1885

There is more said in the Bible about praise than prayer, and music and song have not only accompanied all Scriptural revivals, but are essential in deepening spiritual life. Singing does at least as much as preaching to impress the Word of God upon people's minds. Ever since God first called me, the importance of praise expressed in song has grown upon me.

D. L. Moody, 19th century evangelist

It is regrettable that so few congregations ever fully capture in vibrant singing of praise to God the potential that exists within their hymnals.

William J. Reynolds–*A Survey of Christian Hymnody*

Hymnology study, commonly called the "romance of sacred song," should include a reasonable knowledge of the lives of those who wrote the texts, information about the times and conditions in which they wrote, an awareness of the personal experiences that prompted the writing of particular hymns, an understanding of the doctrinal and spiritual intents of the hymn, and a knowledge of the origins and composers of the music.

The purpose of this book is to provide pastor and worshiping people alike with the informative and inspirational highlights of our hymnals, in order that our "sacrifices of praise" might become more acceptable to our God (Hebrews 13:15). Moreover, it is my personal concern that young people who are preparing to serve God will take time to gain genuine appreciation for the hymnal. Such appreciation will help them become worthy leaders in the important activity of congregational singing.

It is, then, my sincere prayer that the Holy Spirit will use this study of our church hymnals to encourage a renewed awareness of the importance of congregational singing in our local evangelical churches. In doing so, we together may truly heed the scriptural admonition of "singing with the Spirit and with the UNDERSTANDING also."

> Praise ye the Lord: For it is good to sing praises unto our God;
> for it is pleasant; and praise is comely.
>
> Psalm 147:1

KEN OSBECK

Chapter One

UNDERSTANDING–The Hymnal's Structure

A look at the hymnal's
organization and indexes

CHAPTER ONE

UNDERSTANDING–The Hymnal's Structure

1. Hymnal Category

2. Name of Hymn

HYMNS OF WORSHIP: THE FATHER

4. Author of Words

5. Composer of Music

A Mighty Fortress Is Our God

MARTIN LUTHER, 1483-1546
Trans. by Frederick H. Hedge, 1805-1890

EIN' FESTE BURG

MARTIN LUTHER, 1483-1546

3. Name of Tune

3

6. Ownership of Hymn

SINGING WITH UNDERSTANDING

Using the first hymn listed in this book, "A Mighty Fortress Is Our God," the following information seeks to clarify the use of the various indexes found in most church hymnals.

1. *The Hymnal Category*

This subject classification was given to the hymn by the editors of the hymnal. All hymns of the same type are placed together in this grouping. At the front of the hymnal is usually placed the Table of Contents, which shows the broad organization of the book. An example might be:

> Hymns of Worship
> God the Father
> Jesus Our Savior
> The Holy Spirit
> The Word of God
> The Church
> The Christian Experience
> Others

These general classifications are in turn divided into more detailed categories in the Topical Index listings, usually inserted in the back of the book. Here the editors have further classified each hymn on the basis of more specific subject matter. For example, "A Mighty Fortress Is Our God" might be found under such topics as:

Assurance, Christian Warfare, Church, God our Father, Providence, Security, Victory, Worship

2. *The Name of the Hymn*

Usually following the Topical Index is the General Index, which lists all of the titles alphabetically in SMALL CAPS with the familiar first lines generally given in lower case type.

3. *The Name of the Tune*

The melody for this tune is called "Ein' Feste Burg." In the early days of publishing, tune names had much importance since only the words were printed in a hymnal. Leaders of a service would announce not only the hymn text to be sung but also the particular tune to be used. Many of these tune names have a very interesting history associated with them.

UNDERSTANDING the Hymnal's Structure

Some were named after the person who wrote the tune or words; others stated the location in which the hymns were written; often they were dedicated to certain individuals, churches, etc., while some were simply named by a hymnal editorial committee.

After the Tune Index there is usually another closely related index known as the Metrical Index. This index shows the metrical forms for the hymns. The number of digits shown indicates the number of lines per stanza, while each digit indicates the number of syllables receiving an accent in each line of poetry.

"A Mighty Fortress Is Our God" has a metrical form of 87.87.66.667.

	1	2	3	4	5	6	7	8
Line 1	A	might-	y	for-	tress	is	our	God

	1	2	3	4	5	6	7
Line 2	A	bul-	wark	nev-	er	fail-	ing;

	1	2	3	4	5	6	7	8
Line 3	Our	help-	er	He	a-	mid	the	flood

	1	2	3	4	5	6	7
Line 4	Of	mor-	tal	ills	pre-	vail-	ing.

	1	2	3	4	5	6
Line 5	For	still	our	an-	cient	foe

	1	2	3	4	5	6
Line 6	Doth	seek	to	work	us	woe—

	1	2	3	4	5	6
Line 7	His	craft	and	pow'r	are	great,

	1	2	3	4	5	6
Line 8	And,	armed	with	cru-	el	hate,

	1	2	3	4	5	6	7
Line 9	On	earth	is	not	his	e-	qual.

The following are the most widely used meters:

Number of Lines	Meter Names	Number of Syllables for each Line
Four	Short Meter (SM)	6.6.8.6.—Usually used for texts that are emphatic and tense. i.e. "I Love Thy Kingdom, Lord" No. 36
Four	Common Meter (CM)	8.6.8.6.—Provides more flexibility to a text, i.e., "Amazing Grace" No. 6
Four	Long Meter (LM)	8.8.8.8.—Used for texts that are more stately and dignified, i.e., "Jesus Shall Reign" No. 48
Four	10's	10.10.10.10.
Six	Long Perfect Meter (L.P.M.)	8.8.8.8.8.8.

6

When a *D* is added (L.M.D., C.M.D., S.M.D., etc.), it simply denotes that the entire pattern has been doubled. When the pattern differs from any of the above structures, the meter is indicated with Arabic numerals. Example–8.7.8.7; 10.10.10.11.11.11. Other meter indications include:

With Refrain–	Indicates that after each verse there is an additional phrase or short portion of the song to be sung.
With Alleluias–	Indicates that the verses of the hymn include an expression of an "alleluia." Example–"Christ The Lord Is Risen Today." 7.7.7.7 with Alleluias.
Irregular–	Indicates that the lines of the different verses do not always contain the same number of syllables.

The Metrical Index lists the various meters with the hymn tunes listed below them. It will be noted that one tune may serve as music for several hymn texts. For the leader of congregational singing, one of the interesting uses of the Metrical Index is the occasional interchange of various tunes for hymns sharing the same meter. This use of a different tune will quicken a congregation's awareness of texts that have often become too familiar and routine.

4. *The Author of the Words (Text)*

This information is always shown in the upper left hand side of the page. In our example, it is indicated that "A Mighty Fortress Is Our God" was written by Martin Luther (1483-1546). In the index section of most hymnals is another index called Index of Authors, Composers and Sources, including translators and arrangers. This is an alphabetical listing of all the people who wrote the words and music of each hymn, with the dates of birth and death of each hymn writer designated. If the hymn was originally written in a language other than English, the translator and source are shown as well–as in the case of Luther's hymn, where Frederick H. Hedge translated the hymn from German to English.

5. *The Composer of the Music*

This information is always shown in the upper right hand side of the page. For our sample hymn, the tune also was composed by Martin Luther. As mentioned above, all composers and arrangers of these hymns are, as a rule, listed in the Index of Composers, Arrangers and Sources. Like the authors of the texts, these individuals will have all of their contributions in the hymnal listed after their names. The index also gives the sources of the original tune, if known, since many of our hymn tunes have been borrowed from older melodies, folk tunes or carols from other lands.

6. *The Ownership of the Hymn*

A copyright is a legal protection for the person or the company owning the hymn. The copyright law insures that no one else can publish, reproduce, or arrange a hymn without the owner's permission. This protection was first provided by the United States Copyright Act of 1831 and later by the Copyright Act of 1909 as amended. Under the 1909 law, a copyrighted hymn was protected for 28 years. Before the expiration of that period, the owner was able to apply for a renewal of copyright for another 28 year period. After 56 years, the hymn then became known as "public domain" meaning that anyone was then free to use and publish that hymn.

A new Copyright Law was signed on October 19, 1976 which became effective on January 1, 1978. Under this law a copyright renewed after the initial 28 year period may now be extended for an additional 47 years for a total copyright protection of 75 years. Under the provisions of this new law, hymns written and copyrighted after January 1, 1978 will have a term of protection for the life of the author, plus an additional 50 years.

If the copyright is still in effect this information is found at the bottom of the hymn score. "A Mighty Fortress Is Our God" is no longer under any copyright and is now in public domain.

8

Chapter Two

UNDERSTANDING–The Hymnal's Development

A sketch of the historical growth
of hymnody from ancient to present times

CHAPTER TWO

UNDERSTANDING–The Hymnal's Development

Protestant congregational singing as it is known today began with the Reformation Movement of the sixteenth century. It is true that in most hymnals there are a number of important hymns from such earlier sources as the Greek, Hebrew, and medieval Latin cultures, since every religious movement throughout history has always been accompanied with song. Even such early groups as the Waldenses, the Hussites, and the Lollards had their own distinctive hymnody. Several of these pre-Reformation hymns still widely used today include (see Contents of this book chapter 4, no. 3 etc.):

> "All Creatures of Our God and King"–No. 3
> "Jesus, the Very Thought of Thee"–No. 49
> "O Come, O Come, Emmanuel"–No. 64
> "The Day of Resurrection"–No. 89
> "The God of Abraham Praise"–No. 90

However, congregational singing was almost eliminated in the Roman churches after the fourth century Laodicean Council's Decree: "If laymen are forbidden to preach and interpret the Scriptures, much more are they forbidden to sing publicly in church." Not until more than one thousand years later, with Martin Luther's insistence upon the importance of congregational singing, was it eventually restored to its rightful place in the worship of God. Luther said, "Let God speak to His people through the Scriptures; let His people respond with the singing of their hymns."

From the sixteenth century Reformation Movement flowed two main streams of Protestant hymnody: the chorale hymn and the metrical Psalm. Luther was the advocate of the chorale hymn, while John Calvin and his followers promoted the use of the psalter. Of these two leaders, Luther made greater use of music to promote his doctrinal beliefs and practices. Even his opponents admitted that he won more converts through his encouragement of singing than he did through his forceful preaching and teaching. Luther once remarked, "Next to theology, I give the first and highest honor to music."

Luther's greatest hymn, "A Mighty Fortress Is Our God" (No. 1), written in 1529, is a paraphrase of Psalm 46 and has been called the "Marseillaise Hymn of the Reformation." This hymn has been translated and sung in practically every known language in the world, with at least sixty translations in the English language alone. Luther is credited with writing a total of thirty-seven hymns. Of these, eleven are translations from Latin sources, four are revisions of pre-Reformation hymns, seven are versifications of Psalms, six are paraphrases of other Bible selections and nine are classified as original hymns. Luther was an accomplished musician, being noteworthy for his fine tenor voice as well as for his skillful playing of the lute. It is not known for certain just how many original tunes he actually composed for his hymns by borrowing and adapting themes and tunes of a considerable number of the old Latin hymns and even secular melodies. But he gave his selections their striking originality both in content and expression.

One of Luther's expressed concerns was that "the Word of God might dwell in the hearts of believers by means of song." His followers were known for their lusty singing of the chorales in unaccompanied unison. Luther also retained the choir for the church service after the Roman Catholic tradition. These singers, better trained than most members of the congregations, performed the more complicated and sophisticated polyphonic settings of the chorale melodies. In 1524 the first collection of eight Protestant hymns was published, four of which were written by Luther. The little hymn book became widely known throughout Europe. Luther's enemies often commented, "The people are singing themselves into his doctrines!"

Within a year this first Protestant hymnal was increased to twenty-five hymns, bringing fourteen new hymns by Luther. It was called *Erfurt Enchiridon*. These and subsequent hymnal publications did much to further the rise of congregational singing. Two fine German musicians, Johann Walther and Conrad Rupff, were invaluable assistants to Luther in laying these foundations for Lutheran hymnody.

A cursory look at German history in the seventeenth century reveals that one of the important influences affecting the development of German hymnody was the Thirty Years' War (1618–1648). This began as a Catholic-Protestant conflict but soon developed into a larger political struggle, involving at one time or another the entire continent. The extreme hardships suffered by great numbers of people during this time produced a hymnody expressing, with greater emphasis than ever before, man's personal relationship with God. The encouragement of cell Bible study and prayer groups became known as the Pietistic Movement. The main concern of this movement was to counteract the arid scholasticism and cold formalism that characterized the state Lutheran Church. An important German hymn writer of the period was Martin Rinkart (1586–1649), "Now Thank We All Our God" (No. 62).

John Calvin (1509–1564), whose theology emphasized the authority of the Scriptures and the sovereignty of God, was firm in his conviction that congregational singing should employ only the Psalms. He was opposed to the use of the organ or even singing in harmony, claiming that such practices were popish. However, he did not oppose music as an art form when it was used outside of the church service.

One of Calvin's chief aides in versifying the Psalms and making musical settings was Louis Bourgeois. Through the influence of Calvin and Bourgeois, the *Genevan Psalter,* a monumental musical publication, was completed and published in 1562. It has been said that no other hymnal has ever influenced Christendom as much as the *Genevan Psalter.* The well-known "Doxology" (No. 20) is from that collection.

Hymnologists estimate that through the seventeenth century nearly one hundred additional psalters were published. In Great Britain one of the most notable psalter publications was *The Sternhold-Hopkins Psalter and the Whole Book of Psalms,* published in 1562. This psalter and the *Book of Common Prayer,* containing the entire ritual of the Anglican Church, provided the basis of public worship until 1696, when *The New Version* was compiled by two Irishmen, Nahum Tate and Nicholas Brady. Other important psalters included *The Scottish Psalter* in 1564, under the leadership of John Knox; *The Thomas Este's Psalter* in 1592, a significant publication because it first used specific names for tunes; and the *Thomas Ravenscroft Psalter* in 1621, important because it attempted to collect existing Psalm tunes from various sources into one book. This last collection became widely used by future church musicians as a source book of tunes.

Although Psalm singing was the dominant expression of congregational singing throughout Great Britain following the Reformation Movement, hymn singing gradually developed within various congregations. One of the encouragements for this practice came from an important injunction issued by Queen Elizabeth in 1559 when she declared: "In the beginning, or at the end of Common Prayer, there may be sung a hymn or such like song to the praise of Almighty God, in the best sort of melody and music that may be conveniently devised." Eventually some of the newer psalters began including hymns with Scriptural content other than the Psalms. The *1700 Supplement* to Tate and Brady's *New Version* contained sixteen hymns, including Tate's well-known Christmas carol, "While Shepherds Watched Their Flocks By Night" (No. 101).

As is true with most changes, however, the transition from Psalms to hymns was slow and met with strong resistance by many Anglicans, Presbyterians, Baptists and other churchmen. There were many instances of church divisions and controversies over this issue alone. During those unsettled times the change from Psalms to hymns often progressed as follows: A free paraphrasing of the Psalms, rather than an adherence to a strict translation, appeared first. This was followed by the gradual use of other Scriptures for hymn material. Eventually any devotional material was used resulting in what became known as "hymns of human composure." These freely composed hymns were generally first sung for home devotions; then were used sparingly for special purposes in public worship, perhaps in communion services. The practice was justified by this Scripture reference, "And when they had sung an hymn, they went out

13

into the Mount of Olives. . . ." (Matthew 26:30). Toward the close of the seventeenth century, however, some individual evangelical congregations were making a rather general free use of hymn singing in their weekly public services.

The Development of Hymnody in England

With the writings of Isaac Watts (1674–1748) in the early part of the eighteenth century, a new epoch of congregational singing began. At an early age Watts became concerned with the deplorable state to which congregational singing had degenerated in most English-speaking churches. He proceeded to write new metrical versions of the Psalms, with a concern for Christianizing them with the New Testament message and style. In 1719 he published *The Psalms of David Imitated in the Language of the New Testament and Applied to the Christian State and Worship*. Several of Watts's well-known hymns based on Psalm settings are still widely used today. They include "Jesus Shall Reign" Psalm 72 (No. 48) and "O God, Our Help in Ages Past" Psalm 90 (No. 66).

Isaac Watts not only united the Hebrew and Christian ideals with his new metrical Psalmody, but he also believed that writers should be free to express praise and devotion in their own words. These controversial hymns continued the development of texts that were known as "hymns of human composure." One of the best-known of these by Isaac Watts is "When I Survey the Wondrous Cross" (No. 100). Watts, often called the "father of English hymnody," used these hymns to summarize his sermons and to express his strong Calvinistic theology. It must be remembered that many of the hymns of this period were written not primarily to be sung but rather to be read, usually by ministers in finalizing their sermons. This explains why the musical settings which are used with so many of the seventeenth, eighteenth and early nineteenth century hymns were written at a much later time than the texts.

14

In addition to Isaac Watts, John Wesley (1703–1791) and Charles Wesley (1707–1788) should be considered important contributors to the development of English hymnody. The Wesleyan Movement was the spark that set off great religious fervor both in England and in the American Colonies. In America, this spiritual revival, known as The Great Awakening, was spearheaded by the "hell- and heaven-storming preaching" of Jonathan Edwards (1703–1758), pastor of the Congregational Church in Northampton, Massachusetts. In Great Britain, George Whitefield (1714–1770) and the Wesleys were the leading revivalists. This revived emphasis on personal salvation did much to combat the prevailing spirit of agnosticism, the corruptness that was creeping into many of the established churches, the lack of evangelical concern among many of the dissenting groups, as well as the general moral and social degeneration that was rampant in society.

Evangelist John Wesley and his brother Charles, the poet and musician, wrote and translated approximately 6,500 hymns, with about thirty of these titles still in active use today. Their theology was strongly opposed to Calvin's teachings of election and limited atonement; instead, they emphasized the unlimited efficacy of Christ's atonement and the freewill of man. With warmth and personal conviction they wrote hymns related to almost every phase of Christian experience. Many of their hymns had their origin in Moravian hymnody since these zealous, missionary-minded Moravians–Hussites or Bohemian Brethren, as they were known–had a strong influence in the early ministries of the Wesleys. The Wesleys' first hymnbook, *Collection of Psalms and Hymns,* was published in Charlestown in 1737 and contained seventy selections by Isaac Watts and other writers, with five translations by John Wesley. Between 1737 and 1786 the Wesleys published a total of sixty-three different hymnals. John, though not a musician, wrote twenty-seven hymns and translations of hymns from the Greek, Latin and German languages. In his writings he also gave much attention to matters of correct congregational singing. His instructions to his followers included such advice as:

15

Sing all.   See that you join with the congregation as frequently as you can.

Sing lustily.   Beware of singing as if you are half dead or half asleep.

Sing modestly.   Do not bawl so as to be heard above or distinct from the rest of the congregation. Strive to unite your voices together so as to make one clear melodious sound.

Sing in time.   Whatever time is sung, be sure you keep with it. *Above all,*

Sing spiritually.   Have an eye to God in every word you sing.

The Wesleys' use of the music for their hymn texts is also interesting. Silas H. Paine in his book, *Stories of the Great Hymns of the Church,* states that it was the practice of the Wesleys to "seize upon any song of the theater or the street, the moment it became popular, and make it carry some newly-written text into the homes of the people." Several of the best-known Wesleyan hymns in use today are "O For a Thousand Tongues" (No. 65), "Christ the Lord Is Risen Today" (No. 13), and "Jesus, Lover of My Soul" (No. 45).

Various church groups and individual leaders continued to publish hymnals for their particular use. One of the most popular collections was John Rippon's hymnal, published in 1787 and geared especially for Baptist congregations. The well-known hymn "How Firm a Foundation" (No. 32) is from that collection. This book of evangelical hymns was called *A Selection of Hymns from the Best Authors, Intended to be an Appendix to Dr. Watts' Psalms and Hymns.* Another important eighteenth century hymnal was John Newton and William Cowper's *Olney Hymns,* published in 1779. This collection, containing 280 hymns by Newton and 68 by Cowper, was prepared specifically for Newton's congregation at Olney, England, but it gradually gained wide acceptance throughout evangelical circles. Hymns from this hymnal still widely used today include "There Is a Fountain" (No. 95) and "Amazing Grace" (No. 6).

In addition to Watts, Wesley, Rippon, Newton and Cowper, the eighteenth century produced other well-known English hymn composers: William Williams (1717–1781), "Guide Me, O Thou Great Jehovah" (No. 26); Thomas Olivers (1725–1799), "The God of Abraham Praise" (No. 90); Augustus Toplady (1740–1778), "Rock of Ages" (No. 78); Edward Perronet (1721–1792), "All Hail the Power" (No. 4); John Fawcett (1739–1817), "Blest Be the Tie That Binds" (No. 12).

16   Most of the hymn writers of the seventeenth and eighteenth centuries were primarily concerned with composing hymns that expressed some part of their doctrinal convictions. However, nineteenth century hymnists, influenced by the prevailing spirit of the Romantic Age found in all forms of art, were more concerned with improving the literary quality of hymnody. Musicians, too, worked hard at improving the musical standards of the nineteenth century hymn. A number of new tune books were published with this particular objective. One of the best known collections was William Gardiner's *Sacred Melodies,* published in 1812 and again in 1815. In an attempt to have better tunes for hymn texts, Gardiner borrowed melodies freely from the classic works of master composers such as Haydn, Mozart, Beethoven (see No. 50).

Important English hymn writers whose writings were influenced by nineteenth century Romanticism include Reginald Heber (1783–1826), "Holy, Holy, Holy" (No. 31); Thomas Kelly (1769–1854), "Look, Ye Saints! The Sight is Glorious" (No. 55); James Montgomery (1771–1854), "Sun of My Soul" (No. 85); Henry Francis Lyte (1793–1847), "Abide with Me" (No. 2); Sir John Bowring (1792–1872), "In the Cross of Christ I Glory" (No. 42); Hugh Stowell (1799–1865), "From Every Stormy Wind That Blows" (No. 24); Sir Robert Grant (1779–1838), "O Worship the King" (No. 72); Charlotte Elliott (1789–1871), "Just As I Am" (No. 52).

On July 14, 1833, a new religious movement known as the Oxford or

Tractarian Movement was begun in England with a sermon by John Keble entitled "National Apostasy." The Wesleys had preached a message of warmth and conviction geared to the understanding of the common man; however, leaders of this more sophisticated Oxford movement were of the opinion that a meaningful religious experience could only be gained through better liturgy and ceremonies. The Oxford leaders were concerned with the growing strength of the evangelical faction within the Anglican Church. The Oxford emphasis was also a reaction to many indifferent and careless worship services conducted by the more independent congregations of that time. For a decade the Oxford movement tenaciously directed religious England, and during this time many of the leaders of the Anglican Church either joined the Roman Church or became members of a rejuvenated High Church Party known as the Anglo-Catholics. The Oxford movement's influence was also felt in many other Protestant churches with the rise of boys' choirs, use of vestments, greater use of symbolism, processionals and recessionals, etc. Important hymn writers who were influenced by this movement include John Henry Newman (1801–1890), "Lead, Kindly Light" (No. 53), John Mason Neale (1818–1866), "The Day of Resurrection" (No. 89) and Catherine Winkworth (1827–1878), "Praise Ye the Lord, the Almighty" (No. 75). Both Neale and Winkworth were noted for their scholarly translations of earlier hymns. Other church leaders of this period–such as Frederick William Faber (1814–1863), "Faith of Our Fathers" (No. 22) and Edward Caswall (1814–1878), "May Jesus Christ Be Praised" (No. 57)– later, like Newman, became prominent leaders in the Roman Catholic Church.

17

In 1861 the Oxford Movement produced one of the most important hymnals ever published, *Hymns Ancient and Modern*. This hymnal, intended for High Church use, included 273 hymns of which 131 were of English origin, 132 of Latin origin, and ten of German origin. The tunes were carefully chosen to exclude those of earlier evangelical origin. Subsequent editions and revisions of this hymnal, the latest published in 1950, have made this book a national institution in England and a source book for all future hymnal publications.

At the height of the Oxford Movement, Queen Victoria inherited the throne and ruled England from 1837 to 1901. Hymns written throughout this Victorian Era are generally classified as being High Church Hymns, Evangelical or Low Church Hymns, Broad Church Hymns, Dissenting Hymns, Post-Victorian Hymns.

A. *High Church Hymn Writers of the Victorian Age*

These churchmen were Anglicans who resisted the drift toward Rome as well as toward the spirit of agnosticism, which was prevalent at that time. They were deeply concerned with preserving the integrity of the liturgy, creeds, sacraments and the traditional practices of the Anglican Church. Important hymn composers of this group include Mrs. Cecil Frances Alexander (1818–1895), "There Is a Green Hill Far Away" (No. 96); Folliott S. Pierpoint (1835–1917), "For the Beauty of the Earth" (No. 23); Sabine Baring-Gould (1834–1924), "Onward, Christian Soldiers" (No. 73); Samuel John Stone (1839–1900), "The Church's One Foundation" (No. 88).

B. *The Evangelical or Low Church Hymn Writers of the Victorian Era*
These churchmen were Anglicans who, like the High Church writers, remained in the Anglican Church. But they were further characterized by their greater concern for the spiritual and social welfare of individuals rather than for the maintenance of the integrity and traditions of the church. Important hymn composers of this group include George Croly (1780–1860), "Spirit of God, Descend upon My Heart" (No. 84); Emily Elizabeth Steele Elliott (1836–1897), "Thou Didst Leave Thy Throne" (No. 98); Arabella Katherine Hankey (1834–1889), "I Love to Tell the Story" (No. 37); Frances Ridley Havergal (1836–1878), "Take My Life and Let It Be" (No. 87).

18

C. *Broad Church Hymn Writers of the Victorian Era*
This group of churchmen represented the liberal and modern faction in the Anglican Church. They supported the traditions and practices of the established church but attempted to reconcile its teachings with higher criticism and scientific philosophical findings and developments. Important hymn composers of this group include William Walsham How (1823–1897), "O Word of God Incarnate" (No. 71), and John Ellerton (1826–1893), "Savior, Again to Thy Dear Name" (No. 79).

D. *Dissenting Church Hymn Writers of the Victorian Era*
This group represented those who had broken from the established state churches in England or Scotland. It is estimated that by the year 1800, one-fourth of the people of England had severed their connection with the Established Anglican Church. The strongest dissenting groups were the Presbyterians, Methodists, and Baptist congregations.
Hymn singing recovered a new spiritual vitality within these groups, beginning with a spirit of revival which swept the British Isles during the latter half of the nineteenth century. Important hymn writers of this dissenting group include Horatius Bonar, (1808–1889), "I Heard the Voice of Jesus Say" (No. 35); Elizabeth Douglas Clephane (1830–1869), "Beneath the Cross of Jesus" (No. 10); George Matheson (1842–1906), "O Love That Wilt Not Let Me Go" (No. 68).

E. *Post-Victorian Church Hymn Writers*

These were English hymn writers who wrote important hymn texts after the death of Queen Victoria in 1901 and throughout the reigns of Edward VII (1901–1910), George V (1910–1936), George VI (1936–1952) and Queen Elizabeth II (1952–). It can generally be said that these writers emphasized the social concerns of society rather than doctrinal truths. Their writings also reflect a reaction against what they felt to be sentimentality as well as literary and musical triteness represented in the writings and composers of the earlier Victorian artists. A representative writer of this group is John Oxenham,(1852–1941) author of ''In Christ There Is No East or West'' (No. 41).

The Development of Hymnody in America

In America the early settlers used the psalters to which they had been accustomed in England, still clinging to the idea that God would be insulted if men offered to Him any hymns other than those He had dictated in the Scriptures. The Puritans of Salem used the *Sternhold and Hopkins Psalter* while the Pilgrims at Plymouth brought the *Ainsworth Psalter* in 1620. Within a few short years after their arrival, however, the Puritans published their own psalter, *The Whole Book of Psalms Faithfully Translated into English Metre, 1640*. It is interesting to note that this book, commonly known as the *Bay Psalm Book*, was the first book of any kind published in the American colonies. This psalter enjoyed widespread popularity with its twenty-seven published editions. The ninth edition of the psalter in 1698 was the first to include music with the words. It consisted of thirteen melodies which fit the meter of all 150 Psalms.

One of the interesting techniques used by the congregations of this time was the practice of ''lining out'' the Psalm to be sung. Because of the lack of music and published materials, each congregation appointed a ''qualified'' deacon whose responsibility was to ''line out'' the Psalm. He would first read aloud the words of a line of music, and the congregation would then imitate this line in their best manner. Sometimes it would take as long as thirty minutes to complete the singing of a Psalm. It was also the deacon's responsibility to give the proper pitch and to keep the congregation on the right tune. Any type of lively music was thought to be of the Devil. This tedious, uninspired style of congregational singing was one of the important conditions that led to the decline of Psalm singing in this country and paved the way in the eighteenth and early nineteenth centuries for the gradual acceptance of the ''composure hymns'' of Watts, Wesley, and other English hymn writers. The transition from unaccompanied congregational singing to the use of pump organs also societies were formed, such as the Baptist Missionary Society that was organized in 1792, and hymn writers were quick to respond by writing hymns that would challenge Christian young people with foreign missionary service. The climax of the gospel song development occurred during the last quarter of the nineteenth century through the ministries of evangelists such as Dwight L. Moody (1837–1899), who became active in conducting mass evangelistic campaigns both in this country and in Great Britain. Moody was especially interested in music as a tool that could be used in reaching people with the Gospel of Christ. Though Moody himself did not sing, he once wrote,

> I feel sure that the great majority of people do like singing. It helps to build up an audience–even if you preach a dry sermon. If you have singing that reaches the heart, it will fill the church every time. There is more said in the Bible about praise than prayer, and music and song have not only accompanied all scriptural revivals, but are essential in deepening spiritual life. Singing does at least as much as preaching to impress the Word of God upon people's minds. Ever since God first called me, the importance of praise expressed in song has grown upon me.

22

Through Moody's influence came the establishment of the Moody Bible Institute in 1890. The music department was under the leadership of Daniel B. Towner, a pioneer in the training of talented young people for service in evangelical music. One of the early students of the school was Charles Alexander (1867–1920).

Today Alexander is regarded as the forerunner of the present-day evangelistic song leader. Through his leadership there developed the concept of the song leader as the master of ceremonies for the service as well as the leader of the music. It was Alexander who spoke of "warming up" the audience in order to get mass personal involvement in the service. Charles Alexander also began the idea of using large city-wide choirs as part of campaign meetings. Other well-known and successful song leaders who have built their ministries upon these concepts include Homer Rodeheaver, Homer Hammontree, Cliff Barrows and J. Stratton Shufelt.

From these various influences, then, emerged a new type of sacred music known as the "gospel song." Though the music and the texts of these songs were not completely new, the name "gospel music" generally is associated with the type of music that began during the Moody-Sankey revival campaigns in the last quarter of the nineteenth century.

There have been many attempts to describe and define the gospel song (gospel hymn) and to distinguish it from the more liturgical hymns. The following is such an attempt:

UNDERSTANDING the Hymnal's Development

Liturgical Hymn	Gospel Song
1. Primary purpose is to glorify one or all of the persons of the Triune Godhead. Generally more objective and vertical in character.	1. Primary purpose is to give a testimony or an exhortation, a warning or invitation. Generally very subjective and horizontal in character.
2. Used primarily for Christians in a worship service.	2. Used primarily in evangelistic, revival and fellowship services.
3. Music is stately, dignified and more devotional in character. Harmonically the songs are characterized by more frequent chord changes.	3. Music is usually rhythmically fast or lilting, generating a pervasive enthusiasm. Harmonically the songs are characterized by few chord changes.
4. Notes are generally of even time value. Comparatively few notes of eighth or sixteenth note values.	4. Notes of varied time value with the dotted notes (♪.♪ - ♩♪) especially predominant. Also the use of "lilting" 6/8 rhythm is common.
5. The text is usually set to music so that the verses are complete in themselves without use of chorus or refrain techniques.	5. The text finds its complete expression with the use of a chorus or refrain at the end of each stanza.

23

Edmund Simon Lorenz, in *Church Music: What a Minister Should Know About It*, defines the gospel song as follows:

> A sacred folk song, free in form, emotional in character, devout in attitude, evangelistic in purpose and spirit. These hymns are more or less subjective in their matter and develop a single thought rather than a line of thought. That thought usually finds its supreme expression in the chorus or refrain, which binds the stanza together in a very close unity, just as it does in lyrical poetry where it is occasionally used.

Regardless of how one tries to describe or define the gospel song, it must be recognized that these simple, emotional expressions have been greatly used by God in the furtherance of the gospel. Many critics have attacked these songs for their inferior literary and musical qualities, and it must be admitted that many have been published that deserve such criticism. Yet it cannot be denied that the use of these songs has been one of the important factors in the spread of the evangelical message to the present time.

The publishing of many gospel song collections did much to promote the wide-spread popularity of gospel music. Ira D. Sankey (1840–1908), often called the father of gospel music, aided by Philip P. Bliss (1838–

1876), prepared the well-known collection, *Gospel Songs,* published in 1875 with the sixth concluding volume appearing in 1891. After Sankey's death Marshall, Morgan and Scott of England enlarged the 1891 edition and published *Sacred Songs and Solos* with 1200 numbers. It is estimated that before the close of the nineteenth century more than 1500 gospel songbooks had been published. The wide acceptance of gospel music is demonstrated by the fact that 80 million copies of one collection of Sankey's songs were sold in England alone within fifty years after the initial publication. Today such major publishing companies of gospel music as Singspiration, Word, Hope, Lillenas, Lexicon are names well-known to evangelical Christian people everywhere.

In addition to the names of Ira D. Sankey and Philip P. Bliss, other important writers and composers of early gospel hymnody include Charles H. Gabriel, E. O. Excell, Fanny Crosby, William Bradbury, Robert Lowry, James McGranahan, George Stebbins, William Doane, C. C. Converse, James M. Gray, A. H. Ackley, Haldor Lillenas, William J. Kirkpatrick, W. A. Ogden, C. Austin Miles and Homer Rodeheaver. Many of these people were not formally trained musicians but were imbued with a native musical gift from God. They were highly motivated with the desire to reach, through the appealing media of music, the greatest number of individuals possible with the basic truths of the gospel.

24

Several of the later and more contemporary gospel songwriters whose works are well-known today include John W. Peterson, William Gaither, Merrill Dunlop, Norman Clayton, Harry Dixon Loes, Virgil Brock, Alfred B. Smith, Avis B. Christiansen, Ira F. Stamphill, Oswald J. Smith, Charles Weigle, Otis Skillings, Ralph Carmichael, and Don Wyrtzen. It is interesting to compare the musical and literary expressions of the earlier gospel songwriters with those writing since World War II. In general, it is apparent that more musical interest and literary subtlety characterize these later writers, without the loss of the spiritual fervor and concern that have always marked such devoted individuals.

Other nineteenth century American hymn writers whose works are found in most evangelical hymnals include Phillips Brooks (1853–1893), "O Little Town of Bethlehem" (No. 67); Ernest Warburton Shurtleff (1862–1917), "Lead On, O King Eternal" (No. 54); Maltbie Davenport Babcock (1858–1909), "This Is My Father's World" (No. 97); Henry VanDyke (1852–1933), "Joyful, Joyful, We Adore Thee" (No. 51); Washington Gladden (1838–1918), "O Master, Let Me Walk with Thee" (No. 69).

A Review of the Past, Present and Future

A study of the past reveals that the Christian church has inherited rich musical treasures throughout the centuries from various sources: translations of Greek and medieval Latin hymns; chorale hymns from the sixteenth and seventeenth century German Reformation periods; metrical Psalmody embodied in Calvin and the various psalters of this time; the free verse "human composure" hymns, with their strong doctrinal teachings, by Watts, Wesley and other seventeenth and eighteenth century English composers; the fine literary hymns of the nineteenth century; the American gospel song hymnody of the nineteenth and twentieth centuries, especially useful for evangelistic and devotional endeavors; and the later nineteenth and twentieth century hymns with their greater emphasis on Christian behavior as related to the social responsibilities and implications of the gospel. A worthy church hymnal should be representative of all of these valid sources of hymnody.

A look at the present and the future indicates many favorable trends taking place in evangelical church music. Greater numbers of Christian schools are giving stronger emphasis to instruction in church music than ever before. More churches, both large and small, are beginning graded choir programs, including instrumental groups such as church orchestras and handbell choirs. Especially since the 1960's there has been an abundance of exciting new music published for each age group. These contemporary hymns and anthems have derived more from the folk style traditions than from the more artistic heritage of music. Although composed and therefore not truly folk, this contemporary sacred music uses texts that are generally concerned with the very realistic attitudes and applications involved in practical Christian living. The music is often written in simple unison or duet form with strong, instrumental, syncopated rhythmic patterns. The minor mode has also become popular, with the Pentatonic scale (the avoidance of the fourth and seventh degrees of the scale) again becoming widely used. With much choir music today there is also a greater concern with encouraging more congregational involvement than with treating the congregation merely as spectators.

25

The selection of contemporary music requires careful discernment by consecrated directors. There is a legitimate concern on the part of many evangelical leaders that much of this generation's sacred music is being too strongly influenced and has too close an association with the secular rock beat of this age. There is also the concern that today's music tends to be purely subjective and experiential and is not based on the objective, unchanging truths of God's Word.

Again let it be re-emphasized, however, that sacred music is not automatically good or bad merely because it is traditional or contemporary. Furthermore, a historical study of trends and changes teaches that any new style has always had an initial secular connotation and hence has met with resistance. For example, such developments as the changes from Psalmody to the use of "human composure hymns," from unaccompanied congregational singing to the use of instruments, from the liturgical hymns to the more rhythmical nineteenth century gospel-song hym-nody have caused much turmoil among the generations of the past. To many believers, especially those of the older generation, anything new and unfamiliar is unacceptable. The attitude of many younger people, on the other hand, is that anything traditional is valueless and to be rejected. Neither of these extremes is valid. One of the most challenging tasks for any church music director today is trying to satisfy this wide spectrum of musical tastes found in any typical evangelical congregation.

A church music director, then, has the responsibility of providing a musical program of balanced styles that is God-honoring as well as spiritually and aesthetically satisfying to the majority of his people. To administer such a musical program effectively requires the grace and wisdom of God in full measure.

Conclusion

Although there will be a continual struggle on the part of church music directors for better musical standards as well as more relevant ex-pressions, it should be cautioned that these worthy goals are not mere ends in themselves. The ultimate objectives of a church music program must always be to minister significantly to the spiritual needs of people; to provide textual and musical expressions that inspire, comfort and teach in a manner consistent with the integrity and lofty ideals of the gospel; to challenge individuals of all ages with a personal, saving knowledge of Jesus Christ as Savior and Lord; and to direct believers to a more Spirit-filled Christian life. This is the ministry of music with which we must be earnestly concerned.

26

Chapter Three

UNDERSTANDING–The Hymnal's Use

A presentation of specific suggestions
for leaders of congregation singing

CHAPTER THREE

UNDERSTANDING–The Hymnal's Use

A song leader should have a thorough understanding of the factors involved in these three areas of congregational leadership: musical, psychological, spiritual. In addition, a worthy song leader must be concerned about planning services of praise that are inspiring and creative. The following suggestions are offered:

I. *Musical Factors in Song Leading*

    A. Poise and posture of the song leader.
        1. Clench fists and allow arms to hang naturally at one's side. The arms should then be brought up and bent at the elbows and the fists easily opened so that the palms are facing the floor at chest level and the fingers curved in a graceful manner.
        2. Think continually in terms of vibrancy, lift and buoyancy in your manner.
    B. Conducting techniques.
        1. Patterns. The top number of the time signature indicates the pattern.
          a. Right hand.

2-beat pattern   *3-beat pattern*   *4-beat pattern*   *6-beat pattern*

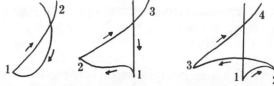

          b. Left hand.

            (Do most of the conducting with your right hand, but be able to change hands for the sake of variety and then be able to use both hands together when there is a need for emphasis.)
          c. Compound rhythms–when the top number of the time signature is either 6, 9, or 12.
          (1) A 6-beat song can be directed either in 6 or in 2,

depending on the tempo of the song, the desired interpretation, or possibly even the place and use of a particular song in a service.

(Directing a song with 6 beats gives an emphasis to the words; directing a song with 2 beats gives an emphasis to the lilt of the rhythm, which is good for praise songs.)

(2) A 9-beat song will invariably be conducted with a 3-beat pattern ("Blessed Assurance") while a 12-beat song will use the 4-beat pattern ("Saved, Saved").

2. Cut-offs. The releases or cut-offs in a song are indicated with the following movements:

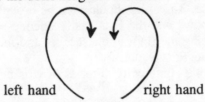

left hand   right hand

II. *Psychological Factors in Leading a Song Service.*

30

A. General suggestions.

1. Don't become fixed in your position. However, use controlled platform movements. Generally, direct from either behind the pulpit or to the right of the pulpit.

2. Direct with a "contagious enthusiasm," yet with mature dignity. Keep in mind that there is a manner of conducting oneself–e.g. dress, speech, decorum, etc. that must always be appropriate for the platform. Yet this must be done without becoming "stuffy" and affectatious.

3. Establish a personal, sympathetic contact with your audience by not being tied to the book. Be conscious of individuals not yet singing.

4. Be the song leader and not the preacher. Don't feel that you have to say some obvious truism between every verse or every song, yet be able to give a meaningful comment about the song when it is appropriate.

5. Strive to have a lively and interesting voice quality in giving instructions. Speak slowly and firmly enough to be distinct even for the elderly. When announcing a hymn, give the instructions at least twice.

6. Guard against annoying mannerisms in your leading (practice with a mirror) as well as in your speaking. This

includes gross grammatical errors or ambiguous expressions such as "Let us *stand* as we *sing,*" "hymn number two hundred *and* sixty," "Let's have a *word* of prayer," or, "sing it like you really mean it," etc.

7. Don't wear out the audience by excessive standing and singing. As a general rule, plan to have the audience stand twice before the message.

8. Don't get into a monotonous routine with your congregation by using the same songs all of the time. (Keep a record of the music you use.)

9. Keep a sense of movement to the service, yet make the congregation feel relaxed and at ease. Be conscious of not wasting time with trivials: small talk, undue announcements, etc.

10. Be inspirational. Never allow the service to become dull and mechanical.

B. Starting the service. Always a challenge for any song leader is the matter of starting the service. It is the director's responsibility to say or do the right thing so that the audience becomes quickly unified and ready to offer praise. In addition to his own general manner-"contagious enthusiasm"-most directors will have a planned approach for starting a service to include:

1. A warm, friendly greeting and welcome to the congregation.

2. A short, personal, enthusiastic testimony which leads directly into the first song.

3. Quoting a Scripture passage which has to do with singing-i.e., Psalm 149:1, Colossians 3:16, Ephesians 5:19, etc.

4. Quoting the verse of a familiar hymn, then having the congregation join in spontaneously with their hymnals.

5. Invite the congregation to stand and remain standing for prayer and the singing of the first number.

6. Have a theme song or chorus for a specified period of time-special meetings, a month, etc.

7. Begin with an unannounced special number or musical package. Or, a 10-15 minute mini-concert preceding the service.

C. Maintaining and building interest throughout the song service. This is basically achieved if the song leader is able to preserve a balance of *unity* and *variety* within the service. Although

31

there should be a unified theme or plan to the service, there need to be contrasting tempos, moods, rhythms, change of keys, etc. Other possibilities for keeping interest are:

1. Use various groups of people or sections of the congregation to sing or play verses or parts of a song.
2. Use medleys–a chain of several songs or choruses for the purpose of getting a spontaneous response from the people.
3. Occasionally give the story or background of a song.
4. Occasionally have the congregation sing unaccompanied.
5. Occasionally have the audience merely read the words of a verse of a song or perhaps hum while the words are read or sung by a soloist.
6. Occasionally have "audience favorites"–just one verse of various individuals' favorite hymns.
7. Teach new hymns or choruses by featuring a special song of the month.

III. *Spiritual Factors in Leading a Song Service.*

32

A. Have a conviction that something spiritual can be accomplished in the lives of your people by a song service.
B. Prepare and pray as earnestly for this portion of the service as you do for the spoken portion. Know in advance which verses are to be sung and which are to be omitted.
C. Know your hymnal objectively as well as subjectively.
   1. Objectively:
      a. Be acquainted with every song in your hymnal.
      b. Try to memorize as many familiar hymns as you can.
      c. Learn to use the indexes in the book.
   2. Subjectively:
      a. Get an emotional grasp and sensitive appreciation of the text.
      b. Make use of the hymnal as part of your daily devotions. Throughout the week live with the songs that you will be leading on Sunday.
      c. Do extensive reading on the backgrounds and experiences that inspired the writing of these hymns.

IV. *Service Planning.*

A. Basic Premises:
   1. Not only should the congregational singing be a prepara-

tion for the spoken word, but the song service can and should be a vital spiritual experience in itself.

    2. The hymnal is a thrilling source of materials for preparing creative, spiritual services of congregational praise and worship.

B. Seven models for different types of services that can be planned from the hymnal:

    1. Building a service on a particular topic or theme.

    2. Building a service on a particular hymn writer.

    3. Building a service around one particular hymn.

    4. Relating the individual verses of a hymn to their scriptural setting.

    5. Song sermons. Developing and integrating an entire service around one particular verse of scripture.

    6. Hymn dramatizations.

    7. Congregational choirs.

1. Building a Service on a Particular Topic or Theme.

Example–"Praise–A Believer's Spiritual Sacrifice"

"By Him, therefore let us offer the sacrifice of praise to God continually, that is, the fruit of our lips giving thanks to His name."

Hebrews 13:15

33

Introduction

One of the basic characteristics of our Christian experience should be our singing of praises to God, for sacred music is truly the expression of the redeemed soul. We are told that there are more than 575 references in the Bible to such words as *singing* and *songs*. One whole Book, the Psalms, was originally a collection of Hebrew songs. Atheism has its arguments but no songs. The heathen religions have their rituals and minor chants but no vibrant melodies. The entertainment world introduces thousands of new lyrics and melodies each year, but few meet the heart-felt needs of the human soul and thereby survive the test of time.

Have you ever thought how dull life would be if we didn't have the capacity to sing, whistle, hum or just enjoy the sounds of music? The Psalmist David wrote in Psalm 147:1 that "it is a good thing to sing praises unto God for it is pleasant." There is an enjoyment from music that is an integral part of our God-given humanity, but even more important than our own enjoyment is the realization that singing is "comely"–it is an activity that honors our Heavenly Father. "Whoso offereth praise glorifieth me . . ." (Psalm 50:23a).

SINGING WITH UNDERSTANDING

It must be admitted, however, that we as Christians often take our "praise privileges" all too lightly and carelessly. These lines of verse by Ronald K. Wells characterize many believers:

Sing Unto the Lord
Ronald K. Wells

He listened as the pastor spoke,
He bowed his head for prayer;
And when the off'ring plate was passed
He gladly gave his share.

But when a hymn was wont to sing,
He tightly sealed his tongue,
Till songs of praise that cried for strength
Were weak and feebly sung.

Not just because he failed to sing,
But others joined him, too,
And mocked with hollow silence
The praises of the few.

Forgive us, Lord, who fail to see
The glory of the song,
That nobly lifts the name of Christ
Above all sin and wrong.

And tune our hearts to sing Thy praise
Until each sincere soul
Shall stand condemned within his heart
To shrink back from our goal—

The goal that each heart born anew
May gladly join our song;
Not just within the worship hour,
But through the whole day long.

Published in *742 Heart-Warming Poems*
Compiled and edited by John R. Rice. Used by permission.

The Praise of Creation
  Read Job 38:7
  Congregation will sing hymns such as:
    "Joyful, Joyful We Adore Thee"
    "I Sing the Mighty Power of God"

The Praise of Christ's First Advent
  Read Luke 2:13,14

34

Congregation will sing hymns such as:
"Angels We Have Heard on High"
"Angels, From the Realms of Glory"

The Praise of Redemption
Read Psalm 40:1–3
Congregation will sing hymns such as:
"Amazing Grace"
"And Can It Be That I Should Gain?"

The Praise of Christ's Second Advent
Read I Thessalonians 4:16
Congregation will sing hymns such as:
"He Is Coming Again"
"Christ Returneth"

The Praise of the Redeemed Throughout Eternity
Read Revelation 5:9–14
Congregation will sing hymns such as:
"Look Ye Saints"
"Rejoice–The Lord Is King!"

35

2. Building a Service on a Particular Hymn Writer.

Example–Robert Lowry

Introduction

Our hymnals are truly amazing collections of poetic and musical expressions born out of many unusual circumstances. Through the centuries God has used the talents of pastors, lay people from all walks of life, and trained and untrained musicians to bless and inspire His people. Names such as Isaac Watts, Charles Wesley, Ira Sankey, Philip P. Bliss, Fanny Crosby have greatly enhanced the ministry of the Christian church with their musical contributions.

In this service we would like to focus our attention on an American Baptist pastor and hymn writer, whose name, though not as familiar as the others we have mentioned, has blessed the evangelical church with many fine gospel hymns. His name is Robert Lowry.

Robert Lowry composed the music for other writers' texts as well as his own. Isaac Watts, called the father of English hymnody, wrote the text for "We're Marching to Zion" in the eighteenth century, and one century later Robert Lowry provided the lilting tune which has made this hymn a joyous favorite with God's people everywhere.

Congregation will sing–"We're Marching to Zion"

Robert Lowry was recognized and honored as an outstanding Baptist minister in his various pastorates throughout the Eastern area of our country. He was born in Philadelphia on March 12, 1826. Lowry served Baptist churches in Pennsylvania, New York City, Brooklyn and New Jersey. He was known as a man of rare administrative ability, an excellent preacher, and a thorough Bible student. Music and hymnology were his favorite studies, but he always thought of them as avocations. Later, however, with the death of William Bradbury in 1868, the Biglow Publishing Company selected Robert Lowry as its music editor. In typical fashion, Lowry applied himself vigorously to the study of music and became highly knowledgeable in the field. It is said that the quality of his publications did much to stimulate and improve the cause of sacred music in this country.

Once when he was asked about his method for writing songs, Lowry replied:

I have no one method. Sometimes the music comes and the words follow . . . I watch my moods, and when anything strikes me, whether words or music, no matter where I am, at home or on the street, I jot it down . . . my brain is sort of a spinning machine, I think, for there is music running through it all the time. I do not pick out my music at the keyboard. The tunes of nearly all the hymns I have written have been completed on paper before I tried them on the organ. Frequently the words of the hymn and the music have been written at the same time.

And from the soul and pen of this dedicated pastor-musician have come such other gospel hymn favorites as listed below:

Congregation will sing one or two stanzas of the following:
"Christ Arose"
"Nothing But the Blood"

During the summer of 1864, a severe epidemic swept through New York City while Lowry was serving the Hanson Place Baptist Church of Brooklyn. People died in great numbers. Dr. Lowry was extremely busy during these days visiting the sick and comforting bereaved loved ones. One day, when the conditions were at their worst, Lowry came home one night completely exhausted. While resting in his living room he let his imagination take flight. He pictured the throne of heaven, the heavenly river, the gathering of the saints of all ages, and the cessation of all sickness and death.

36

Almost subconsciously, both words and music of the hymn "Shall We Gather At the River?" came spontaneously to his mind and fingers. Out of these sad circumstances came a hymn that has brought consolation to many a bereaved and stricken heart even to the present time.

It has been well said that Robert Lowry's preaching reached thousands with the gospel but his simply stated hymns have moved and inspired millions for more than a century.

Congregation will sing–"Shall We Gather At the River?"

3. Building a Service Around One Particular Hymn.

Example–"Amazing Grace"

Introduction

(Give background information about this hymn–see No. 6.)

Congregation will sing the first stanza–*Grace that Provides Believing Faith*

Speak about the utter amazement that overwhelms a believer when he ponders the undeserved favor that an omnipotent God bestowed upon lost mankind in providing a provision for personal salvation.

37

Congregation will sing the second stanza–*Grace that Produces the Response of Faith*

Speak about the paradoxical picture of the ministry of grace in salvation:

1. Grace that was necessary to arrest one's attention and cause a reverential awe and fear of a Holy God.
2. Yet the grace that caused one to fear God prior to conversion is the same grace that produces liberty and freedom from all fear commencing with the very hour one "first believes."

Congregation will sing the third stanza–*Grace that Protects the Believer Throughout Life*

Speak about the assurance a believer can have regarding the fact that the grace that accomplished one's personal salvation will also guide the child of God safely through this life and will eventually usher him into the eternal kingdom.

Congregation will sing the fourth stanza–*Grace that Prepares the Believer for Heaven*

Speak about the thrilling truth for all believers to contemplate that through the ages of eternity, this will still be the dominant theme of our praise–the Amazing Grace of our Lord.

Congregation will sing all four stanzas again in closing.

4. Relating the Individual Verses of a Hymn to Their Scriptural Setting.

Example–"How Firm a Foundation"

Introduction (see No. 32).

Like so many of our fine hymns, this hymn text is really a sermon in verse. In the first stanza the sure foundation of the Christian faith is established as being the Word of God, with this challenging question posed: What more can God do than give us His very Word as a completed revelation of Himself to man? The succeeding verses then personalize and amplify precious promises that God has documented in His Word.

Congregation will sing the first stanza.

The second verse provides a promise of comfort based on Isaiah 41:10–"Fear thou not, for I am with thee, be not dismayed, for I am thy God."

Congregation will sing the second stanza.

The third verse provides a promise for those passing through the crisis experiences of life. It is based on Isaiah 43:2–"When thou passest through the waters, I will be with thee."

Congregation will sing the third stanza.

The fourth verse is based on a New Testament promise found in 2 Corinthians 12:9–"My grace is sufficient for thee; For my strength is made perfect in weakness."

Congregation will sing the fourth stanza.

The powerful fifth verse is based on one of the glorious, eternal promises given in Hebrews 13:5–"I will never leave thee, nor forsake thee."

Congregation will sing the fifth stanza.

5. Song Sermons. Developing and Integrating an Entire Service Around One Particular Verse of Scripture.

Example–John 3:16

38

"For God So Loved the World"... *the object of love*

  Pastor will speak to this point
  Congregation will sing a related hymn
    i.e. "How Great Thou Art"
      "This Is My Father's World"

"That He Gave His Only Begotten Son"... *the gift of love*

  Pastor will speak to this point
  Congregation will sing a related hymn
    i.e. "Amazing Grace"
      "Ivory Palaces"

"That Whosoever Believeth in Him... *the breadth of love*

  Pastor will speak to this point
  Congregation will sing a related hymn
    i.e. "Whosoever Will May Come"
      "Christ Receiveth Sinful Men"

"Should Not Perish but Have Everlasting Life"... *the reward of love*   39

  Pastor will speak to this point
  Congregation will sing a related hymn
    i.e. "Verily, Verily"
      "I Stand Amazed In the Presence"

Congregation will sing chorus "For God So Loved the World;" or possibly the choir closes with John Stainer's "God So Loved the World."

6. Hymn Dramatizations.

Example—"Blest Be The Tie That Binds"

Introduction (see No. 12)

Reader No. 1: One of the important blessings of the Christian life is the fellowship we enjoy here and now with other believers. Oh, I know that sometimes we have our times of tensions and disagreements, and we are quite ready to agree with these good-natured lines:

Reader No. 2: "To dwell up above with the saints that we love, will be for us endless glory;
But to dwell here below with the saints that we know—is quite a different story."

Reader No. 1: Well, we can laugh at ourselves now as we recall some trivial upset that we have had with a fellow believer in the past, but wouldn't we have to agree that when we have experienced some deep sorrow or difficulty in our lives, the strong bond of prayerful concern by fellow Christians has been a most meaningful and undergirding help for such an hour?

Reader No. 2: It was this feeling and appreciation of Christian fellowship that prompted a Baptist pastor, John Fawcett, to write "Blest Be the Tie That Binds," in the little village of Wainsgate in northern England in 1782.

(Several poorly dressed people gather with baskets and bundles at the village meeting place)

No. 1 ——— : Oh ———, have you heard the terrible news? Pastor Fawcett is going to leave us!

No. 2 ——— : Not really! What would we ever do without him? He is such a fine preacher . . . and we all love him so much.

No. 3 ——— : He just can't leave us . . . where is he going?

No. 1 ——— : He has just received a call to pastor that large Carter's Lane Baptist Church in London. It will be a much better position for him. He will take the place of that famous preacher, Dr. Gill.

No. 4 ——— : But doesn't our pastor know how much we've all loved him and Mrs. Fawcett ever since they arrived here just after their marriage with nothing but their clothing and a few books?

No. 2 ——— : He was only 26 years of age when he came and his helpfulness and kindness have made us all so devoted to him and his dear family ever since.

No. 1 ——— : Yes, and his preaching has been so inspiring and helpful these past years that now those people in that large, rich church in London have heard about him and want him as their pastor.

No. 3 ——— : I have been fearful, ———, that this might someday happen to us. We can't just compete with other churches like Carter's Lane.

No. 2 ——— : But what will we ever do here at Wainsgate when the Fawcett family finally do leave us?

No. 4 ——— : Let's pray earnestly that God will keep our pastor and his family with us for at least a little longer.

Reader No. 1: But moving day soon came. Pastor Fawcett's farewell sermon had been preached and the wagons were being loaded with the family's belongings. The parishioners

40

	were gathered around the family saying their tearful goodbyes.
John Fawcett:	There . . . that finishes it–books, furniture and all the trunks of clothing . . . I think we're finally ready to move on. God bless you all, my dear people!
No. 2 ———— :	But Pastor Fawcett . . . you just can't leave us . . . please, we all love you and need you too much.
No. 3 ———— :	Our hearts are broken because of your leaving. You have done so much for all of us–you have taught us most of all what it really means to love and trust God. (moments of silence)
Mary Fawcett:	Oh, John, I cannot bear this. I do not know how we can leave this place and these dear people. (hesitation)
John Fawcett:	Nor can I either, Mary. (long pause). We shall remain here with our people. Unload those wagons and let us get on with our work.
No. 1 ———— :	God bless you, pastor and sister Mary. We shall see to it that you never will regret this day.
Everyone:	Glory be to God . . . God bless our pastor and his family . . . Let God's name be ever praised . . . etc.
John Fawcett:	My dear friends, let this experience ever remind us of the truth of God's Word that the fellowship of kindred minds is like to that above. I feel that God would have me write my feelings of this day in a poem for all of you to remember. I will share these thoughts with you in one of my sermons very soon.
Reader:	During one of his ensuing sermons and while the farewell experience was still vivid in his mind, the pastor shared this next text with his congregation.
John Fawcett:	Blest be the tie that binds our hearts in Christian love; The fellowship of kindred minds is like to that above. Before our Father's throne we pour our ardent prayers; Our fears, our hopes, our aims are one, our comforts and our cares. We share our mutual woes, our mutual burdens bear; And often for each other flows the sympathizing tear. When we asunder part, it gives us inward pain; But we shall still be joined in heart, and hope to meet again.
Reader No. 1:	John Fawcett continued his faithful ministry to these humble people at Wainsgate until a paralytic stroke caused his death on July 25, 1817, at the age of 77. His salary was estimated at never more than $200 per

41

year, despite his growing reputation as an outstanding evangelical preacher and scholar. In recognition of his ministry and many accomplishments including the establishment of a school for the training of the nonconformist men for the ministry, Brown University in our own country conferred the Doctor of Divinity Degree upon him in 1811.

Reader No. 2: John Fawcett's life can certainly be cited as an example of a spiritual leader who sacrificed ambition and personal gain for Christian devotion to God and His people.

Congregation will sing all four stanzas of "Blest Be The Tie That Binds."

7. Congregational Choirs

Example-"It Is Well With My Soul"

(Have a page such as this duplicated and distributed to the congregation.)

Introduction (see No. 44).

Horatio Spafford was a successful Chicago attorney and business man but one deeply committed to the person and cause of Jesus Christ. Despite his financial success, he always maintained a keen interest in Christian activities. He enjoyed a close and active relationship with D. L. Moody and many of the other evangelical leaders of this period.

Some months prior to the great Chicago fire in 1871, Spafford had invested heavily in real estate on the shore of Lake Michigan and his holdings were virtually wiped out by this disaster. Just before this he had experienced the death of his son. Desiring a rest for his wife and four daughters as well as wishing to join and assist in the evangelistic endeavors of Moody's campaign in Great Britain, Spafford planned a European trip for his family during the fall of 1873. Due to unexpected last minute business developments, he had to remain in Chicago, but he sent his wife and four daughters on ahead as scheduled on the *S. S. Ville du Harve*. It was Spafford's intent to follow in a few days and to rejoin his family in Europe.

On November 22, 1873, the ship was struck by the *Lochearn*, an English vessel, and twelve minutes later it sank. On December first the few survivors were finally landed at Cardiff, Wales, and Mrs. Spafford cabled her anxious husband, "Saved alone." Mr. Spafford left immediately to join his bereaved wife. It is said that on the sea near the area where it was thought that his four daughters had drowned, Spafford penned these words so significantly describing his personal grief as well as his personal faith in the ways of an omnipotent God.

Instruments will play first three measures of the refrain followed by everyone singing:

42

It is well, it is well with my soul!

Vs. 1. Solo with congregation humming:
> When peace, like a river, attendeth my way, when sorrows like
> sea-billows roll;
> Whatever my lot, Thou hast taught me to say:

Congregation–It is well, it is well with my soul!

Vs. 2. Ladies:
> 'Tho Satan should buffet, 'tho trials should come, Let this blest
> assurance control.

Men:
> That Christ hath regarded my helpless estate.

Everyone:
> And hath shed His own blood for my soul.

Vs. 3. Men:
> My sin–O, the bliss of this glorious thought,
> My sin–not in part but the whole.

Ladies:
> Is nailed to the cross, and I bear it no more–Praise the Lord!

Men:
> Praise the Lord!

Everyone:
> O my soul!

(Instrumental Interlude of Refrain)

43

Vs. 4. Everyone (faster):
> And, Lord, haste the day when my faith shall be sight. The clouds be
> rolled back as a scroll. The trump shall resound and the Lord shall
> descend, Even so–it is well with my soul.
> Ladies. It is well. . . .   Men . . . It is well
> Ladies. . . . With my soul. . . .   Men. . . . With my soul
> Everyone.   It is well, it is well with my soul.

Chapter Four

UNDERSTANDING–The Hymnal's Contents

Inspiring, factual backgrounds and experiences that prompted the writing of 101 selected favorite hymns.

UNDERSTANDING–The Hymnal's Contents

1 ## A Mighty Fortress Is Our God

EIN' FESTE BURG

MARTIN LUTHER, 1483-1546
Trans. by Frederick H. Hedge, 1805-1890

MARTIN LUTHER, 1483-1546

1. A might-y for-tress is our God, A bul-wark nev-er fail - ing;
2. Did we in our own strength con-fide Our striv-ing would be los - ing,
3. And tho this world,with dev-ils filled, Should threaten to un - do us,
4. That word a - bove all earth-ly pow'rs–No thanks to them-a - bid - eth;

Our help-er He a - mid the flood Of mor-tal ills pre - vail - ing.
Were not the right Man on our side, The Man of God's own choos - ing.
We will not fear, for God hath willed His truth to tri-umph thru us.
The Spir-it and the gifts are ours Thru Him who with us sid - eth.

For still our an-cient foe Doth seek to work us woe — His craft and
Dost ask who that may be? Christ Je-sus, it is He— Lord Sab - a -
The prince of dark-ness grim— We trem-ble not for him; His rage we
Let goods and kin-dred go, This mor-tal life al - so; The bod-y

pow'r are great, And,armed with cru-el hate, On earth is not his e - qual.
oth His name, From age to age the same— And He must win the bat - tle.
can en-dure, For lo! his doom is sure— One lit-tle word shall fell him.
they may kill: God's truth a - bid-eth still— His king-dom is for - ev - er.

47

A Mighty Fortress Is Our God

Author-Martin Luther, 1483–1546
English Translation-Frederick H. Hedge, 1805–1890
Composer-Martin Luther, 1483–1546
Tune Name-"Ein' Feste Burg"
Meter-87.87.66.667
Scripture Reference-Psalm 46

> The Lord is my rock, and my fortress, and my deliverer; my God, my strength, in whom I will trust; my buckler, and the horn of my salvation, and my high tower.
>
> Psalm 46

Martin Luther was born on November 10, 1483 in Eisleben, Saxony, Germany. He was educated at the University of Erfurt, later becoming an Augustinian monk, teaching philosophy and theology at the University of Wittenberg. On October 31, 1517, sometimes called the "4th of July of Protestantism," Martin Luther nailed his ninety-five theses to the door of the Cathedral of Wittenberg, Germany. These theses condemned various practices and teachings of the Roman church. After several years of stormy disputes with the Pope and other church leaders, Martin Luther was finally excommunicated from the fellowship of the Roman Catholic church in 1520.

One of the important benefits of the Reformation Movement was the rediscovery of congregational singing. Luther had strong convictions about the use and power of sacred music. He expressed his convictions in this way, "If any man despises music, as all fanatics do, for him I have no liking; for music is a gift and grace of God, not an invention of men. Thus it drives out the devil and makes people cheerful. Then one forgets all wrath, impurity and other devices." Again, "The Devil, the originator of sorrowful anxieties and restless troubles, flees before the sound of music almost as much as before the Word of God." In another place, "I wish to compose sacred hymns so that the Word of God may dwell among the people also by means of songs." Finally, Luther wrote, "I would allow no man to preach or teach God's people without a proper knowledge of the use and power of sacred song."

The single most powerful hymn of the Protestant Reformation Movement was Luther's "A Mighty Fortress Is Our God," based on Psalm 46. This hymn became the battle cry of the people, a great source of strength and inspiration even for those who were martyred for their convictions. This hymn has been translated into practically every known language and is regarded as one of the noblest and most classic examples of Christian hymnody. It is said there are no less than sixty translations of this text in English alone. In England the version by Thomas Carlyle is in general

48

use, while in this country the translation by Frederick H. Hedge, a professor at Harvard University, is used most frequently. This translation was not made until 1852 and first appeared in a book entitled *Gems of German Verse* by W. H. Furness, published in 1853.

The first line of this national hymn of Protestant Germany is fittingly inscribed on the tomb of the great reformer at Wittenberg, and may still be read with appreciation by travellers to that historic spot.

49

Martin Luther

2

Abide with Me

EVENTIDE

HENRY F. LYTE, 1793-1847

WILLIAM H. MONK, 1823-1889

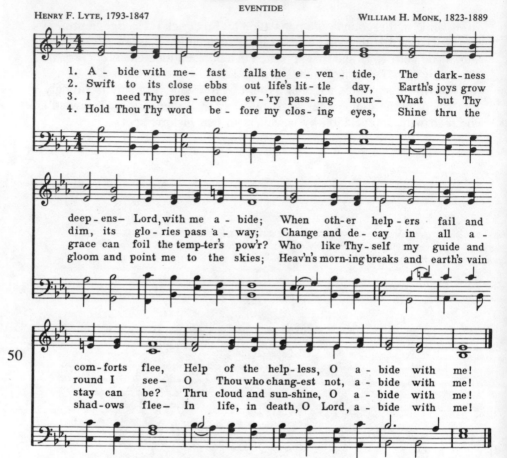

1. A - bide with me— fast falls the e - ven - tide, The dark - ness
2. Swift to its close ebbs out life's lit - tle day, Earth's joys grow
3. I need Thy pres - ence ev - 'ry pass - ing hour— What but Thy
4. Hold Thou Thy word be - fore my clos - ing eyes, Shine thru the

deep - ens— Lord, with me a - bide; When oth - er help - ers fail and
dim, its glo - ries pass a - way; Change and de - cay in all a -
grace can foil the temp-ter's pow'r? Who like Thy - self my guide and
gloom and point me to the skies; Heav'n's morn-ing breaks and earth's vain

50

com - forts flee, Help of the help - less, O a - bide with me!
round I see— O Thou who chang-est not, a - bide with me!
stay can be? Thru cloud and sun-shine, O a - bide with me!
shad - ows flee— In life, in death, O Lord, a - bide with me!

Author–Henry F. Lyte, 1793–1847
Composer–William H. Monk, 1823–1889
Tune Name–"Eventide"
Meter–10 10. 10 10
Scripture Reference–Luke 24:29

Yea, though I walk through the valley of the shadow of death, I will fear no evil: For Thou art with me; Thy rod and Thy staff they comfort me.   Psalm 23:4

It has been stated that only the person who can face the prospect of death realistically is able to live this life with purpose and confidence. Such was the conviction of a rather obscure English pastor, Henry F. Lyte, when he wrote the text for this hymn in 1847, shortly before his own home-going. It has since become one of the favorite hymns for Christians everywhere during times of sorrow and deep distress.

Henry F. Lyte was born in Scotland on June 1, 1793. He was educated at Trinity College, Dublin, Ireland, and was a member of the Church of England all of his life. Throughout his lifetime he was known as a man frail in body but strong in faith and spirit. His health was continually threatened by asthma and tuberculosis. Despite his physical frailties he was a tireless worker with an established reputation as a poet, musician and minister. It was he who coined the phrase, "It is better to wear out than to rust out." Wherever he ministered, he was greatly loved and admired by his people.

For the last twenty-three years of his life Lyte pastored a poor parish church among fishing people at Lower Brixham, Devonshire, England. During these later years his health became progressively worse so that he was forced to seek a warmer climate in Italy. For the last sermon with his poor parishioners on September 4, 1847, it is recorded that Lyte nearly had to crawl to the pulpit and his message came as from a dying man. His final words made a deep impact upon his people when he said that it was his desire to "induce you to prepare for the solemn hour which must come to all by a timely appreciation and dependence on the death of Christ." On his way to Rome, Italy, he was overtaken by death at Nice, France, and was buried there in the English cemetery on November 20, 1847.

Lyte is said to have written this text along with his own tune shortly before his last Sunday at the Lower Brixham Church. It never became widely used in England until it was first published in a book, *Lyte's Remains,* in 1850, London. Its first appearance in America was in Henry Ward Beecher's *Plymouth Collection* in 1855 with the notation that "this hymn was meant to be read and not sung." Later it was discovered by William Henry Monk, music editor of the well-known Anglican Church hymnal, *Hymns Ancient and Modern,* and it was included in the first edition of that hymnal published in 1861.

51

Altogether William Monk personally contributed fifty original tunes for the hymnal. It is said that in less than half an hour he composed for Lyte's text a tune named "Eventide." He was inspired by the beauty of a glorious sunset while yet experiencing a deep personal sorrow. In addition to his work as editor of this hymnal, considered by hymnologists to be one of the most important hymnals ever published, William Monk was also choir director and organist at King's College, London.

William H. Monk also supplied the music for the hymn, "Look, Ye Saints! The Sight Is Glorious" (No. 55).

Henry Lyte's text for this hymn was taken from the account of Christ's appearance with the two disciples on the way to Emmaus and their statement, "Abide with us: for it is toward evening and the day is far spent" (Luke 24:29). Although Lyte did not write a great quantity of hymns, others from his pen include such congregational favorites as "Praise My Soul, the King of Heaven" and "Jesus, I My Cross Have Taken."

3 All Creatures of Our God and King

LASST UNS ERFREUEN

FRANCIS OF ASSISI, 1182-1226
Trans. by William H. Draper, 1855-1933

From *Geistliche Kirchengesäng*, 1623
Arr. by Norman Johnson, 1928-

1. All creatures of our God and King, Lift up your voice and with us
2. Thou rush-ing wind that art so strong, Ye clouds that sail in heav'n a-
3. Dear moth-er earth, who day by day Un-fold-est bless-ings on our
4. And all ye men of ten-der heart, For-giv-ing oth-ers, take your
5. Let all things their Cre-a-tor bless, And wor-ship Him in hum-ble-
Praise God, from whom all bless-ings flow, Praise Him, all crea-tures here be-

sing Al-le-lu-ia, Al-le-lu-ia! Thou burn-ing sun with gold-en
long, O praise Him! Al-le-lu-ia! Thou ris-ing morn, in praise re-
way, O praise Him! Al-le-lu-ia! The flow'rs and fruits that in thee
part, O sing ye! Al-le-lu-ia! Ye who long pain and sor-row
ness— O praise Him! Al-le-lu-ia! Praise, praise the Fa-ther, praise the
low, Al-le-lu-ia, Al-le-lu-ia! Praise Him a-bove, ye heav'n-ly

beam, Thou sil-ver moon with soft-er gleam: O praise Him,
joice, Ye lights of eve-ning, find a voice: O praise Him,
grow, Let them His glo-ry al-so show: O praise Him,
bear, Praise God and on Him cast your care: O praise Him,
Son, And praise the Spir-it, Three in One: O praise Him,
host, Praise Fa-ther, Son and Ho-ly Ghost: Al-le-lu-ia,

O praise Him! Al-le-lu-ia, Al-le-lu-ia! Al-le-lu- ia!
Al-le-lu-ia! Al-le-lu-ia, Al-le-lu-ia! Al-le-lu- ia!

52

All Creatures of Our God and King

Author–Francis of Assisi, 1182–1226
English Translation–William H. Draper, 1855–1933
Music–From the *Geistliche Kirchengesäng* of 1623
Tune Name–"Lasst Uns Erfreuen"
Meter–LMA (88.88 with Alleluias)
Scripture Reference–Psalm 145

> All Thy works shall praise Thee, O Lord; and Thy saints shall bless Thee. They shall speak of the glory of Thy kingdom, and talk of Thy power.   Psalm 145:10,11

This inspiring expression of praise found in nearly every hymnal was originally written in 1225 by one of the most interesting figures in all of church history. Giovanni Bernardone, who was better known as Saint Francis of Assisi, was a mystic, medieval monk who spent his lifetime as an itinerant evangelist, preaching and helping the poor people of Italy.

Saint Francis was born in Assisi, Italy, in 1182. After an early indulgent life as a soldier, he reformed his ways dramatically, at the age of twenty-five, and determined to serve God by imitating the selfless life of Christ in all that he did. Although his family were people of considerable means, Francis scorned the possession of material goods, denounced his inherited wealth, denied himself everything but the most meager necessities, and devoted himself completely to moving about his area as Christ's representative. At the age of twenty-eight Francis founded the influential Franciscan Order of Friars, which developed into a large movement of young men and some women who adopted his religious beliefs and ascetic style of life.

53

Saint Francis was known as a great lover of nature, seeing the hand of God in all creation. One of the well-known master paintings from this time was done by the famous Italian artist, Giotto, and shows Saint Francis feeding the birds. The following well-known verse was written in tribute to this man:

Saint Francis came to preach–with smiles he met the friendless, fed the poor, freed a trapped bird, led home a child; Although he spoke no word–his text, God's love, the town did not forget.

Another familiar verse that has become especially popular in recent years is the thoughtful prayer written by this medieval monk during the early years of his life:

Lord, make me an instrument of Thy peace. Where there is hatred, let me sow love.

Where there is injury, pardon. Where there is discord, unity.

Where there is doubt, faith. Where there is error, truth.

Where there is despair, hope. Where there is sadness, joy. Where there is darkness, light.

O divine master, grant that I may not so much seek to be consoled, as to console.

To be understood, as to understand. To be loved, as to love.

For it is in giving, that we receive. It is in pardoning, that we are pardoned. It is in dying, that we are born to eternal life.

There are many interesting but strange incidents and legends associated with the life of Saint Francis which are difficult to explain. Historical accounts relate various visitations that Saint Francis is supposed to have had with the Lord. One of those occasions was while Francis was fasting for forty days in the lofty mountain of LaVerne. It is said that this encounter left him for the remainder of his life bearing on his hands, feet and body the stigmata or painful wounds of the crucified Lord. Another account, whether fact or fiction, states that as his soul was being committed to the creator, a flock of larks gathered unmistakably about his little hut and rose, singing a beautiful song in the still evening air.

54

"All Creatures of Our God and King" is from another of Saint Francis's writings entitled "Canticles of the Sun," said to have been written one hot summer day in 1225, one year before his death, while Francis was very ill and suffering the loss of his eyesight. Throughout his life Saint Francis made much use of singing and believed strongly in the importance of church music. In all he wrote more than sixty hymns for use in the monastery. This beautiful expression of praise is one that has survived the passing of these several hundred years.

The English translation of this text was made by William Draper, a village rector in England, who prepared this paraphrased version for a children's choir festival at some time between 1899-1919. The tune for this text first appeared in a Roman Catholic hymnal in Cologne, Germany, in 1623. After being forgotten for a time, the tune was revived in the present century and appeared in the *English Hymnal,* published in London, England, in 1906. An interesting congregational use of this hymn is to sing it as a two, three, or four part round or canon. This can be done simply by disregarding the hold or fermata at the end of the second line. Another interesting practice is to sing the alternating phrases antiphonally.

Although there is much that is difficult to understand and explain about the author of this text, we certainly can be thankful that God ordained the birth, translation and the preservation of this fine expression of praise for His people to enjoy even to the present time.

It should be noted that the Keswick Doxology, "Praise God from Whom All Blessings Flow," with the alleluias, can be used effectively with this tune.

*   *   *

"Art is man's nature: nature is God's art."

Philip James Bailey

"At home with Nature, and one with God!"

Florence Earle Coates

"Nature is but a name for an effect whose cause is God."

55

William Cowper

"The man who can really, in living union of the mind and heart, converse with God through nature, finds in the material forms around him, a source of power and happiness inexhaustible, and like the life of angels. The highest life and glory of man is to be alive unto God; and when this grandeur of sensibility of Him, and this power of communion with Him is carried, as the habit of the soul, into the forms of nature, then the walls of our world are as the gates of heaven."

George B. Cheever

All Hail the Power

CORONATION

4

EDWARD PERRONET, 1726-1792
Alt. by John Rippon, 1751-1836

OLIVER HOLDEN, 1765-1844

56

1. All hail the pow'r of Je-sus' name! Let an-gels pros-trate fall;
2. Ye cho-sen seed of Is-rael's race, Ye ran-somed from the fall,
3. Let ev-'ry kin-dred, ev-'ry tribe, On this ter-res-trial ball,
4. O that with yon-der sa-cred throng We at His feet may fall!

Bring forth the roy-al di-a-dem, And crown Him Lord of all!
Hail Him who saves you by His grace, And crown Him Lord of all!
To Him all maj-es-ty as-cribe, And crown Him Lord of all!
We'll join the ev-er-last-ing song, And crown Him Lord of all!

MILES LANE

Alternate tune

WILLIAM SHRUBSOLE, 1760-1806

1. All hail the pow'r of Je-sus' name! Let an-gels prostrate fall; Bring forth the royal di-a-dem, And crown Him, crown Him, crown Him, Crown Him Lord of all!

All Hail the Power

Author-Edward Perronet, 1726–1792. Altered by John Rippon, 1751–1836
"Coronation" Tune-Oliver Holden, 1765–1844
"Miles Lane" Tune-William Shrubsole, 1760–1806
Meter-CM (86.86)
Scripture Reference-Revelation 19:12, 16

> Thou art worthy, O Lord, to receive glory and honor and power: For Thou hast created all things, and for Thy pleasure they are and were created.   Revelation 4:11

This hymn is often called the "National Anthem of Christendom." The hymn first appeared in the November, 1779, issue of the *Gospel Magazine,* edited by Augustus Toplady, author of "Rock of Ages" (No. 78). This text has been translated into almost every language where Christianity is known; and wherever it is sung, it communicates to the spiritual needs of human hearts. One writer has said, "So long as there are Christians on earth, it will continue to be sung; and after that, in heaven."

Edward Perronet was born at Sundridge, Kent, England, in 1726. He was a descendant of a distinguished French Huguenot family who had fled to Switzerland and later to England because of the religious persecution in France. Edward's father, a pastor in the State Church of England, was strongly sympathetic with the evangelical movement spearheaded by the Wesleys and George Whitefield. Edward, too, became a minister in the Anglican Church but was always critical of its ways. Once he wrote, "I was born and I am likely to die in the tottering communion of the Church of England, but I despise her nonsense." Soon, however, he broke from the Church and threw himself strenuously into the evangelistic endeavors of the Wesleys during the 1740's and 1750's. It was during this time that the Wesleys and their followers suffered much persecution and even violence from those who disagreed with their ministry. Concerning these experiences, Wesley made the following notation in his diary:

> From Rockdale we went to Bolton, and soon found that the Rockdale lions were lambs in comparison with those of Bolton. Edward Perronet was thrown down and rolled in mud and mire. Stones were hurled and windows broken.

Another interesting account regarding the relationship between the Wesleys and Perronet concerns the incident when John Wesley announced to a congregation that Edward Perronet would preach at the next

57

service. Being eighteen years younger than Wesley, Perronet had always refused to preach in the elder statesman's presence. Desiring to avoid a public conflict with Wesley, Perronet mounted the pulpit but quickly explained that he had never consented to preach. "However," he added, "I shall deliver the greatest sermon that has ever been preached on earth." He then read the Sermon on the Mount and sat down without comment.

Eventually, Perronet's strong-mindedness and free spirit caused a break with the Wesleys, especially on the issue of whether the evangelists as well as the regular ministers could administer the sacraments. Perronet continued to the end of his days as pastor of an independent church at Canterbury, England. His last words have also become classic:

> Glory to God in the height of His divinity!
> Glory to God in the depth of His humanity!
> Glory to God in His all-sufficiency!
> Into His hands I commend my spirit.

Though Perronet wrote many other hymns and forms of poetry, most of which he published anonymously, this is his only work to survive. The success of this text has, no doubt, been furthered by three fine tunes. "Coronation," composed by Oliver Holden, a Massachusetts carpenter, self-taught musician and respected singing-school teacher, is most widely used in America. "Miles Lane" by William Shrubsole, Perronet's personal friend, is the most popular in Great Britain, while the festive "Diadem" tune, composed in 1838 for this text by James Ellor, an English layman, is frequently used as a choir number.

Many interesting accounts have been associated with the use of this hymn. One of the most remarkable is a story told by E. P. Scott, a pioneer missionary to India. One day he was waylaid by a murderous band of tribesmen who were closing in on him with spears. On impulse the missionary took his violin out of his luggage and began to play and sing this hymn. When he reached the stanza "let every kindred, every tribe," he saw to his surprise every spear lowered and many of these tribesmen moved to tears. Scott spent the remaining years of his life preaching and ministering God's love and redemption to these people. God in His providence used a simple hymn as a means of introducing the gospel to a group of needy pagans.

58

5   All the Way My Savior Leads Me

FANNY J. CROSBY, 1820-1915

ROBERT LOWRY, 1826-1899

1. All the way my Sav-ior leads me— What have I to ask be - side?
2. All the way my Sav-ior leads me— Cheers each wind-ing path I tread,
3. All the way my Sav-ior leads me— O the full - ness of His love!

Can I doubt His ten-der mer - cy, Who thru life has been my Guide?
Gives me grace for ev -'ry tri - al, Feeds me with the liv - ing bread.
Per - fect rest to me is prom-ised In my Fa - ther's house a - bove.

Heav'n - ly peace, di - vin - est com-fort, Here by faith in Him to dwell!
Tho my wea - ry steps may fal - ter And my soul a-thirst may be,
When my spir - it, clothed im - mor-tal, Wings its flight to realms of day,

59

For I know, what-e'er be - fall me, Je-sus do - eth all things well; well.
Gush-ing from the Rock be - fore me, Lo! a spring of joy I see; see.
This my song thru end-less a - ges: Je-sus led me all the way; way.

SINGING WITH UNDERSTANDING

All the Way My Savior Leads Me

Author-Fanny J. Crosby, 1820–1915
Composer-Robert Lowry, 1826–1899
Meter-87.87 Doubled

The steps of a good man are ordered by the Lord: And He delighteth in his way.
Psalm 37:23

This beloved gospel hymn was the expression of gratitude to God after a direct answer to prayer. It is reported that one day Fanny Crosby desperately needed five dollars and did not know where she could obtain this amount. As was her custom, she began to pray about this matter. Within a few minutes a stranger appeared at her door with just the right amount. "I have no way of accounting for this," she wrote, "except to believe that God, in answer to my prayer, put it into the heart of this good man to bring the money. My first thought was, it is so wonderful the way the Lord leads me. I immediately wrote the poem and Dr. Lowry set it to music." The hymn first appeared in a Sunday School collection, *Brightest and Best,* compiled by William H. Doane and Robert Lowry in 1875.

60   Fanny Jane Crosby was born of humble parents at Southeast, New York, on March 24, 1823. She was blinded at the age of six weeks by improper medical treatment. Throughout her lifetime she was a faithful member of the St. John's Methodist Episcopal Church in New York City. She was educated at the New York School for the Blind. From 1847 to 1858 she served as a teacher at this school. In 1858 she married a blind musician, Alexander Van Alstyne, a highly respected teacher of music at the blind institution. Her early verse writing was primarily of a secular nature. One of her popular songs, "Rosalie, the Prairie Flower," brought her almost three thousand dollars in royalties, a considerable amount for that day. Through the influence of a well-known church musician, W. B. Bradbury, she began, in her early forties, to write gospel song lyrics in earnest and became the "happiest creature in all the land." It is said that Fanny Crosby never wrote a hymn text without first kneeling in earnest prayer and asking for divine guidance. She was also characterized by the little American flag that she always carried along with her Bible. Throughout her career she was associated in her writing with such leading gospel musicians of her time as Ira D. Sankey, Wm. H. Doane, John Sweney, George Stebbins, George Root, William Kirkpatrick, and others.

Other hymns by Fanny J. Crosby include "Blessed Assurance" (No. 11), "My Savior First of All" (No. 60), and "Rescue the Perishing" (No. 76).

UNDERSTANDING the Hymnal's Contents

Robert Lowry was born on March 12, 1826, in Philadelphia, Pennsylvania. He later became known as a brilliant preacher and pastor of a number of leading Baptist churches throughout the East. Music and hymnology were his favorite studies, but always as an avocation. Later, upon the death of William Bradbury, Lowry was selected as music editor of the Biglow Publishing Company. It is said that the quality of his publications did much to stimulate the cause of sacred music in this country during the latter part of the past century (see page 35).

*   *   *

"More like Jesus would I be, Let my Savior dwell in me;
Fill my soul with peace and love, make me gentle as a dove;
More like Jesus while I go, pilgrim in this world below;
Poor in spirit would I be; let my Savior dwell in me.

"If He hears the raven's cry, if His ever watchful eye   61
Marks the sparrows when they fall, surely He will hear my call;
He will teach me how to live, all my sinful thoughts forgive;
Pure in heart I still would be; let my Savior dwell in me.

"More like Jesus when I pray, more like Jesus day by day;
May I rest me by His side, where the tranquil waters glide;
Born of Him, through grace renewed, by His love my will subdued,
Rich in faith I still would be; let my Savior dwell in me."

Written by Fanny J. Crosby in 1867

6

Amazing Grace

AMAZING GRACE

American melody
From Carrell & Clayton's *Virginia Harmony*, 1831
Arr. by Norman Johnson, 1928-

JOHN NEWTON, 1725-1807

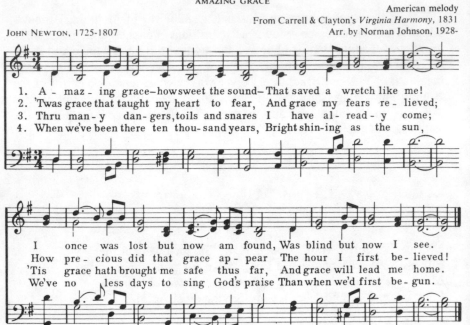

1. A - maz - ing grace—how sweet the sound—That saved a wretch like me!
2. 'Twas grace that taught my heart to fear, And grace my fears re - lieved;
3. Thru man - y dan-gers,toils and snares I have al - read - y come;
4. When we've been there ten thou- sand years, Bright shin-ing as the sun,

I once was lost but now am found, Was blind but now I see.
How pre - cious did that grace ap - pear The hour I first be - lieved!
'Tis grace hath brought me safe thus far, And grace will lead me home.
We've no less days to sing God's praise Than when we'd first be - gun.

62

Author-John Newton, 1725-1807
Music-From Carrell and Clayton's "Virginia Harmony," 1831
Tune Name-"Amazing Grace"
Meter-CM (86.86)
Scripture Reference-1 Chronicles 17:16,17

> For by grace are ye saved through faith; and that not of yourselves; it is the gift of God: not of works, lest any man should boast. Ephesians 2:8,9

In a small cemetery of a parish churchyard in Olney, England, stands a granite tombstone with the following inscription: "John Newton, clerk, once an infidel and Libertine, a servant of slavers in Africa, was, by the rich mercy of our Lord and Savior Jesus Christ, preserved, restored, pardoned, and appointed to preach the Faith he had long labored to destroy." This fitting testimonial, written by Newton himself prior to his death, describes aptly the unusual and colorful life of this man, one of the great evangelical preachers of the eighteenth century.

John Newton's mother, a Godly woman, died when he was not quite seven years of age. When his father remarried and after several brief years of formal education away from home; John left school and joined his father's ship, at the age of eleven, to begin life as a seaman. His early years were one continuous round of rebellion and debauchery. After serving on several ships as well as working for a period of time on the islands and mainland of the West African coast collecting slaves for sale to visiting traders, Newton eventually became a captain of his own slave ship. Needless to say, the capturing, selling and transporting of black slaves to the plantations in the West Indies and America was a cruel and vicious way of life.

On March 10, 1748, while returning to England from Africa during a particularly stormy voyage when it appeared that all would be lost, Newton began reading Thomas a Kempis's book, *Imitation of Christ*. Kempis was a Dutch monk, 1380–1471, who belonged to an order called the Brethren of the Common Life. This book is still printed today as a religious classic. The message of the book and the frightening experience at sea were used by the Holy Spirit to sow the seeds of Newton's eventual conversion and personal acceptance of Christ as his Savior.

For the next several years he continued as a slave ship captain, trying to justify his work by seeking to improve conditions as much as possible, even holding public worship services for his hardened crew of thirty each Sunday. Eventually, however, he felt convicted of the inhuman aspects of this work and became a strong and effective crusader against slavery. Newton returned to England, established a home with his youthful sweetheart, Mary Catlett, whom he had married on February 12, 1750, and became a clerk at the Port of Liverpool for the next nine years. During this period he felt the call of God increasingly to preach the gospel and began to study diligently for the ministry. He was greatly aided and influenced by the evangelist George Whitefield as well as the Wesleys, but he decided to stay within the established Anglican Church rather than to join forces with these Dissenters. At the age of thirty-nine, John Newton was ordained by the Anglican Church and began his first pastorate at the little village of Olney, near Cambridge, England. His work for the next fifteen years (1764–1779) was a most fruitful and influential ministry.

63

Especially effective was the use of the story of his early life and conversion experience, which he told often. In addition to preaching for the stated services in his own church, Newton would hold services regularly in any large building he could secure in the surrounding area. This was an unheard of practice for an Anglican clergyman of that day. Wherever he preached, large crowds gathered to hear the "Old Converted Sea Captain."

Another of Newton's extremist practices at the Olney Church was the singing of hymns that expressed the simple, heartfelt faith of his preaching rather than the staid singing of the Psalms from the *Sternhold and*

Hopkins Psalter, which was practiced in other Anglican churches. When Newton couldn't find enough available hymns for this purpose, he began writing his own. To assist him in this endeavor, he enlisted the aid of his friend and neighbor, William Cowper, a well-known writer of classic literature of this period. In 1779 their combined efforts produced the famous *Olney Hymns* hymnal, one of the most important single contributions made to the field of evangelical hymnody. In this ambitious collection of 349 hymns, sixty-seven were written by Cowper with the remainder by Newton. The purpose of the hymnal, according to Newton's Preface, was "a desire to promote the faith and comfort of sincere Christians."

Since 1947, an interesting ancient tradition has been revived at the Olney Church. It is the annual pancake race that is held on the Tuesday (Shrove Tuesday) prior to the beginning of Lent. The ladies of the parish race from the center of town to the church flipping pancakes. At the service the winner is announced followed by the congregation singing "Amazing Grace" and other Olney Hymnal favorites.

After concluding his ministry at Olney, Newton spent the remaining twenty-eight years of his life as pastor of the influential St. Mary Woolnoth Church in London. Among his converts there was Claudius Buchanan, who became a missionary to the East Indies, and Thomas Scott, the Bible commentator. By this time Newton had also established a strong relationship with William Wilberforce and other political leaders engaged in the crusade for the abolition of the slave trade. It is interesting to note that the year of Newton's death, 1807, was the same year that the British Parliament finally abolished slavery throughout all of its domain.

In 1790 Newton's wife, beloved companion for forty years, died of cancer. Mary had been a wife of true devotion and encouragement, but now John faced the next seventeen long years without her. In 1893 John and Mary's remains were re-interred in the Olney Church graveyard, where the massive granite monument can still be viewed.

Until the time of his death at the age of eighty-two, John Newton never ceased to marvel at God's mercy and grace that had so dramatically changed his life. This was the dominant theme of his preaching and writing. Shortly before his death a spokesman for the church suggested that he consider retirement because of failing health, eyesight and memory. Newton replied, "What, shall the old Africa blasphemer stop while he can still speak?" On another occasion before his death he is quoted as proclaiming with a loud voice during a message, "My memory is nearly gone, but I remember two things: 'That I am a great sinner and that Christ is a great Savior!'"

Undoubtedly, the most representative expression of John Newton's life is his appealing hymn, "Amazing Grace." The hymn, originally consisting of six stanzas and entitled "Faith's Review and Expectation," was

64

based on 1 Chronicles 17:16, 17. Three interesting additional verses written by Newton that are not included in most hymnals are as follows:

1. The Lord has promised good to me, His Word my hope secures;
   He will my shield and portion be as long as life endures.
2. Yes, when this heart and flesh shall fail, and mortal life shall cease,
   I shall possess within the veil, a life of joy and peace.
3. The earth shall soon dissolve like snow, the sun forbear to shine;
   But God, who called me here below, will be forever mine.

The tune, "Amazing Grace," is an early American folk melody. It was first known as a plantation melody entitled "Loving Lambs." The earliest known publication of this tune was found in a book entitled *The Virginia Harmony,* compiled by James P. Carrell and David S. Clayton and published in 1831 in Winchester, Virginia. Scarcely a hymnal appeared throughout the South during the remainder of the nineteenth century that did not include this hymn (see page 37).

65

The author at Newton's tombstone

7

Angels, from the Realms of Glory

REGENT SQUARE

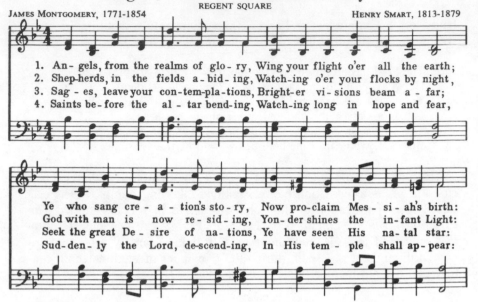

JAMES MONTGOMERY, 1771-1854

HENRY SMART, 1813-1879

1. An- gels, from the realms of glo- ry, Wing your flight o'er all the earth;
2. Shep-herds, in the fields a-bid-ing, Watch-ing o'er your flocks by night,
3. Sag- es, leave your con-tem-pla-tions, Bright-er vi-sions beam a- far;
4. Saints be-fore the al- tar bend-ing, Watch-ing long in hope and fear,

Ye who sang cre- a- tion's sto-ry, Now pro-claim Mes- si- ah's birth:
God with man is now re- sid-ing, Yon- der shines the in-fant Light:
Seek the great De- sire of na-tions, Ye have seen His na- tal star:
Sud-den- ly the Lord, de-scend-ing, In His tem- ple shall ap-pear:

Author–James Montgomery, 1771–1854
Composer–Henry Smart, 1813–1879
Tune Name–"Regent Square"
Meter–87.87.87

66

And, lo, the angel of the Lord came upon them, and the glory of the Lord shone round
about them: and they were sore afraid.   Luke 2:9

When one recalls important contributors to the development of English
hymnody, the names of Isaac Watts, generally titled the father of English
hymnody, and Charles Wesley, provider of approximately 6,500 hymn
texts, are usually acclaimed the most important. Next to these two
spiritual leaders, however, it is commonly agreed by students of hymnology that no writer has made a greater contribution to English hymnody
than has James Montgomery. A foremost authority in hymnology, John
Julian, has written,

Montgomery's devotional spirit was of the noblest type. With the faith
of a strong man he united the beauty and simplicity of a child. Richly
poetic without exuberance, dogmatic without uncharitableness, tender
without sentimentality, elaborate without diffusiveness, richly musical
without apparent effort, he has bequeathed to the church wealth which
could only come from true genius and a sanctified heart.

James Montgomery was born at Irvine, Ayrshire, Scotland, on
November 4, 1771. His parents were Moravian missionaries to the West

Indies. While attending a Moravian seminary in England, young James received word of the sudden death of both of his parents on the mission field. James left the seminary suddenly and, for a period, lived a life of aimless discouragement. Soon he became interested in newspaper work and writing. At the age of twenty-three he was appointed editor of the weekly *Sheffield Register* in London, maintaining this position for the next thirty-one years. As editor of this paper Montgomery championed many different causes, such as the abolition of slavery. He was ever ready to assist the poor and defend the rights of the down-trodden. Twice he was imprisoned for writing on controversial issues. In 1797 he published a volume of poems called *Prison Amusements,* so named from the fact that many of these works had been written in prison. In 1825 he gave up his paper to devote himself solely to literary and philanthropic pursuits, including the promotion of foreign missions, a cause always dear to his heart. By 1833 his integrity and worth were widely recognized throughout his homeland, and he was awarded an annual pension of $1,000 by the British government as a reward for his many contributions to English society.

"Angels, From the Realms of Glory" first appeared as a poem in Montgomery's newspaper on December 24, 1816. Later it was published in a hymnal entitled *Montgomery's Original Hymns* and was known as "Good Tidings of Great Joy to All People." Many students of hymnody have acclaimed this as one of our finest Advent hymns; for example, one writer claims that "for comprehensiveness, appropriateness of expression, force and elevation of sentiment, it may challenge comparison with any hymn that was ever written in any language or country" (*English Hymns–Their Authors and History* by Samuel Duffield). In all Montgomery wrote approximately 400 hymns.

67

The composer of this tune, known as "Regent Square," was Henry Smart, born on October 26, 1813, in London, England. Although largely self-taught, Smart was recognized as one of the finest organists and composers in the British Isles in his day. He was totally blind for the last fifteen years of his life, yet he continued to play and write some of his finest music. "Regent Square" was written during this period of blindness. The tune was composed especially for a hymnal being compiled by Dr. Hamilton, pastor of London's Regent Square Presbyterian Church, known as the "Cathedral of Presbyterianism" in London. Smart dedicated his new tune to this church. Smart's advice in new organ installations was also frequently sought in both England and Scotland. He designed and built some of England's finest organs. Henry Smart also served as music editor for such hymnal publications as *Psalms and Hymns for Divine Worship,* 1867, *The Presbyterian Hymnal,* 1875, and the *Hymnal of the United Presbyterian Church of Scotland.* Smart is also the composer of the "Lancashire" tune, used for the hymn text, "Lead On, O King Eternal" (No. 54).

8

Battle Hymn of the Republic

JULIA WARD HOWE, 1819-1910

American melody, c. 1852

1. Mine eyes have seen the glo-ry of the com-ing of the Lord, He is
2. I have seen Him in the watch-fires of a hun-dred cir-cling camps, They have
3. He has sound-ed forth the trum-pet that shall nev-er sound re-treat, He is
4. In the beau-ty of the lil-ies Christ was born a-cross the sea, With a

tram-pling out the vin-tage where the grapes of wrath are stored; He hath loosed the
build-ed Him an al-tar in the eve-ning dews and damps; I can read His
sift-ing out the hearts of men be-fore His judg-ment seat; O be swift, my
glo-ry in His bos-om that trans-fig-ures you and me; As He died to

68

fate-ful light-ning of His ter-ri-ble swift sword—His truth is march-ing on.
right-eous sen-tence by the dim and flar-ing lamps—His day is march-ing on.
soul, to an-swer Him! be ju-bi-lant, my feet!— Our God is march-ing on.
make men ho-ly, let us die to make men free, While God is march-ing on.

REFRAIN

Glo-ry! glo-ry, hal-le-lu-jah! Glo-ry! glo-ry, hal-le-lu-jah!

Glo-ry! glo-ry, hal-le-lu-jah! His truth is march-ing on.

Battle Hymn of the Republic

Author–Julia Ward Howe, 1819–1910
Music–American melody, c. 1852
Meter–Irregular

> Some trust in chariots, and some in horses: but we will remember the name of the Lord
> our God.   Psalm 20:7

Music always had a unique way of stirring strong feelings of patriotism. Of our several fine national hymns, this particular hymn has been unrivaled for inspiring these noble responses.

The words for this hymn first appeared in the February, 1862, issue of *The Atlantic Monthly* magazine and were published as the Civil War battle song of the Republic. The author, Julia Ward Howe, received the grand total of five dollars for her literary efforts. Mrs. Howe and her doctor husband had recently moved from Boston to Washington, D.C., where he was involved in medical service for the government. Julia became deeply anguished as she noted the growing angry mood of the nation and its frenzied preparations for the tragic war between the northern and southern states. Day after day Mrs. Howe watched the troops go by as they marched off to war and heard them singing the strains of "John Brown's Body"–named for a self-styled abolitionist who was hanged for his efforts to have the slaves freed.

One day, while witnessing a parade of soldiers singing this catchy tune, a visiting friend and her former pastor, the Rev. James Freeman Clarke of Boston, turned to Mrs. Howe and said, "Why don't you write some decent words for that tune?" "I will," answered Mrs. Howe, and the words came to her that same evening. She has left the following account:

> I awoke in the grey of the morning, and as I lay waiting for dawn, the long lines of the desired poem began to entwine themselves in my mind, and I said to myself, "I must get up and write these verses, lest I fall asleep and forget them!" So I sprang out of bed and in the dimness found an old stump of a pen, which I remembered using the day before. I scrawled the verses almost without looking at the paper.

Soon the entire nation was united in singing, "Mine eyes have seen the glory of the coming of the Lord. . ." rather than the many derisive phrases coined about "John Brown's Body." Julia Ward Howe's text, written in response to a challenge to make better words for an existing Southern American camp meeting tune, was destined for immortality.

Julia Ward Howe was born on May 27, 1819, in New York City, into a wealthy family that had a distinguished lineage on both sides. Her ances-

69

tors were famous leaders in Revolutionary history. She was raised in a conservative, Episcopalian home, with a father who was an ardent Calvinist in his beliefs. Julia rebelled against these doctrines, however, and increasingly became very liberal in her religious convictions. In 1848 she married the well-known humanitarian, Dr. Samuel Gridley Howe, who was twenty years her senior. In his younger days he had fought in the Greek War of Independence and had written the book, *Historical Sketches of the Greek Revolution*. Later he served as the director of the Perkins Institute for the Blind in Boston, Massachusetts. After marriage Mrs. Howe became even more involved in her humanitarian pursuits. She was especially vehement in her opposition to slavery. She joined the Radical Club, studied modern philosophies and became a member of the Unitarian Church, often filling the pulpits for these churches. She stated her religious convictions vigorously, "Nothing of what I have heard or read has shaken my faith in the leadership of Christ in a religion which makes each man the brother of all, and God the beneficent Father of each and all." Even as a liberal thinker, however, she always maintained her belief in the presence of a personal God and His over-ruling power and truth in controlling the affairs of mankind. In addition to her role as a leader in the Woman's Suffrage Movement in this country, she organized in 1870 an international crusade for all women of the world to unite for the purpose of ending war for all time. In 1910, just twelve days before her death, she was awarded an honorary Doctor of Laws Degree from Smith College for her life-long accomplishments.

70

Although this Civil War hymn gave Mrs. Howe her first national acclaim, she was also known for other publications, including three volumes of poetry–*Passion Flowers*, 1854; *Words of the Hour*, 1856; and *Later Lyrics*, 1866. This remarkable woman was also the mother of four children, all of whom became eminently successful in fields of science and literature. Mrs. Howe continued her active life in causes of human betterment until her death in Newport, Rhode Island, on October 17, 1910, at the age of ninety-one.

It is recorded that this hymn was sung at a large patriotic rally attended by President Lincoln. After the singer had finished, the audience responded with tumultuous applause. The President, with tears in his eyes, cried out, "Sing it again," and it was sung again. It soon became accepted as one of our finest national hymns, finding its way into almost every American hymnal. Its original purpose of serving as a battle song for the Northern Republic during the Civil War was soon forgotten.

9   Be Still, My Soul

FINLANDIA

KATHARINA VON SCHLEGEL, 1697-?
Trans. by Jane L. Borthwick, 1813-1897

JEAN SIBELIUS, 1865-1957

1. Be still, my soul— the Lord is on thy side! Bear pa-tient-ly the
2. Be still, my soul— thy God doth un-der-take To guide the fu-ture
3. Be still, my soul— the hour is has-t'ning on When we shall be for-

cross of grief or pain; Leave to thy God to or-der and pro-vide—
as He has the past; Thy hope, thy con-fi-dence let noth-ing shake—
ev-er with the Lord, When dis-ap-point-ment, grief, and fear are gone,

In ev-'ry change He faith-ful will re-main. Be still, my soul— thy
All now mys-te-rious shall be bright at last. Be still, my soul— the
Sor-row for-got, love's pur-est joys re-stored. Be still, my soul— when

best, thy heav'n-ly Friend Thru thorn-y ways leads to a joy-ful end.
waves and winds still know His voice who ruled them while He dwelt be-low.
change and tears are past, All safe and bless-ed we shall meet at last.

71

Be Still, My Soul

Author-Katharine von Schlegel, 1697-?
English Translation-Jane L. Borthwick, 1813-1897
Music-Jean Sibelius, 1865-1957
Tune Name-"Finlandia"
Meter-10 10. 10 10. 10 10.
Scripture Reference-Psalm 46:10

In quietness and in confidence shall be your strength.   Isaiah 30:15

Spiritual revivals have always been accompanied by an outburst of song. This was especially true of the sixteenth century Reformation Movement when, following centuries of dormancy during the Middle Ages, congregational singing was rediscovered. However, by the seventeenth century the Church was once more cold and non-evangelistic. Again God lit the fires of revival in the latter half of this century with a movement known as the Pietistic revival in Germany, which was similar to the Puritan and Wesleyan movements in England.

72   The leader of this German movement was Philipp Jacob Spener, pastor of a Lutheran Church in Berlin, Germany. Although not a noted hymn writer himself, Spener's encouragement of singing gave birth to a great revival in hymnody in Germany during this time. All of the hymns coming out of this movement were characterized by genuine piety, depth of feeling, rich Christian experience, and faithfulness in Scriptural expression.

Katharina von Schlegel was the outstanding woman of this revival movement. Little is known of her other than that she was a Lutheran and may have been the canoness of an evangelical women's seminary in Germany. She, however, did contribute a number of lyrics to a collection of spiritual songs published in 1752. She wrote many additional verses for this particular hymn, but not all were translated. Most hymnals use just the three stanzas included above.

This hymn was translated into English approximately one hundred years after it was written by Jane Borthwick, who ranks second only to Catherine Winkworth for excellent translations of German hymns into English. Miss Borthwick was born in Edinburgh, Scotland, on April 9, 1813 and was a member of the Free Church of Scotland and a noble supporter of home and foreign missions.

Jean Sibelius was Finland's best-known composer. His music is generally characterized by a nationalistic fervor. This hymn tune is an arrangement of one movement of "Finlandia," a tone poem written in 1899 depicting the majestic natural beauty of the composer's native land.

10

Beneath the Cross of Jesus

ST. CHRISTOPHER

ELIZABETH C. CLEPHANE, 1830-1869   FREDERICK C. MAKER, 1844-1927

1. Be - neath the cross of Je - sus I fain would take my stand,
2. Up - on that cross of Je - sus Mine eye at times can see
3. I take, O cross, thy shad - ow For my a - bid - ing - place —

The shad - ow of a might-y Rock With - in a wea - ry land;
The ver - y dy - ing form of One Who suf - fered there for me;
I ask no oth - er sun-shine than The sun-shine of His face;

A home with-in the wil - der - ness, A rest up - on the way
And from my smit-ten heart with tears Two won-ders I con - fess —
Con - tent to let the world go by, To know no gain nor loss,

From the burn-ing of the noon-day heat And the bur-den of the day.
The won-ders of His glo-rious love And my own worth-less-ness.
My sin - ful self my on - ly shame, My glo - ry all the cross.

Beneath the Cross of Jesus

Author-Elizabeth C. Clephane, 1830-1869
Composer-Frederick C. Maker, 1844-1927
Tune Name-"St. Christopher"
Meter-76.86.86.86
Scripture Reference-Isaiah 32:2

> For the preaching of the cross is to them that perish foolishness; but unto us which are saved it is the power of God.   I Corinthians 1:18

This meaningful hymn was written by a frail Scottish, Presbyterian woman of the past century, who, despite her physical frailties, was known throughout her community for her helpful, cheery nature. Elizabeth Cecilia Douglas Clephane, one of the few women hymn writers of Scotland, was born in Edinburgh, Scotland, but grew up in Melrose, Scotland, in the lovely area of Abbotsford, near the old bridge described by the well-known Scottish writer, Sir Walter Scott, in his book, *The Abbot and the Monastery*. Her father was a county sheriff, her mother a descendant of the famous Douglas family. Elizabeth was one of three sisters, but she was known as the delicate, retiring member of the family. Yet within the limits of her strength she served the poor and sick of her community, and she and her sisters gave to charity all they did not actually require for their daily needs. Throughout the Melrose area Elizabeth was affectionately known to the townspeople as "the sunbeam." Elizabeth enjoyed writing poems and had several published in a Scottish Presbyterian Magazine entitled *The Family Treasury*. However, the majority of her writings appeared anonymously in this magazine in 1872, three years after her early death at the age of thirty-nine.

"Beneath the Cross of Jesus" was written by Miss Clephane in 1868, one year before her death. It was not published, however, until 1872, when it appeared anonymously in *The Family Treasury* with several of her other poems. The original poem consisted of five stanzas, but today only three are used in most hymnals. It is obvious that Elizabeth, like most Scottish Presbyterians of her day, was an ardent Bible student for her hymn is replete with Biblical symbolism and imagery. For example, in stanza one:

The reference to "the mighty Rock" is taken from Isaiah 32:2.
The reference to "the weary land" is taken from Psalm 63:1.
The reference to "home within the wilderness" is taken from Jeremiah 9:2.
The reference to "rest upon the way" is taken from Isaiah 28:12.
The reference to "noontide heat" is taken from Isaiah 4:6.
The reference to "burden of the day" is taken from Matthew 11:30.

74

Elizabeth Clephane is also the author of "The Ninety and Nine" (No. 91).

The tune for this text, named "St. Christopher," etymologically means "bearer of Christ." It was composed for this text by Frederick Charles Maker, one of the outstanding organists in the English, non-conformist churches of that day. Maker was born in Bristol, England, and he spent his entire active life playing in the various churches of that city. Frederick Maker contributed a number of hymn tunes to the 1881 edition of a hymnal called *The Bristol Tune Book*.

*   *   *

"Go to dark Gethsemane, Ye that feel the tempter's power;
Your Redeemer's conflict see; watch with Him one bitter hour;
Turn not from His griefs away; learn of Jesus Christ to pray.

"See Him at the judgment hall, beaten, bound, reviled, arraigned;
See Him meekly bearing all; love to man His soul sustained;
Shun not suffering, shame or loss; learn of Christ to bear the cross.

"Calvary's mournful mountain climb; there adoring at His feet,
Mark that miracle of time, God's own sacrifice complete:
"It is finished!" hear Him cry; learn of Jesus Christ to die."

Written by James Montgomery in 1822
(See No. 7)

75

11 Blessed Assurance

FANNY J. CROSBY, 1820-1915

PHOEBE P. KNAPP, 1839-1908

1. Blessed as-sur-ance, Jesus is mine! O what a fore-taste of
2. Per-fect sub-mis-sion, per-fect de-light! Vi-sions of rap-ture now
3. Per-fect sub-mis-sion—all is at rest, I in my Sav-ior am

glo-ry di-vine! Heir of sal-va-tion, pur-chase of God,
burst on my sight; An-gels de-scend-ing bring from a-bove
hap-py and blest; Watch-ing and wait-ing, look-ing a-bove,

CHORUS

Born of His Spir-it, washed in His blood.
Ech-oes of mer-cy, whis-pers of love. This is my sto-ry,
Filled with His good-ness, lost in His love.

this is my song, Prais-ing my Sav-ior all the day long; This is my

sto-ry, this is my song, Prais-ing my Sav-ior all the day long.

76

Blessed Assurance

Author-Fanny J. Crosby, 1820–1915
Composer-Phoebe P. Knapp, 1839–1908
Meter-9 10. 9 10. with Chorus

> Let us draw near with a true heart in full assurance of faith, having our hearts sprinkled from an evil conscience, and our bodies washed with pure water.   Hebrews 10:22

Gospel music as an important form of Christian hymnody had its beginning in the latter half of the nineteenth century and is associated with such well-known names as Moody, Sankey, Bliss and Frances Jane Crosby. Crosby, perhaps more than any other writer, however, truly captured the spirit of the American gospel song movement. As one author has written,

> Gospel hymnody has the distinction of being America's most typical contribution to Christian song. Gospel hymnody has been a plough digging up hardened surfaces of pavemented minds. Its very obviousness has been its strength. It is the music of the people.
> Robert M. Stevenson-*Patterns of Protestant Church Music*

77

It is estimated that Fanny Crosby wrote more than 8,000 gospel song texts in her lifetime. Her hymns have been and are still being sung more frequently than those of any other gospel hymn writer. Her many favorites have been an important part of evangelical worship for the past century.

It is truly amazing that anyone, and especially a blind person, could write on this variety of spiritual truths and experiences with such proliferation. For a considerable period during her life, while under contract to a music publisher, she wrote three new hymns each week. She used over 200 pen names besides her own. Many of her original texts are still being uncovered and no doubt will be published in the near future. Often the themes for her hymns were suggested by visiting ministers wishing to have a new song on a particular subject. At other times musician friends would first compose the music and then ask Fanny Crosby for the words.

Such was the case for the hymn, "Blessed Assurance." The music for the hymn was composed by Mrs. Joseph Knapp, an amateur musician, wife of the founder of the Metropolitan Life Insurance Company, and a close personal friend of Fanny Crosby. One day Mrs. Knapp played this melody for the blind poetess and asked, "What does this tune say?" Fanny responded immediately, "Why, that says: 'Blessed Assurance, Jesus Is Mine.'"

Mrs. Knapp published more than 500 gospel songs herself, including the popular gospel classic, "Open the Gates of the Temple."

Fanny Crosby died at the age of ninety-five. Only eternity will disclose the host of individuals who have been won to a saving faith in Jesus Christ or those whose lives have been spiritually enriched through the texts of her many hymns.

Engraved on Fanny J. Crosby's tombstone at Bridgeport, Connecticut, are these significant words taken from our Lord's remarks to Mary, the sister of Lazarus, after she had anointed Him with costly perfume,

She hath done what she could.

Other hymns by Fanny J. Crosby include "All the Way My Savior Leads Me" (No. 5), "My Savior First of All" (No. 60), and, "Rescue the Perishing" (No. 76).

* * *

78

"You may trust the Lord too little, but you can never trust Him too much."

Anonymous

"Beware of despairing about yourself: you are commanded to put your trust in God, and not in yourself."

St. Augustine

"All I have seen teaches me to trust the Creator for all I have not seen."

Ralph Waldo Emerson

"We trust as we love, and where we love—If we love Christ much, surely we shall trust Him much."

Thomas Benton Brooks

12 Blest Be the Tie That Binds

DENNIS

JOHN FAWCETT, 1740-1817   HANS G. NAEGELI, 1773-1836

1. Blest be the tie that binds Our hearts in Chris-tian love! The
2. Be - fore our Fa-ther's throne We pour our ar - dent prayers; Our
3. We share our mu - tual woes, Our mu - tual bur - dens bear; And
4. When we a - sun - der part It gives us in - ward pain; But

fel - low-ship of kin - dred minds Is like to that a - bove.
fears, our hopes, our aims are one, Our com-forts and our cares.
oft - en for each oth - er flows The sym - pa-thiz - ing tear.
we shall still be joined in heart, And hope to meet a - gain.

Author-John Fawcett, 1740–1817   79
Composer-Hans G. Naegeli, 1773–1836
Tune Name-"Dennis"
Meter-SM (66.86)

> He that loveth his brother abideth in the light, and there is none occasion of stumbling in him.   I John 2:10

John Fawcett was born of poor parents in Lidget Green, Yorkshire, England, in 1740. He was converted to Christ at the age of sixteen through the ministry of George Whitefield. At the age of twenty-six he was ordained as a Baptist minister. He accepted a call to pastor a small and impoverished congregation at Wainsgate in Northern England. After spending several years at Wainsgate where his salary was meager and his family growing, he received a call to the large and influential Carter's Lane Baptist Church in London to succeed the well-known Dr. Gill.

As the day for the scheduled departure from Wainsgate arrived, with the saddened parishioners gathered around the wagons, Mrs. Fawcett finally broke down and said, "John, I cannot bear to leave. I know not how to go!" "Nor can I either," said the saddened pastor. The order was soon given to unpack the wagons.

During one of his ensuing sermons Fawcett shared this hymn text with his congregation. The poem was first printed in 1782 under the title "Brotherly Love," in a collection containing 166 of Fawcett's poems.

Fawcett continued his faithful ministry to these humble people at Wainsgate for more than fifty years at a salary estimated at never more than $200.00 a year. Soon he became well-known as an outstanding preacher and scholar. In 1777 he opened a school for young preachers. In 1793 he was invited to become principal of the Baptist Academy at Bristol, England, but he declined the offer. He wrote a number of books on various aspects of practical Christianity, some of which had a very large circulation. In recognition of his ministry and accomplishments, Brown University in the United States conferred the Doctor of Divinity Degree upon him in 1811. Yet he remained with his beloved parishioners at Wainsgate until a paralytic stroke caused his death on July 25, 1817. John Fawcett's life can certainly be cited as an example of a spiritual leader who sacrificed ambition and personal gain for Christian devotion.

The composer of the music, Hans G. Naegeli, was born on May 26, 1773, near Zurich, Switzerland. He was a music publisher and president of the Swiss Association for the Cultivation of Music. He was known as a pioneer in the field of music education. His progressive teaching methods had much influence on Lowell Mason, often called the father of public school and church music in the United States. The tune, "Dennis," originated in Switzerland and was later purchased by Lowell Mason while he was travelling and studying in Europe in 1837. The music first appeared in *The Psaltery,* edited in 1845 by Mason and George J. Webb, with the notation, "arranged from H. G. Naegeli" (see page 39).

80

The author at the Wainsgate Baptist Church

13   # Christ the Lord Is Risen Today

EASTER HYMN

CHARLES WESLEY, 1707-1788   From *Lyra Davidica,* 1708

1. Christ the Lord is ris'n to - day,   Al - le - lu - ia!
2. Lives a - gain our glo - rious King,   Al - le - lu - ia!
3. Love's re - deem - ing work is done,   Al - le - lu - ia!
4. Soar we now where Christ has led,   Al - le - lu - ia!

Sons of men and an - gels say: Al - le - lu - ia!
Where, O death, is now thy sting?   Al - le - lu - ia!
Fought the fight, the bat - tle won,   Al - le - lu - ia!
Fol - l'wing our ex - alt - ed Head,   Al - le - lu - ia!

Raise your joys and tri - umphs high,   Al - le - lu - ia!
Dy - ing once He all doth save,   Al - le - lu - ia!
Death in vain for - bids Him rise,   Al - le - lu - ia!
Made like Him, like Him we rise,   Al - le - lu - ia!

Sing, ye heav'ns, and earth re - ply: Al - le - lu - ia!
Where thy vic - to - ry, O grave?   Al - le - lu - ia!
Christ has o - pened Par - a - dise,   Al - le - lu - ia!
Ours the cross, the grave, the skies,   Al - le - lu - ia!

Christ the Lord Is Risen Today

Author–Charles Wesley, 1707–1788
Music–From *Lyra Davidica,* 1708
Tune Name–"Easter Hymn"
Meter–77.77 with Alleluias

> He is not here: For He is risen, as He said. Come, see the place where the Lord lay.
>   Matthew 28:6

The first Wesleyan Chapel in London, England, was a deserted iron foundry. It became known as the Foundry Meeting House. This hymn was written by Charles Wesley for the first service in this chapel in 1739, just one year after Charles's dramatic Aldersgate conversion experience. The hymn was first published in the *Foundry's Collection*–which contained "hymns set to music as they are commonly sung at the Foundry." The book had approximately fifty hymns with an additional Psalm Supplement. This hymn was originally entitled "Hymn for Easter Day" and consisted of eleven four-line stanzas.

The popularity of this hymn is due in part to the fine tune with which it has been wedded for many years. The composer of the music has never been identified. The tune first appeared anonymously in the *Lyra Davidica* hymnal, published in London in 1708. The joyous "alleluia" at the end of each line was not written by Wesley but was added by some editor to make the text fit the tune. "Hallelujah" or "alleluia" is from the ancient Hebrew worship service and was a common expression of praise in the early Christian Church. Jerome, an important leader of the early church who translated the Bible into the Latin language and died c. 420 A.D., wrote that in his day the very ceilings of houses of worship were often shaken with the reverberating "Hallelujahs" when believers sang their praises to God.

Charles Wesley is also the author of "Jesus, Lover of My Soul" (No. 45) and "O For a Thousand Tongues" (No. 65).

14

Come, Thou Almighty King

ITALIAN HYMN

Source unknown, c. 1757

FELICE DE GIARDINI, 1716-1796

1. Come, Thou Al - might - y King, Help us Thy name to sing,
2. Come, Thou In - car - nate Word, Gird on Thy might - y sword,
3. Come, Ho - ly Com - fort - er, Thy sa - cred wit - ness bear
4. To the great One in Three E - ter - nal prais - es be,

Help us to praise: Fa - ther, all - glo - ri - ous, O'er all vic -
Our prayer at - tend: Come and Thy peo - ple bless, And give Thy
In this glad hour: Thou who al - might - y art, Now rule in
Hence ev - er - more: His sov - 'reign maj - es - ty May we in

to - ri - ous, Come and reign o - ver us, An - cient of Days.
word suc-cess— Spir - it of ho - li - ness, On us de - scend.
ev - 'ry heart, And ne'er from us de - part, Spir - it of pow'r.
glo - ry see, And to e - ter - ni - ty Love and a - dore.

83

Author-Source unknown, c. 1757
Composer-Felice de Giardini, 1716-1796
Tune Name-"Italian Hymn"
Meter-664.6664

Lift up your heads, O ye gates; even lift them up, ye everlasting doors; and the King of glory shall come in. Who is this King of glory? The Lord of Hosts, He is the King of Glory.   Psalm 24:9,10

This is one of our most popular "opening" hymns, yet little is known of its background. It appeared anonymously in London, England, about 1757 to commemorate Trinity Sunday. About fifteen years earlier the British national hymn, "God Save Our Gracious King," first came into general use. Both of these hymn texts were sung to the same tune for a period of time. Today, however, that tune, "America," is used exclusively in this country for our national hymn, "My Country, 'Tis of Thee" (No. 58). The "Italian Hymn" tune has been wedded permanently with "Come, Thou Almighty King." It has been suggested that the newer text was written as an act of rebellion and as a substitute for the words of the royal hymn, and that for this reason the author wished to remain anonymous. Other writers have felt that this text was written as a sequel to the earlier text, with one a prayer for an earthly ruler, the other a prayer to a heavenly King.

"Come, Thou Almighty King" has often been attributed to Charles Wesley since it first appeared in 1757 in a pamphlet, published by John Wesley, which also contained an original hymn text by Charles Wesley. However, many students of hymnology argue that this could not be a Wesleyan text since the Wesleys were never known to use an odd meter for their texts–which this hymn has.

An interesting account is told of this hymn's use during the time of the Revolutionary War. A group of British troops invaded an American church service one Sunday morning and demanded that the congregation sing "God Save our Gracious King." The people responded with the requested tune but sang "Come, Thou Almighty King" instead.

84

This is a hymn that must always be sung with all four stanzas. To omit any of the first three verses would be to slight one of the members of the Godhead. The fourth stanza is a grand affirmation of the mysterious doctrine of the Trinity, that God is One yet Three. The late A. W. Tozer, in his book, *The Knowledge of the Holy* (Harper and Row, 1961), has left these choice words,

> The doctrine of the Trinity . . . is truth for the heart. The fact that it cannot be satisfactorily explained, instead of being against it, is in its favor. Such a truth had to be revealed; no one could have imagined it.

The tune, "Italian Hymn," was composed especially for this anonymous text by Felice de Giardini in 1769. This Italian composer was born in Turin, Italy, on April 12, 1716. He moved to London, England, where he became a popular violinist in London operatic circles. Later he spent time in Moscow, Russia, as an operatic conductor and died there in 1796.

15 Come, Thou Fount

NETTLETON

ROBERT ROBINSON, 1735-1790

JOHN WYETH, 1770-1858
Arr. by Norman Johnson, 1928-

1. Come, Thou Fount of ev-'ry bless-ing, Tune my heart to sing Thy grace;
2. Here I raise mine Eb-en - e - zer— Hith-er by Thy help I'm come;
3. O to grace how great a debt-or Dai - ly I'm con-strained to be!

Streams of mer - cy, nev-er ceas-ing, Call for songs of loud-est praise.
And I hope by Thy good pleas-ure Safe-ly to ar rive at home.
Let Thy good-ness like a fet-ter Bind my wan-d'ring heart to Thee:

Teach me some me - lo-dious son - net Sung by flam-ing tongues a - bove;
Je - sus sought me when a strang-er Wan - d'ring from the fold of God;
Prone to wan - der—Lord, I feel it— Prone to leave the God I love;

Praise the mount—I'm fixed up - on it— Mount of Thy re-deem-ing love.
He to res - cue me from dan-ger In - ter-posed His pre-cious blood.
Here's my heart— O take and seal it, Seal it for Thy courts a - bove.

85

Come, Thou Fount

Author-Robert Robinson, 1735-1790
Composer-John Wyeth, 1770-1858
Tune Name-"Nettleton"
Meter-87.87 Doubled
Scripture Reference-I Samuel 7:12

> O Lord, Thou art my God: I will exalt Thee, I will praise Thy name; for Thou hast done wonderful things; Thy counsels of old are faithfulness and truth.   Isaiah 25:1

Robert Robinson was born of lowly parents in Swaffham, Norfolk, England, on September 27, 1735. His father died when Robert was eight, and at the age of fourteen he was sent by his mother to London to learn the barbering trade. Here for the next few years he was associated with a notorious gang of hoodlums and lived a debauched life. At the age of seventeen he attended a meeting where George Whitefield was preaching. Robinson and his friends went for the purpose of "scoffing at the poor, deluded Methodists." However, Whitefield's strong evangelistic preaching so impressed young Robinson that he was converted to Christ. Several years later he felt called to preach and entered the ministry of the Methodist Church. Subsequently, he left the Methodist Church when he moved to Cambridge and became a Baptist pastor. Here he became known as an able theologian through his writing of many theological works as well as several hymns.

This hymn text, written when Robinson was only twenty-three years of age, contains an interesting expression in the second stanza, "Here I raise mine Ebenezer-Hither by Thy help I'm come." This language is taken from I Samuel 7:12, where the Ebenezer is a symbol of God's faithfulness. An expression in the third verse, "Prone to wander-Lord, I feel it-Prone to leave the God I love," seems to have been prophetic of Robinson's later years, as once again his life became characterized by lapses into sin, unstableness, and an involvement with the doctrines of Unitarianism.

The story is told that Robinson was one day riding a stagecoach when he noticed a woman deeply engrossed with a hymn book. During an ensuing conversation the lady turned to Robinson and asked what he thought of the hymn she was humming. Robinson burst into tears and said, "Madam, I am the poor unhappy man who wrote that hymn many years ago, and I would give a thousand worlds, if I had them, to enjoy the feelings I had then."

The tune, "Nettleton," was named for the Rev. Asahel Nettleton, noted American evangelist of the early eighteenth century. Its composer,

86

John Wyeth, born in Cambridge, Massachusetts, March 31, 1770, was a printer and lay musician. This hymn first appeared in his hymnal, *Wyeth's Repository of Sacred Songs,* published in 1813.

This hymn can be used effectively with other tunes of the same 87.87 Doubled Meter.

Robert Robinson

87

16   Count Your Blessings

JOHNSON OATMAN, JR., 1856-1922   EDWIN O. EXCELL, 1851-1921

1. When up-on life's bil-lows you are tem-pest-tossed, When you are dis-
2. Are you ev-er bur-dened with a load of care? Does the cross seem
3. When you look at oth-ers with their lands and gold, Think that Christ has
4. So a-mid the con-flict, wheth-er great or small, Do not be dis-

cour-aged, think-ing all is lost, Count your man-y bless-ings—name them
heav-y you are called to bear? Count your man-y bless-ings— ev-'ry
prom-ised you His wealth un-told; Count your man-y bless-ings— mon-ey
cour-aged—God is o-ver all; Count your man-y bless-ings— an-gels

one by one, And it will sur-prise you what the Lord hath done.
doubt will fly, And you will be sing-ing as the days go by.
can-not buy Your re-ward in heav-en nor your home on high.
will at-tend, Help and com-fort give you to your jour-ney's end.

CHORUS

Count your bless-ings—name them one by one; Count your
Count your man-y bless-ings— name them one by one; Count your man-y

bless-ings— see what God hath done; Count your bless-ings—
bless-ings— see what God hath done; Count your man-y bless-ings—

name them one by one; Count your man-y bless-ings—see what God hath done.

88

Count Your Blessings

Author-Johnson Oatman, Jr., 1856-1922
Composer-Edwin O. Excell, 1851-1921
Meter-11 11. 11 11. with Chorus

> Blessed be the God and Father of our Lord Jesus Christ, who hath blessed us with all spiritual blessings in heavenly places in Christ.   Ephesians 1:3

This hymn certainly ranks as one of the most familiar numbers in our hymnals. It is one of the songs that many of us first sang with gusto during our early Sunday School days, yet one that we still enjoy singing in our gospel type of services.

Rev. Johnson Oatman, Jr., was one of the important and prolific gospel song writers of the late nineteenth and early twentieth centuries. He was born near Medford, New Jersey, on April 21, 1856. As a child he became acquainted with the hymns of the church through the singing talents of his father.

At the age of nineteen Oatman joined the Methodist Church and several years later was granted a license to preach in local Methodist congregations. Though he wrote over 5,000 hymn texts, Oatman was busily engaged throughout his life in a mercantile business and later as an administrator for a large insurance company in New Jersey.

"Count Your Blessings" is generally considered to be Oatman's finest hymn. It first appeared in *Songs for Young People,* compiled and published by Edwin O. Excell in 1897. It has been sung all over the world. One writer has stated, "Like a beam of sunlight it has brightened up the dark places of the earth."

Perhaps no American hymn was ever received with such enthusiasm in Great Britain as this hymn. *The London Daily,* in giving an account of a meeting presided over by Gypsy Smith, reported, "Mr. Smith announced the hymn 'Count Your Blessings.' Said he, 'In South London the men sing it, the boys whistle it, and the women rock their babies to sleep on this hymn.'" During the great revival in Wales it was one of the hymns sung at every service along with such Welsh favorites as "Guide Me, O Thou Great Jehovah" (No. 26) and "O That Will be Glory" (No. 70).

The composer of the music, E. O. Excell, is a well-known name in early gospel hymnody. He was born in Stark County, Ohio, on December 13, 1851. At the age of twenty he became a singing teacher, traveling around the country establishing singing schools. For twenty years he was associated with Sam Jones, a well-known Southern revivalist. Excell was recognized as one of the finest song leaders of his day. In addition to

89

writing and composing more than 2,000 gospel songs as well as publishing about fifty songbooks, he administered a successful music publishing business in Chicago. While assisting Gypsy Smith in an evangelistic campaign in Louisville, Kentucky, in 1921, he was suddenly stricken at the age of seventy and taken home to join the immortal heavenly chorus.

17 Day by Day

LINA SANDELL BERG, 1832-1903
Trans. by Andrew L. Skoog, 1856-1934

OSCAR AHNFELT, 1813-1882

1. Day by day and with each pass-ing mo-ment, Strength I find to
2. Ev - 'ry day the Lord Him-self is near me With a spe - cial
3. Help me then in ev - 'ry trib - u - la - tion So to trust Thy

meet my tri - als here; Trust-ing in my Fa-ther's wise be - stow-ment,
mer - cy for each hour; All my cares He fain would bear, and cheer me,
prom - is - es, O Lord, That I lose not faith's sweet con-so - la - tion

I've no cause for wor - ry or for fear. He whose heart is kind be -
He whose name is Coun-sel-lor and Pow'r. The pro - tec - tion of His
Of - fered me with-in Thy ho - ly word. Help me, Lord, when toil and

yond all meas-ure Gives un - to each day what He deems best— Lov - ing -
child and treas-ure Is a charge that on Him-self He laid; "As thy
trou - ble meet-ing, E'er to take, as from a fa - ther's hand, One by

ly, its part of pain and pleas-ure, Min-gling toil with peace and rest.
days, thy strength shall be in meas - ure," This the pledge to me He made.
one, the days, the mo-ments fleet-ing, Till I reach the prom-ised land.

91

SINGING WITH UNDERSTANDING

Day by Day

Author-Lina Sandell Berg, 1832–1903
English Translation-Andrew L. Skoog, 1856–1934
Music-Oscar Ahnfelt, 1813–1882
Meter-10 9. 10 9. 10 9. 10 7.

> Be not afraid, neither be thou dismayed: For the Lord Thy God is with thee whither-
> soever thou goest.   Joshua 1:9

The waves of revival that swept the Scandinavian countries during the latter half of the nineteenth century were greatly influenced by the wealth of fine hymns which flowed from the pen of Lina Sandell, born on October 3, 1832 at Fröderyd, Sweden. She was a daughter of the pastor of the parish church of that community. Being a frail youngster, she usually preferred to spend her time in her father's study rather than to join her comrades in play. When she was twenty-six years of age, she accompanied her father on a journey to Gothenburg, but tragedy occurred before the destination was reached. The ship gave a sudden lurch and Lina's father fell overboard and drowned before the eyes of his devoted daughter.

Although she had written hymns prior to this tragic experience, more songs began to flow out of her broken heart which reflect a simple, child-like trust in Christ and a deep sense of His abiding presence in her life.

The remarkable popularity attained by her hymns has been due, to a large extent, to the simple but melodious music written for them by such musicians as Oscar Ahnfelt. He was known as a "spiritual troubadour" in his day. Not only did he possess the gift of writing pleasing melodies that caught the fancy of the Swedish people, but he also traveled from place to place throughout the Scandinavian countries singing these folk-like songs to the accompaniment of his home-made ten-string guitar. Miss Sandell once said, "Ahnfelt has sung my songs into the hearts of the people."

Not only Ahnfelt, but also Jenny Lind, affectionately known as the "Swedish Nightingale," used her sweet voice in the singing of these heart-warming hymns. Though she was internationally known for her formal concertizing, it is said that she would sit with the common workmen at their crude benches and sing these simple hymns about the Savior she loved and served.

It is often true that whenever revival fires begin to glow, there is Satanic opposition. The account is given that at one time King Karl XV was petitioned to forbid Ahnfelt's preaching and singing throughout Scandinavia. The king called for Ahnfelt to appear before him. Being considerably perturbed as to what he should sing to his monarch, Ahnfelt requested Lina Sandell to write a special hymn. She was equal to the occasion, and within a few days the song was ready. With his guitar under his arm and the new hymn in his pocket, Ahnfelt appeared at the palace and sang these words:

Who is it that knocketh upon your heart's door in peaceful eve?
Who is it that brings to the wounded and sore the balm that can heal and relieve?
Your heart is still restless, it findeth no peace in earth's pleasures;
Your soul is still yearning, it seeketh release to rise to the heavenly treasures.

The king listened with moist eyes. When Ahnfelt had finished, King Karl gripped him by the hand and exclaimed, "You may sing as much as you desire in both of my kingdoms."

The name of Andrew L. Skoog, the translator of this hymn, was well-known to the immigrant Swedish community in midwestern America in the late nineteenth and early twentieth centuries. He was born in Sweden and moved to St. Paul, Minnesota, at the age of twelve. He had only a sixth grade education, yet he edited seven hymnals, numerous works of the masters, and wrote a textbook on theory. For the last fifty years of his life he was active in the religious life of the Minneapolis-St. Paul area where he was associated with the illustrious Pastor E. August Skogsberg. The two men were frequently described as the Swedish counterpart of the Moody and Sankey team.

Lina Sandell was married to a Stockholm merchant, C. O. Berg, in 1867, but she continued to sign her hymns with the initials "L. S." by which she was affectionately known throughout Sweden. She has often been called the "Fanny Crosby of Sweden" for her many fine contributions to gospel hymnody.

93

18 Day Is Dying in the West

CHAUTAUQUA

MARY A. LATHBURY, 1841-1913

WILLIAM F. SHERWIN, 1826-1888

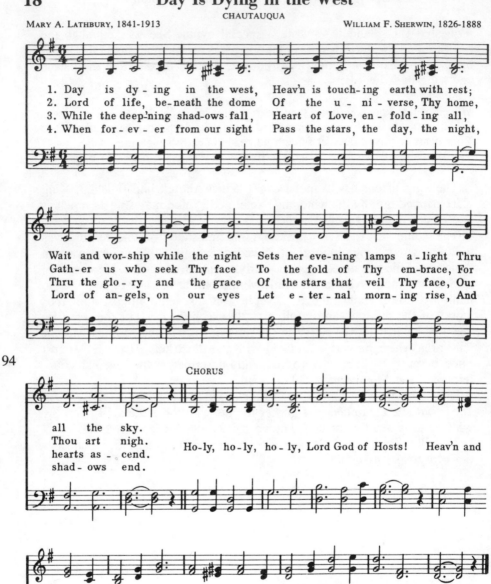

1. Day is dy-ing in the west, Heav'n is touch-ing earth with rest;
2. Lord of life, be-neath the dome Of the u-ni-verse, Thy home,
3. While the deep'-ning shad-ows fall, Heart of Love, en-fold-ing all,
4. When for-ev-er from our sight Pass the stars, the day, the night,

Wait and wor-ship while the night Sets her eve-ning lamps a-light Thru
Gath-er us who seek Thy face To the fold of Thy em-brace, For
Thru the glo-ry and the grace Of the stars that veil Thy face, Our
Lord of an-gels, on our eyes Let e-ter-nal morn-ing rise, And

94

CHORUS

all the sky.
Thou art nigh. Ho-ly, ho-ly, ho-ly, Lord God of Hosts! Heav'n and
hearts as-cend.
shad-ows end.

earth are full of Thee! Heav'n and earth are prais-ing Thee, O Lord most high!

Day is Dying in the West

Author-Mary A. Lathbury, 1841–1913
Composer-William F. Sherwin, 1826–1888
Tune Name-"Chautauqua"
Meter-77.774 with Chorus

> Ye shall have a song, as in the night when a holy solemnity is kept; and gladness of heart, as when one goeth with a pipe to come into the mountain of the Lord, to the mighty One of Israel.   Isaiah 30:29

The Chautauqua Movement was an important religious and cultural force in our country during the later nineteenth and early twentieth centuries. The headquarters and conference grounds for this movement are located on beautiful Lake Chautauqua near Jamestown, New York, often described as one of the most picturesque spots in the world. The purposes of this movement were to give religious education and to provide cultural development to the American people. When the conference was at its height, many thousands of people gathered each summer to hear the finest speakers and artists available. The Movement also sponsored lectures and concerts all throughout our country. Though not as influential as in former days, this movement is still very much operative at its lovely New York site.

95

Mary Artemisia Lathbury was born into a prominent Methodist family in Manchester, New York, on August 10, 1841; her father and two brothers were all ordained ministers. She became an artist by profession and for a period of time taught art in the schools of Vermont and New York. Increasingly, however, her life became more involved with religious work and in writing. Eventually, she served as the general editor of the Methodist Sunday School materials. In relating the story of her call into full-time Christian service, Miss Lathbury recalled that one day a voice from God seemed to say to her, "Remember, my child, that you have a gift of weaving fancies into verse and a gift with the pencil of producing visions that come to your heart; consecrate these to Me as thoroughly as you do your inmost spirit."

Along with Methodist Bishop John H. Vincent, Miss Lathbury is credited with being one of the founders of the Chautauqua Movement. She became affectionately known as the "Poet Laureate and Saint of Chautauqua." During the summer meetings of 1877 the leaders felt the need for an appropriate evening vesper hymn of their own. Miss Lathbury was asked by Dr. Vincent to write such a hymn text. The inspiration is said to have come to her as she was watching the setting sun on the lake with all of its magnificent colors. The final two stanzas were not added until two years later at the suggestion of her friends for a more complete text. The tune for these words was also supplied in the summer of 1877 by Professor William Fisk Sherwin, the music director of Chautauqua. Sherwin was well-known for his ability to organize and direct amateur choirs and for his skillful congregational leading, which produced beautiful sounds from large and enthusiastic audiences.

George C. Stebbins, noted gospel musician of that era, described the occasion of the first use of this hymn:

> On Saturday evening, in August, about 2,000 people gathered on the shores of Lake Chautauqua. On the water near the shore was a boat in which were the Professor and I. About this central boat were thirty other little boats filled with men, women and children. It was a beautiful scene and a very impressive sight as we sang this lovely hymn together.

"Day is Dying in the West" has been used as the Vesper Hymn for all evening services at Chautauqua ever since it was first written. It has been described by some students of hymnology as "one of the finest and most distinctive hymns of modern times." The poetic language of the verses, "Heaven is touching earth with rest," ". . . night sets her evening lamps alight"–combined with the worshipful and majestic expressiveness of the chorus make this an excellent hymn for both choir and congregational use.

96

*   *   *

"A thing of beauty is a joy forever."

John Keats

"Music, the greatest good that mortals know,
And all of heaven we have below."

John Milton

19

Deeper and Deeper

OSWALD J. SMITH, 1890-

OSWALD J. SMITH, 1890-

1. In-to the heart of Je-sus Deep-er and deep-er I go,
2. In-to the will of Je-sus Deep-er and deep-er I go,
3. In-to the cross of Je-sus Deep-er and deep-er I go,
4. In-to the joy of Je-sus Deep-er and deep-er I go,
5. In-to the love of Je-sus Deep-er and deep-er I go,

Seek-ing to know the rea-son Why He should love me so—
Pray-ing for grace to fol-low, Seek-ing His way to know;
Fol-low-ing thru the gar-den, Fac-ing the dread-ed foe;
Ris-ing, with soul en-rap-tured, Far from the world be-low;
Prais-ing the One who brought me Out of my sin and woe;

97

Why He should stoop to lift me Up from the mir-y clay,
Bow-ing in full sur-ren-der Low at His bless-ed feet,
Drink-ing the cup of sor-row— Sob-bing with bro-ken heart,
Joy in the place of sor-row, Peace in the midst of pain,
And thru e-ter-nal a-ges Grate-ful-ly I shall sing,

Sav-ing my soul, mak-ing me whole, Tho I had wan-dered a-way.
Bid-ding Him take, break me and make, Till I am mold-ed and meet.
"O Sav-ior, help! dear Sav-ior, help! Grace for my weak-ness im-part."
Je-sus will give, Je-sus will give— He will up-hold and sus-tain.
"O how He loved! O how He loved! Je-sus, my Lord and my King!"

Deeper and Deeper

Author–Oswald J. Smith, 1890–
Composer–Oswald J. Smith, 1890–
Meter–7 7. 7 6. 7 6 4 4 7

> I delight to do Thy will, O my God: Yea, Thy law is within my heart. Psalm 40:8

This hymn is from the pen of one of the great evangelical preachers and missionary statesmen of our day, Oswald J. Smith. For many years now this name has been associated with the Peoples Church of Toronto, Canada, a church that contributes more than a quarter-of-a-million dollars annually toward the support of over 300 missionaries. Dr. Smith is presently the Minister of Missions while his son, Paul, is pastor of the church.

In addition to his preaching and promoting of missionary activities, Dr. Smith has authored a number of books and has composed more than 1200 hymns and religious verses. Several of his other well-known gospel songs include "God Understands," "Joy in Serving Jesus," "The Glory of His Presence," "The Song of the Soul Set Free," "The Savior Can Solve Every Problem," "Then Jesus Came."

98

Dr. Smith gives the following account of the writing of "Deeper and Deeper" in his book, *The Story of My Hymns:* "I was traveling secretary of the Pocket Testament League, founded by Mrs. Charles M. Alexander. Arriving in Woodstock, Ontario, one day in the year 1911, I was invited to preach one Sunday morning in the largest Methodist Church in that city.

"As I walked along the street on my way to the church, the melody of this hymn sang itself into my heart and with it the words, 'Into the heart of Jesus, deeper and deeper I go.' I can still recall the joy and buoyancy of youth, the bright sunshine overhead, and the thrill with which I looked forward to my service that Sunday morning, as again and again I hummed over the words. I wondered if I could retain the music in my mind until the service was over. I was then just twenty-one years of age.

"After preaching, I returned to my rented room, and the first thing I did was to write out the melody as God had given it to me. I had been able to remember it, and it has never changed from that day to this.

"The verses were much more difficult. I worked on them at Belwood, Ontario, but it was three years later, in the First Presbyterian Church of South Chicago, of which I was pastor, that I completed them. It was then 1914, and I was twenty-four years of age.

"The writing of the hymn afforded me much joy, nor has it ever grown old. I still love it and always will, for it was the child of my youth. It proves conclusively that God can impart His deepest truths to the hearts of the young, for I doubt if I have ever written anything more profound since.

"There are five steps portrayed in 'Deeper and Deeper'–the heart, the will, the cross, joy and love. What an experience! But it is the note of triumph in the last verse that transports the soul to heights sublime."

In his book, *The Story of My Life*, Dr. Smith relates many heart-breaking experiences, especially in the early years of his ministry. Out of such experiences and disappointments flowed many of his deeper life songs. He emphasizes continually the importance of spending time alone with God each day, a time he calls his "morning watch":

For half a century now I have walked the floor morning by morning with God. It was when I walked alone with God that I learned the lessons He would teach. I set aside a time and a place to meet Him, and I have never been disappointed.

*   *   *

"Alone, dear Lord, ah, yes! alone with Thee!   99
    My aching heart at rest, my spirit free;
  My sorrow gone, my burdens all forgotten,
    When far away I soar alone with Thee."

Oswald J. Smith

20

Doxology
OLD 100TH L.M.

Thomas Ken, 1637–1711   Louis Bourgeois c. 1510–c. 1561

Praise God from whom all bless-ings flow; Praise Him, all crea-tures here be-low;

Praise Him a-bove, ye heav'n-ly host; Praise Fa-ther, Son, and Ho-ly Ghost. A-men.

100

Author–Thomas Ken, 1637–1711
Composer–Louis Bourgeois, c. 1510–c. 1561
Tune Name–"Old Hundredth"
Meter–LM (88.88)
Scripture Reference–Psalm 100

I will praise Thee, O Lord my God, with all my heart: And I will glorify Thy name forevermore.   Psalm 86:12

The four lines of the Doxology have been the most frequently sung words of any known song for more than three hundred years. Even today nearly every English-speaking Protestant congregation still unites at least once each Sunday in this noble ascription of praise. It has been said that the doxology has done more to teach the doctrine of the Trinity than all the theological books ever written. It has often been called "the Protestant Te Deum Laudamus."

The author of this text was a bold, outspoken seventeenth century Anglican Bishop named Thomas Ken. He was born at Little Berkhampstead, England, in 1637. Left an orphan in early childhood, Ken was educated at Winchester School where he was raised under the care of his older sister and her famous husband, Izaak Walton, distinguished in history as the most eminent angler of his time. Later Ken attended Oxford University and was ordained in 1662 to the ministry of the Church of England. His illustrious career in the ministry was stormy and colorful. Following ordination, he served as chaplain to the Bishop of Winchester.

In 1679 he was sent to Holland, where he was the English chaplain at the royal court at the Hague. Ken, however, was so outspoken in denouncing the corrupt lives of those in authority in the Dutch capital that he was compelled to leave the following year. Upon his return to England Charles II appointed Ken as one of his own chaplains. Ken continued to reveal the same spirit of boldness in rebuking the moral sins of his dissolute English monarch. Despite these rebukes Charles always admired the courageous chaplain. He referred to him as "the good little man" and, when it was chapel time, he would usually say, "I must go in and hear Ken tell me my faults." Eventually, the King rewarded Thomas Ken by appointing him to the Bishopric of the Bath and Wells area.

Just twelve days after Ken was consecrated as a Bishop, his friend Charles II died. Soon Ken incurred the wrath of the new monarch, papist James II, by refusing to read the Royal Declaration of Indulgence, and with six other Anglican Church leaders he was imprisoned in the Tower of London. Although Ken was eventually acquitted, he was later removed from his bishopric in 1691 by the next ruler, William III. The remaining years of Ken's life were spent in quiet obscurity with a devoted friend, Lord Weymouth, at his home in Longleat, Wiltshire, where Ken died in 1711 at the age of seventy-four. The historian Macaulay gave a tribute to Bishop Ken when he stated that he came as near to the ideal of Christian perfection "as human weakness permits."

101

Bishop Ken wrote a number of hymns, and it was always his desire that Christians be allowed to express their praise to God without being limited only to Psalmody and the Bible canticles. He was one of the first English writers to produce hymns that were not merely versifications of the Psalms.

In 1673 Thomas Ken wrote a book entitled *A Manual of Prayers for the Use of the Scholars of Winchester College*. In one of the editions of this manual, Ken included three of his hymns that he wanted the students to sing each day as part of their devotions. These hymns were called "Morning Hymn," "Evening Hymn," and "Midnight Hymn." Each of these hymns closed with the familiar four lines we now know as the Doxology. The text of his "Morning Hymn" became especially popular. Two of the verses from this hymn are as follows:

Awake, my soul, and with the sun
Thy daily course of duty run,
Shake off dull sloth, and early rise,
To pay thy morning sacrifice.

Direct, control, suggest, this day,
All I design, or do, or say;
That all my powers, with all their might,
In Thy sole glory may unite.

It is said that after Bishop Ken had written this hymn, he sang it to his own accompaniment on the lute every morning as part of his private devotions.

The tune for Bishop Ken's text, "Old Hundredth," is said to be the most famous of all Christian hymn tunes. It was composed or adapted by Louis Bourgeois, born in Paris, France, c. 1510. In 1541 Bourgeois moved to Geneva, Switzerland, where he became an ardent follower of John Calvin and the Reformed Reformation Movement. Here he was given the responsibility to provide the tunes for the new metrical psalms which were being prepared at that time. Bourgeois was largely responsible for the Genevan Psalter, a monumental musical publication, completed and published in 1562. The tune was prepared originally for the French version of Psalm 134 and was included in the Anglo-Genevan Psalter of 1551. The first English words to which it was wedded were William Kethe's version of Psalm 100, "All People That on Earth Do Dwell;" accordingly, the tune became known as "The Hundredth." In 1696, when Tate and Brady published their *New Version*, the word "Old" was used to show that the tune was the one in use in the previous Psalter, edited by Sternhold and Hopkins.

102

Thomas Ken

21

Fairest Lord Jesus!

CRUSADERS' HYMN

From *Münster Gesangbuch*, 1677
4th vs. trans. by Joseph A. Seiss, 1823-1904

From *Schlesische Volkslieder*, 1842
Adapted by Richard S. Willis, 1819-1900

1. Fair - est Lord Je - sus! Rul - er of all na - ture!
2. Fair are the mead - ows, Fair - er still the wood - lands,
3. Fair is the sun - shine, Fair - er still the moon - light,
4. Beau - ti - ful Sav - ior! Lord of the na - tions!

O Thou of God and man the Son! Thee will I cher - ish,
Robed in the bloom-ing garb of spring: Je - sus is fair - er,
And all the twink-ling star - ry host: Je - sus shines bright - er,
Son of God and Son of Man! Glo - ry and hon - or,

Thee will I hon - or, Thou my soul's glo - ry, joy and crown!
Je - sus is pur - er, Who makes the woe-ful heart to sing.
Je - sus shines pur - er Than all the an-gels heav'n can boast.
Praise, ad - o - ra - tion Now and for - ev - er - more be Thine!

103

Text–From *Munster Gesangbuch*, 1677. 4th verse translated by Joseph
  A. Seiss, 1823-1904
Music–From *Schlesische Volkslieder*, 1842. Adapted by Richard S.
  Willis, 1819-1900
Tune Name–"Crusaders' Hymn"
Meter–568.558

> For by Him were all things created, that are in heaven, and that are in earth, visible and
> invisible, whether they be thrones, or dominions, or principalities, or powers: All
> things were created by Him, and for Him.   Colossians 1:16

Little is known of the origin of this cherished hymn. Associated with it
are several popular legends which cannot always be substantiated by
research. One of the best-known accounts is that it was called the

"Crusaders' Hymn." Some think that it was sung by the twelfth century German Crusaders, especially by their children, as they made their long and wearisome trek to the Holy Land. Another account, which has more credence, is that it was one of the hymns used by the singing followers of John Hus, a small band of believers who settled in Silesia (now part of Poland) after they were driven out of Bohemia in the bloody anti-Reformation purge of 1620. This hymn, then, is generally said to be a folk song derived from these devout Silesian peasants.

The text for the hymn first appeared in the Roman Catholic *Munster Gesangbuch* of 1677, where it was published as the "first of three beautiful selected new hymns." Later it is said that a man by the name of Hoffman Fallersleben heard a group of Silesians singing the hymn in a service, recorded the words and music from this oral recitation, and published it in his *Schlesische Volkslieder* in 1842. This is the form in which we now know the hymn.

No one knows for certain who first translated the text from German into English. The English adaptation by Richard Storrs Willis, born in Boston, Massachusetts, on February 10, 1819, first appeared in his *Church Chorals and Choir Studies* in 1850. It is interesting to note that in this collection a notation about the origin of the hymn is made stating that it was 104 "sung by the German knights on the way to Jerusalem." This statement undoubtedly did much to foster and popularize the Crusader account.

The fourth verse, a fine translation by Joseph A. Seiss, emphasizes the dual nature of the Savior–"Son of God and Son of Man" as well as the praise that will be eternally His.

*　　*　　*

"God has created man in His own image and therefore God is creative by His very nature. Because of this, man also has communication and expression as a basic part of his humanity. The characteristic common to God and man is the desire to make things as well as to enjoy the creation about him."

Anonymous

22

Faith of Our Fathers

ST. CATHERINE

FREDERICK W. FABER, 1814-1863

HENRI F. HEMY, 1818-1888
Adapted by James G. Walton, 1821-1905

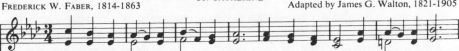

1. Faith of our fa-thers, liv-ing still In spite of dun-geon, fire and sword—
2. Our fa-thers, chained in pris-ons dark, Were still in heart and con-science free;
3. Faith of our fa-thers, we will love Both friend and foe in all our strife;

O how our hearts beat high with joy When-e'er we hear that glo-rious word!
How sweet would be their chil-dren's fate If they, like them, could die for thee!
And preach thee too, as love knows how, By kind-ly words and vir-tuous life.

Author–Frederick W. Faber, 1814–1863
Composer–Henri F. Hemy, 1818–1888
Adapted–James G. Walton, 1821–1905
Tune Name–"St. Catherine"
Meter–88.88.88

105

Our fathers trusted in Thee: They trusted, and Thou didst deliver them. Psalm 22:4

The eleventh chapter of Hebrews has well been called the "great gallery of gallant Christian faith"–a thrilling account of spiritual giants who were willing to give all in defense of their faith in God. There have been martyrs of the Christian faith in every century since this New Testament record was first written. Some writers and historians have estimated that at least fifty million individuals have died a martyr's death since the crucifixion of Christ. Even today, in our civilized culture, there are many who suffer and die because of their faith and profession of Christ as Savior and Lord.

No doubt the hearing and singing of this hymn conjures in many minds various scenes from the great "cloud of witnesses" referred to in Hebrews 12:1, who, with their surrounding but unseen presence, encourage us to "run with patience the race that is set before us." It is good for us to be reminded often that the history of the Christian faith is a rich heritage of countless numbers whose faith in God was counted more dear than life itself. Much could be said about the first century Christians and their persecution by the Roman Empire, or the suffering of the Huguenots in France during the reign of Louis XIV, or even the religious persecution to our forefathers resulting in their quest for a new land where they could enjoy religious freedom.

The "faith of our fathers" referred to in this hymn, however, is the faith of the martyred leaders of the Roman Catholic Church during the sixteenth century. The author of this text, Frederick William Faber, born June 28, 1814, in Calverley, Yorkshire, England, was raised as a strict Calvinist by a father who was an English clergyman. After young Faber's graduation from the renowned Oxford University in 1843, he became a minister in the Anglican Church at a small parish at Elten, England.

In his younger days Faber was strongly opposed to the teachings and practices of the Roman Church. However, this was the time when a movement known as the Oxford or Tractarian Movement was strongly influencing the Anglican Church. Whereas the Wesleys and their evangelical followers preached a message of personal conversion easily grasped by even the illiterate man, leaders of the more sophisticated Oxford Movement were of the persuasion that a meaningful religious experience could only be gained through better liturgical and ceremonial church services. From about 1833 to 1850 the Oxford Movement tenaciously directed religious England, during which time many of the Anglican Church's leaders either joined the Roman Church or developed a rejuvenated high church party known as Anglo-Catholics.

Early in his ministerial training Faber came under the influence of this Oxford Movement. After serving just three years as an Anglican minister, he left the Church and joined the Roman Catholic fold. He became known as Father Wilfrid. Shortly after his secession to the Roman Church Faber noticed the great lack of congregational hymnody that existed within this group. He recalled the important and influential role that congregational singing had in Anglican congregations, especially within the more evangelical parishes. Faber began to make it his life's mission to write hymns that promoted the history and teachings of the Catholic Church. In all Frederick Faber wrote 150 such hymns before his early death at the age of forty-nine. For his efforts in this regard he was honored by the Pope with a Doctor of Divinity Degree.

"Faith of Our Fathers" was written by Faber to remind Catholic congregations of their many leaders who were martyred during the reign of Henry VIII in the early days of the establishment of the Anglican Church in Great Britain. The text first appeared in 1849 in Faber's collection, *Jesus and Mary; or Catholic Hymns for Singing and Reading*. It was always Faber's hope that some day England would be brought back to the papal fold. One of the omitted verses from his original text expresses this thought:

106

Faith of our fathers! Mary's prayers
   Shall win our country back to thee;
And through the truth that comes from God,
   England shall then indeed be free.
Faith of our fathers, holy faith!
   We would be true to Thee till death.

The tune for this hymn, a melody known as "St. Catherine's Tune," was composed by a noted Roman Catholic, Henri Hemy, born at New Castle-Upon-Tyne, England, on November 12, 1818. He was a respected organist and composer at the church at Tynemouth and in 1864 compiled a popular Catholic hymnal, *Crown of Jesus*. The tune was originally composed for a Catholic hymn entitled "St. Catherine, Virgin and Martyr." It was written in honor of Catherine of Alexander, a fourth century martyr. The final eight measures or refrain–"Faith of our fathers, holy faith, we will be true to Thee till death" were added by James G. Walton, when he made a new arrangement and used it for his collection, *Plain Song Music for the Holy Communion Office*, published in 1874.

*   *   *

107

"There's a wideness in God's mercy
   Like the wideness of the sea;
There's a kindness in His justice
   Which is more than liberty.

"There is welcome for the sinner
   And more graces for the good;
There is mercy with the Savior;
   There is healing in His blood.

"For the love of God is broader
   Than the measure of man's mind;
And the heart of the Eternal
   Is most wonderfully kind.

"If our love were but more simple
   We should take Him at His word,
And our lives would be all sunshine
   In the sweetness of our Lord."

Written by Frederick Faber in 1862

23   For the Beauty of the Earth

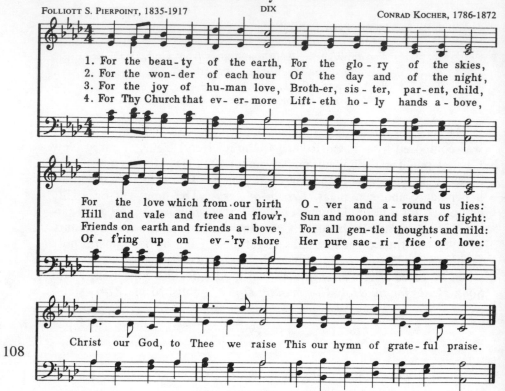

108

Author–Folliott S. Pierpoint, 1835–1917
Composer–Conrad Kocher, 1786–1872
Tune Name–"Dix"
Meter–77.77.77
Scripture Reference–Hebrews 13:15

> Whatsoever things are true, whatsoever things are honest . . . just, . . . pure, . . . love-
> ly, . . . of good report, . . . think on these things.   Philippians 4:8

     This hymn expresses in fine literary style many of the blessings of life
so commonly taken for granted and then directs our "grateful praise" to
God, the giver of every good and perfect gift. The author, Folliott S.
Pierpoint, begins by reminding us of all the physical beauties of the
world–the sun, flowers, and shining stars. He then reminds us of the
social joys of friends and home–those relationships that bring such enriching dimensions to life. Above all, however, he gives thanks for the
ministry of the church, God's ordained agency for accomplishing divine
purposes in this world.

When he was about twenty-nine years of age, Pierpoint wrote this text in the late spring of the year while he was enjoying his native city of Bath, England. He was entranced by the beautiful countryside with its winding river, Avon, in the distance. As his heart welled up with emotion, he expressed with his pen the feelings of gratitude that were within him.

This hymn first appeared in a collection of poems published in 1864. It was entitled "The Sacrifice of Praise." It consisted of eight six-line stanzas of which four are omitted in some hymnals. An interesting verse not included in most hymnals gives thanks for God Himself, who has made all of the joys and beauties of life possible:

> For Thyself, best Gift Divine! To our race so freely given;
> For that great, great love of Thine, peace on earth, and joy in heaven:
> Lord of all, to Thee we raise this our hymn of grateful praise.

Little is known about the author of this text. He was born in the interesting historic town of Bath, England, in 1835, and was a lay member of the Anglican Church. Following his graduation from Queen's College, Cambridge, he taught the classics for a time at Somerset College, and later became an independent writer. Although he published seven volumes of poems and hymn texts, many of them showing his love for nature, he is best remembered for this one beautiful hymn.

109

The tune name "Dix" came from the association of this melody with William Dix's hymn, "As With Gladness Men of Old." Its composer, Conrad Kocher, was born in Wurttëmberg in 1786 and became an important musician and reformer of German church music. The tune produces very interesting effects with this text, because of the antiphonal or answering structures of the music. It has phrases which balance each other, so that one group in the congregation can sing the first couplet, while another group responds with the second, with all of the voices joining to bring out the joyful strength of the refrain.

"For the Beauty of the Earth" was first written for use at a communion service of the church but has since become one of the favorite hymns during the thanksgiving season. It has also proven to be a favorite hymn for children.

* * *

> "Music religious heat inspires,
>   It wakes the soul, and lifts it high,
> And wings it with sublime desires,
>   And fits it to bespeak the Deity."

Joseph Addison

24   **From Every Stormy Wind That Blows**
RETREAT

HUGH STOWELL, 1799-1865

THOMAS HASTINGS, 1784-1872
Arr. by John W. Peterson, 1921-

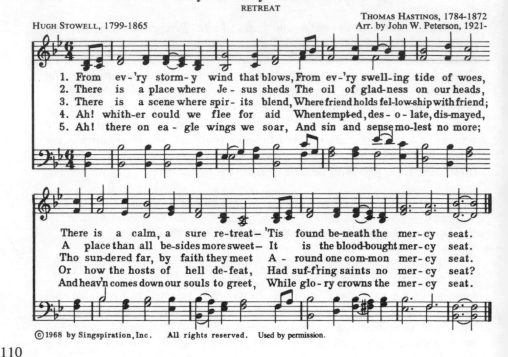

1. From ev-'ry storm-y wind that blows, From ev-'ry swell-ing tide of woes,
2. There is a place where Je-sus sheds The oil of glad-ness on our heads,
3. There is a scene where spir-its blend, Where friend holds fel-low-ship with friend;
4. Ah! whith-er could we flee for aid When tempt-ed, des-o-late, dis-mayed,
5. Ah! there on ea-gle wings we soar, And sin and sense mo-lest no more;

There is a calm, a sure re-treat— 'Tis found be-neath the mer-cy seat.
A place than all be-sides more sweet— It is the blood-bought mer-cy seat.
Tho sun-dered far, by faith they meet A-round one com-mon mer-cy seat.
Or how the hosts of hell de-feat, Had suf-f'ring saints no mer-cy seat?
And heav'n comes down our souls to greet, While glo-ry crowns the mer-cy seat.

110

Author–Hugh Stowell, 1799–1865
Composer–Thomas Hastings, 1784–1872
Tune Name–"Retreat"
Meter–LM (88.88)

> When thou passest through the waters, I will be with thee; and through the rivers, they
> shall not overflow thee: When thou walkest through the fire, thou shalt not be burned;
> neither shall the flame kindle upon thee. For I am the Lord thy God, the Holy One of
> Israel, thy Savior. . . .   Isaiah 43:2,3

Hugh Stowell was born on December 3, 1799 in the Isle of Man,
England. He was known as a strong evangelical Anglican preacher, one
of the truly outstanding evangelical leaders in the Church of England
during his day. Stowell spent most of his life preaching at Christ's Church
in Salford, a suburb of Manchester, England. He was known for his love
of children and always worked hard to have a fine Sunday School in his
own church. At his death he was greatly mourned by his many friends in
the Manchester area. Stowell wrote several books, including a volume of
poems and a collection of hymns published in 1831. To this collection
and subsequent editions he contributed approximately fifty hymn texts.

This hymn text was originally entitled "Peace at the Mercy Seat" and first appeared in an original collection of poems, *The Winter's Wreath*, published in London in 1828.

Thomas Hastings, born on October 15, 1784, in Washington, Connecticut, was a self-taught American musician, who along with Lowell Mason is credited with being very influential in shaping the development of church music in the United States during the nineteenth century. He wrote more than 600 hymns, 1000 hymn tunes, and published more than fifty song-book collections. This tune, "Retreat," was composed for this text in 1840 and was published in *Sacred Songs* in 1842. The tune name is taken from the third line of the hymn, "There is a calm and sure retreat...."

Other hymns by Thomas Hastings include "Majestic Sweetness Sits Enthroned" (No. 56) and "Rock of Ages" (No. 78).

*   *   *

111

"Jesus is our Shepherd, well we know His voice!
How its gentlest whisper makes our heart rejoice:
Even when He chideth, tender is its tone;
None but He shall guide us; we are His alone."

A popular children's hymn by H. Stowell, written in 1849

25 From Greenland's Icy Mountains

MISSIONARY HYMN

REGINALD HEBER, 1783-1826

LOWELL MASON, 1792-1872

1. From Green-land's i - cy moun - tains, From In-dia's cor-al strand,
2. What though the spi - cy breez - es Blow soft o'er Cey-lon's isle,
3. Shall we, whose souls are light - ed With wis-dom from on high,
4. Waft, waft, ye winds, His sto - ry, And you, ye wa-ters, roll,

Where Af-ric's sun-ny foun-tains Roll down their gold-en sand,
Though ev-'ry pros-pect pleas-es And on-ly man is vile;
Shall we to men be-night-ed The lamp of life de-ny?
Till like a sea of glo-ry It spreads from pole to pole,

112

From man-y an an-cient riv-er, From man-y a palm-y plain,
In vain with lav-ish kind-ness The gifts of God are strown,
Sal-va-tion! O sal-va-tion! The joy-ful sound pro-claim,
Till o'er our ran-somed na-ture The Lamb for sin-ners slain,

They call us to de-liv-er Their land from er-ror's chain.
The hea-then in his blind-ness Bows down to wood and stone.
Till earth's re-mot-est na-tion Has learned Mes-si-ah's name.
Re-deem-er, King, Cre-a-tor, In bliss re-turns to reign.

From Greenland's Icy Mountains

Author–Reginald Heber, 1783–1826
Music–Lowell Mason, 1792–1872
Tune Name–"Missionary Hymn"
Meter–76.76 Doubled

> Then saith He unto His disciples, The harvest truly is plenteous, but the laborers are few; pray ye therefore the Lord of the harvest, that He will send forth laborers into His harvest.   Matthew 9:37,38

Written in 1819 by Reginald Heber, this hymn is generally considered one of the finest missionary hymns ever written. Heber himself is ranked as one of the foremost nineteenth century English hymnists. Altogether Heber wrote fifty-seven hymns, with every one still in use, a rare tribute to the genius of this consecrated writer.

Throughout his ministry in the Anglican Church Heber had a keen interest in world missions. His writings and influence did much to promote among Protestant circles the missionary cause that became active during this time. In 1822 his interest in world missions was rewarded with an appointment to the episcopate as a bishop of Calcutta, India. After only three years of arduous work in this position, however, his health failed and he died at the early age of forty-three.

In the summer of 1819 while visiting his father-in-law, Dean Shirley, in the Wrexham Vicarage, Heber was asked if he knew a missionary hymn that could be used at a missionary service on the next Lord's day for Whit-Sunday. It is said that within a few minutes he returned from a quiet meditation and produced the first three verses of this text. The Dean and other members of the family were thrilled, but Heber felt the hymn was incomplete. He returned to his study and shortly produced the triumphant final verse.

Reginald Heber is also the author of the hymn, "Holy, Holy, Holy" (No. 31).

The tune, "Missionary Hymn," was composed specifically for this text by the American educator and church musician, Lowell Mason, in 1824. Like the writing of the text, it is said that Mason composed this tune with a great sense of inspiration within just a very brief time.

Other hymns by Lowell Mason include "Nearer, My God, to Thee" (No. 61) and "When I Survey the Wondrous Cross" (No. 100).

113

26 Guide Me, O Thou Great Jehovah

CWM RHONDDA

WILLIAM WILLIAMS, 1717-1791
Trans. by Peter Williams, 1722-1796, and others

JOHN HUGHES, 1873-1932
Arr. by Norman Johnson, 1928-

1. Guide me, O Thou great Je-ho-vah, Pil-grim thru this bar-ren land;
2. O-pen now the crys-tal foun-tain Whence the heal-ing stream doth flow;
3. When I tread the verge of Jor-dan, Bid my anx-ious fears sub-side;

I am weak, but Thou art might-y— Hold me with Thy pow'r-ful hand:
Let the fire and cloud-y pil-lar Lead me all my jour-ney thru:
Bear me thru the swell-ing cur-rent, Land me safe on Ca-naan's side:

Bread of Heav-en, Bread of Heav-en, Feed me till I want no
Strong De-liv-'rer, strong De-liv-'rer, Be Thou still my strength and
Songs of prais-es, songs of prais-es I will ev-er give to

more, (want no more,) Feed me till I want no more.
shield, (strength and shield,) Be Thou still my strength and shield.
Thee, (give to Thee,) I will ev-er give to Thee.

Guide Me, O Thou Great Jehovah

Author-William Williams, 1717–1791
English Translation-Peter Williams, 1722–1796, and others
Composer-John Hughes, 1873–1932
Tune Name-"Cwm Rhondda"
Meter-87.87.87

> For Thou art my rock and my fortress; therefore for Thy name's sake lead me, and guide me.   Psalm 31:3

Throughout the centuries the Welsh people have been recognized as one of the most enthusiastic groups of singers in the world. From the days of the Druids, Wales has been a land of song. To this day they still conduct an International Eisteddfodd (singing festival) at Llangollen. This hymn is a product of that fine musical heritage.

During the early part of the eighteenth century a young Welsh preacher, Howell Harris, was stirring Wales with his evangelistic preaching and congregational singing. In England the Wesleys and George Whitefield were conducting similar revivals and outdoor campaigns. One of the lives touched by Harris's preaching was William Williams. Prior to this time Williams had been preparing for the medical profession, but upon hearing a sermon by Harris, young Williams gave his heart and life to God and decided to enter the ministry. He served two parishes in the Anglican Church for a time but never felt at ease in the established, ritualistic church. Like Harris, he decided to take all of Wales as his parish and for the next forty-three years traveled nearly 100,000 miles on horseback, preaching and singing the gospel in his native tongue. Though he suffered many hardships, he was affectionately known as the "sweet singer of Wales." Throughout Wales he was respected as a persuasive preacher, yet it is said that the chief source of his influence was his hymns. He wrote approximately 800 of them, all in Welsh. One hymnologist has said, "What Isaac Watts has been to England, that and more has William Williams been to Wales." Unfortunately, most of Williams's hymns are untranslated, and this is the only hymn for which he is widely known today.

"Guide Me, O Thou Great Jehovah" first appeared in a hymnal published by Williams in Bristol, England, in 1745. It originally consisted of five six-line stanzas and was entitled "Strength to Pass Through the Wilderness." In 1771 another hymnal was published by Peter Williams (no relation) in which he translated into English stanzas 1, 3, 5. A year later the original author, William Williams, or possibly his son John, made another English version using Peter Williams's first stanza, then

115

translating stanzas three and four of the original hymn and adding a new fourth verse. Most hymnals today make use of only three of these stanzas.

The imagery of the hymn is drawn wholly from the Bible. The hymn compares the forty-year journey of the Israelites to the promised land with the living of a Christian life as a "pilgrim[age] through this barren land." Note the symbolic phrases used throughout: "bread of heaven" (manna), "crystal fountain" (I Corinthians 10:3, 4), "fire and cloudy pillar," "verge of Jordan," "Canaan's Side."

The tune for this text was written in 1907 by John Hughes, a noted Welsh composer of a number of Sunday School marches, anthems and hymn tunes. This particular tune was written especially for the annual Baptist Cymnfa Ganu (singing festival) at Capel Rhondda, Pontypridd, Wales, and was printed in leaflets for that occasion. The text with this tune is still one of the most popular and widely used hymns in Wales. It is not at all uncommon even today for a large crowd at some public event such as a rugby match to burst into the spontaneous singing of this hymn. The strong symbolic text with its virile tune has had great universal appeal, evidenced by the fact that the hymn has been translated into over seventy-five different languages.

116

William Williams

27   # Great Is Thy Faithfulness

Thomas O. Chisholm, 1866-1960   William M. Runyan, 1870-1957

1. Great is Thy faith-ful-ness, O God my Fa-ther! There is no
2. Sum-mer and win-ter, and spring-time and har-vest, Sun, moon and
3. Par-don for sin and a peace that en-dur-eth, Thine own dear

shad-ow of turn-ing with Thee; Thou chang-est not, Thy com-
stars in their cours-es a-bove, Join with all na-ture in
pres-ence to cheer and to guide, Strength for to-day and bright

pas-sions,they fail not: As Thou hast been Thou for-ev-er wilt be.
man-i-fold wit-ness To Thy great faith-ful-ness, mer-cy and love.
hope for to-mor-row-Bless-ings all mine,with ten thou-sand be-side!

117

Chorus

Great is Thy faith-ful-ness! Great is Thy faith-ful-ness! Morn-ing by

morn-ing new mer-cies I see; All I have need-ed Thy

hand hath pro-vid-ed- Great is Thy faith-ful-ness, Lord, un-to me!

Great is Thy Faithfulness

Author–Thomas O. Chisholm, 1866–1960
Composer–William M. Runyan, 1870–1957
Meter–11 10. 11 10 with Chorus
Scripture Reference–Lamentations 3:22

> Every good gift and every perfect gift is from above, and cometh down from the Father of Lights, with whom is no variableness, neither shadow of turning.   James 1:17

Of the many gospel hymns written in recent times on the theme of God's goodness and faithfulness, this hymn stands out like a beacon light. While many hymns are born out of a particular dramatic experience, this hymn was simply the result of the author's "morning by morning realization of God's personal faithfulness."

Thomas Obadiah Chisholm was born in a humble log cabin in Franklin, Kentucky, on July 29, 1866. Without the benefit of high school or advanced training, he began his career as a school teacher at the age of sixteen in the same country school house where he had received his elementary training. When he was twenty-one, he became the associate editor of his home town weekly newspaper, *The Franklin Favorite*. Six years later he accepted Christ as personal Savior during a revival meeting conducted in Franklin by Dr. H. C. Morrison. At Dr. Morrison's invitation Chisholm moved to Louisville to become office editor and business manager of Morrison's publication, the *Pentecostal Herald*. Later Chisholm was ordained to the Methodist ministry but was forced to resign after a brief pastorate because of poor health. After 1909 he became a life insurance agent in Winona Lake and later in Vineland, New Jersey. Thomas Chisholm retired in 1953 and spent his remaining years at the Methodist Home for the Aged, Ocean Grove, New Jersey.

Mr. Chisholm wrote more than 1200 poems, many of which have appeared frequently in such religious periodicals as the *Sunday School Times, Moody Monthly, Alliance Weekly* and others. A number of these poems have become prominent hymn texts.

In a letter dated 1941, Mr. Chisholm writes, "My income has not been large at any time due to impaired health in the earlier years which has followed me on until now. Although I must not fail to record here the unfailing faithfulness of a covenant-keeping God and that He has given me many wonderful displays of His providing care, for which I am filled with astonishing gratefulness."

In 1923 Mr. Chisholm sent several of his poems to the Rev. W. M. Runyan, a musician associated with the Moody Bible Institute and an editor with the Hope Publishing Company until his death July 29, 1957. Mr. Runyan has written as follows:

118

UNDERSTANDING the Hymnal's Contents

This particular poem held such an appeal that I prayed most earnestly that my tune might carry over its message in a worthy way, and the subsequent history of its use indicates that God answered prayer. It was written in Baldwin, Kansas, in 1923, and was first published in my private song pamphlets.

This hymn was the favorite of the late Dr. Will Houghton, former beloved president of the Moody Bible Institute. It has since been an all-time favorite with students at the school and as a result its usefulness has spread to evangelical churches everywhere. Bev Shea states that this hymn was first introduced to audiences in Great Britain in 1954 by the Billy Graham Crusades and has since been a favorite there as well.

*   *   *

"He leads us on by paths we did not know;   119
Upward He leads us, though our steps be slow,
Though oft we faint and falter on the way,
Though storms and darkness oft obscure the day;
  Yet when the clouds are gone,
  We know He leads us on.

"He leads us on through all the unquiet years;
Past all our dreamland hopes, and doubts and fears,
He guides our steps, through all the tangled maze
Of losses, sorrows, and o'erclouded days;
  We know His will is done;
  And still He leads us on."

    Nicolaus L. von Zinzendorf, 1700–1760
    (See No. 50)

He Leadeth Me

Joseph H. Gilmore, 1834-1918

William B. Bradbury, 1816-1868

1. He lead - eth me! O bless - ed thought! O words with heav'n - ly
2. Some-times 'mid scenes of deep-est gloom, Some-times where E - den's
3. Lord, I would clasp Thy hand in mine, Nor ev - er mur - mur
4. And when my task on earth is done, When by Thy grace the

com - fort fraught! What - e'er I do, wher - e'er I be, Still
bow - ers bloom, By wa - ters still, o'er trou - bled sea, Still
nor re - pine; Con - tent, what - ev - er lot I see, Since
vic - t'ry's won, E'en death's cold wave I will not flee, Since

CHORUS

'tis God's hand that lead - eth me.
'tis His hand that lead - eth me! He lead - eth me, He
'tis my God that lead - eth me!
God thru Jor - dan lead - eth me.

120

lead - eth me, By His own hand He lead-eth me; His faith - ful

fol - l'wer I would be, For by His hand He lead - eth me.

He Leadeth Me

Author-Joseph H. Gilmore, 1834–1918
Composer-William B. Bradbury, 1816–1868
Meter-8 8. 8 8 with Chorus
Scripture Reference-Psalm 23

> He maketh me to lie down in green pastures: He leadeth me beside the still waters. Psalm 23:2

This beloved gospel hymn was written on March 26, 1862. The author, Joseph H. Gilmore, has left the following account:

I had been speaking at the Wednesday evening service of the First Baptist Church in Philadelphia, Corner of Broad and Arch Streets, about the 23rd Psalm, and had been especially impressed with the blessedness of being led by God.... At the close of the service we adjourned to Deacon Watson's pleasant home where we were being entertained. During our conversation the blessedness of God's leading so grew upon me that I took out my pencil, wrote the hymn just as it stands today, handed it to my wife, and thought no more of it. She sent it without my knowledge to the *Watchman and Reflector* magazine, and there it first appeared in print.

Three years later I went to Rochester, New York, to preach as a candidate for the Second Baptist Church. Upon entering the chapel I took up a hymnbook, thinking, "I wonder what they sing." The book opened up at "He Leadeth Me," and that was the first time I knew that my hymn had found a place among the songs of the church.

121

Joseph H. Gilmore was born in Boston, Massachusetts, on April 29, 1834. His father was the governor of the state of New Hampshire for a period of time. Joseph graduated from the Newton Theological Seminary in 1861. Throughout his lifetime he pastored several Baptist churches, served as a secretary to his father the governor, was a professor of Hebrew at Newton Seminary, and later taught English literature at Rochester University, where he published several college texts in these subjects. He also wrote other hymns, but none ever gained the acceptance that "He Leadeth Me" did. Although Gilmore was highly respected both in religious and educational circles, he is best remembered for this hurriedly written text when he was just twenty-eight years of age and a visiting supply preacher in Philadelphia.

William B. Bradbury, an important contributor to the development of early gospel hymnody, saw this text in the *Watchman and Reflector*

Magazine in 1863 and wrote this fitting melody to match the words. He also added two additional lines to the chorus, "His faithful follower I would be, for by His hand He leadeth me."

Other hymns by William B. Bradbury include "Jesus Loves Me" (No. 47) and "Just As I Am" (No. 52).

This hymn, perhaps more than any other modern hymn, has been translated into many different languages. Servicemen during World War II were greatly surprised to find it one of the favorite hymns sung by the primitive Polynesians in the South Pacific.

When the First Baptist Church building of Philadelphia at the busy Broad and Arch intersection was demolished in 1926, it was replaced by a large office building. In the corner of the building was placed a bronze tablet, which still remains today, containing the words of the first verse of "He Leadeth Me." This was done, states the inscription, "in recognition of the beauty and fame of this beloved hymn, and in remembrance of its distinguished author."

*   *   *

122

"... The sweetest words of the whole is that monosyllable, my. He does not say, The Lord is the shepherd of the world at large, and leadeth forth the multitude as His flock. If He be a shepherd to no one else, He is a Shepherd to me. He cares for me, watches over me, and preserves me. The words are in the present tense. Whatever be the believer's position, he is even now under the pastoral care of Jehovah ..."

Charles Haddon Spurgeon—*Treasury of David*

29 Hiding in Thee

WILLIAM O. CUSHING, 1823-1902

IRA D. SANKEY, 1840-1908

1. O safe to the Rock that is high - er than I My
   soul in its con - flicts and sor - rows would fly; So sin - ful, so
   wea - ry—Thine, Thine would I be: Thou blest "Rock of
   A - ges," I'm hid - ing in Thee.

2. In the calm of the noon-tide, in sor - row's lone hour, In
   times when temp-ta - tion casts o'er me its pow'r, In the tem - pests of
   life, on its wide, heav - ing sea, Thou blest "Rock of
   A - ges," I'm hid - ing in Thee.

3. How oft in the con - flict, when pressed by the foe, I have
   fled to my Ref - uge and breathed out my woe; How oft - en, when
   tri - als like sea - bil - lows roll, Have I hid - den in
   Thee, O Thou Rock of my soul.

CHORUS

Hid - ing in Thee, Hid - ing in Thee, Thou blest "Rock of A - ges," I'm hid - ing in Thee.

123

Hiding in Thee

Author–William O. Cushing, 1823–1902
Composer–Ira D. Sankey, 1840–1908
Meter–Irregular
Scripture Reference–Psalm 31:2

> But the Lord is my defense; and my God is the Rock of my refuge.   Psalm 94:22

William O. Cushing was for more than twenty years a successful pastor in the eastern areas of our country. Following the death of his wife in 1870, ill health forced his retirement from the active ministry. During this time he became intensely interested in hymn writing and wrote more than three hundred hymns, cooperating with such gospel musicians as Ira Sankey, Robert Lowry, George Root, and others.

Mr. Cushing has left the following account regarding the writing of "Hiding in Thee":

"Hiding in Thee" was written at Moravia, New York, in 1876. It must be said of this hymn that it was the outgrowth of many tears, many heart conflicts, and yearnings of which the world can know nothing. The history of many battles is behind it. But the occasion which gave it being was the call of Mr. Sankey. He said, "Send me something new to help me in my gospel work." A call from such a source, and for such a purpose, seemed to be a call from God. I so regarded it and prayed, "Lord, give me something that may glorify Thee." It was while thus waiting that "Hiding in Thee" pressed to make itself known. Mr. Sankey called forth the tune, and by his genius gave the hymn wings, making it useful in the Master's work.

124

William O. Cushing is also the author of "Ring the Bells of Heaven" (No. 77).

Ira D. Sankey is often called the "father of the gospel song" because he made extensive use of this new type of music in his evangelistic campaigns with D. L. Moody, and he worked hard in widely publishing and distributing gospel songbook collections. One collection alone, *Sacred Songs and Solos,* is said to have sold more than eighty million copies in the first fifty years following its initial publication. This book is still being published and used today. This collection, as well as a series of publications in which Sankey collaborated with P. P. Bliss and George C. Stebbins, *Gospel Hymns Numbers 1–6,* has had an extraordinary influence on evangelical church music to the present time.

Although the singing of Psalms, hymns, and spiritual songs had always been an important part of public worship since the time of the sixteenth century Protestant Reformation, Sankey introduced a style of congregational singing that was "calculated to awaken the careless, to melt the hardened, and to guide the inquiring souls to Jesus Christ." It was frequently said that Sankey was as effective a preacher of the gospel of salvation with his songs as his associate, D. L. Moody, was with his sermons.

For nearly thirty years Sankey and Moody were inseparable in the work of the gospel, both in this country and throughout Great Britain. Sankey's smooth, cultured ways complemented and made up for Moody's poor English and impulsiveness. They were often referred to as the "David and Jonathan of the gospel ministry."

Ira Sankey had little or no professional voice training. He generally accompanied himself on a small reed organ, singing simply but with careful enunciation and much feeling and expression. His voice was described as an exceptionally strong baritone of moderate compass. An English newspaper once wrote the following review:

As a vocalist, Mr. Sankey has not many equals. Possessed of a voice of great volume and richness, he expresses with exquisite skill and pathos the gospel message, in words very simple but replete with love and tenderness, and always with marked effect on the audience. It is, however, altogether a mistake to suppose that the blessing which attends Mr. Sankey's efforts is attributed only or chiefly to his fine voice and artistic expression. These, no doubt, are very attractive, and go far to move the affections and gratify the taste for music; but the secret of Mr. Sankey's power lies, not in his gift of song, but in the spirit of which the song is only the expression.

125

Another writer wrote as follows regarding Sankey's manner of singing:

There was something about his baritone voice that was enormously affecting. He had a way of pausing between lines of the song, and in that pause the vast audience remained absolutely silent.

"Hiding in Thee" first appeared in a collection entitled *Welcome Tidings,* compiled by Robert Lowry, William H. Doane, and Ira Sankey in 1877. It was prefaced with the Scriptural text, "My strong rock for a house of defense" (Psalm 31:2).

Ira D. Sankey is also the composer of the hymn, "The Ninety and Nine" (No. 91).

30 Hold the Fort

PHILIP P. BLISS, 1838-1876   PHILIP P. BLISS, 1838-1876

1. Ho, my com-rades, see the sig-nal Wav-ing in the sky!
2. See the might-y host ad-vanc-ing, Sa-tan lead-ing on;
3. See the glo-rious ban-ner wav-ing! Hear the trum-pet blow!
4. Fierce and long the bat-tle rag-es, But our help is near;

Re - in-force-ments now ap-pear-ing, Vic-to-ry is nigh.
Might-y men a-round us fall-ing, Cour-age al-most gone!
In our Lead-er's name we tri-umph O - ver ev-'ry foe.
On - ward comes our great Com-mand-er— Cheer, my com-rades, cheer!

CHORUS

126

"Hold the fort, for I am com-ing," Je-sus sig-nals still;

Wave the an-swer back to heav-en, "By Thy grace we will."

Author–Philip P. Bliss, 1838–1876
Composer–Philip P. Bliss, 1838–1876
Meter–8 5. 8 5. with Chorus
Scripture Reference–Revelation 2:25

But that which ye have already hold fast till I come.   Revelation 2:25

As was true of so many of P. P. Bliss's gospel songs, this stirring hymn was inspired by an illustration used by Major Whittle, an officer in the American Civil War, while addressing a YMCA meeting on the text from

Revelation 2:25. Major Whittle's illustration was about a small Northern force of soldiers in charge of guarding a great quantity of supplies. They were being hard pressed by greatly superior Confederate forces. Finally, the Confederate general, General French, commanded the Federal troops to surrender. At that moment the troops saw a signal from their leader, General Sherman, on a hill some miles away which said, "Hold the fort, I am coming. Sherman." The story so captivated Bliss's interest that he could not retire that evening until he had completed both the text and the music for this rousing gospel song.

At the next day's YMCA service, Bliss introduced his new hymn to all of the delegates and the response was immediate and enthusiastic. Later it became a great favorite in the Moody-Sankey campaigns both in Great Britain and in the United States. As Moody and Sankey were leaving the British Isles in 1874, Lord Shaftesbury, presiding at the final service remarked, "If Mr. Sankey has done no more than teach the people to sing 'Hold the Fort,' he has conferred inestimable blessing on the British Empire, and it would have been worth all the expense of these meetings."

Although Philip Bliss did not consider this to be one of his better songs, his monument at Rome, Pennsylvania, bears this inscription: "P. P. Bliss, author of 'Hold the Fort.' "

Other hymns by P. P. Bliss include "I Gave my Life for Thee" (No. 34), "It Is Well with My Soul" (No. 44), "Jesus Loves Even Me" (No. 46) and "My Redeemer" (No. 59).

127

31
Holy, Holy, Holy
NICAEA

REGINALD HEBER, 1783-1826

JOHN B. DYKES, 1823-1876

1. Ho-ly, Ho-ly, Ho-ly, Lord God Al-might-y! Ear-ly in the
2. Ho-ly, Ho-ly, Ho-ly! All the saints a-dore Thee, Cast-ing down their
3. Ho-ly, Ho-ly, Ho-ly! Tho the dark-ness hide Thee, Tho the eye of
4. Ho-ly, Ho-ly, Ho-ly, Lord God Al-might-y! All Thy works shall

morn - ing our song shall rise to Thee; Ho-ly, Ho-ly, Ho-ly!
gold-en crowns a-round the glass-y sea; Cher-u-bim and ser-a-phim
sin-ful man Thy glo-ry may not see; On-ly Thou art ho-ly—
praise Thy name in earth and sky and sea; Ho-ly, Ho-ly, Ho-ly!

128

Mer - ci-ful and Might-y! God in Three Per-sons, bless-ed Trin-i-ty!
fall - ing down be-fore Thee, Which wert and art and ev-er-more shalt be.
there is none be-side Thee Per-fect in pow'r, in love and pur-i-ty.
Mer - ci-ful and Might-y! God in Three Per-sons, bless-ed Trin-i-ty!

Author–Reginald Heber, 1783–1826
Composer–John B. Dykes, 1823–1876
Tune Name–"Nicaea"
Meter–11 12, 12 10.
Scripture Reference–Revelation 4:8–11

O come, let us worship and bow down: Let us kneel before the Lord our maker. For He is our God; and we are the people of His pasture.   Psalm 95:6,7

Reginald Heber was born in the area of Cheshire, England, on April 21, 1783, of scholarly and well-to-do parents. At the age of seventeen he entered Oxford University, where his scholarship and literary abilities received much attention. Following his ordination to the ministry of the

Anglican Church, he served for the next sixteen years at an obscure parish church in the little village of Hodnet in western England. Throughout his ministry he was known and respected as a man of rare refinement and noble Christian character. Heber was also noted as a prolific literary writer, making frequent contributions to magazines with his poetry, essays and hymns.

In 1823, just three years before his early death at the age of forty-three, Heber was sent to India to serve as the Bishop of Calcutta. This responsibility included not only India but the Island of Ceylon and all of Australia as well. The pressures of this work along with the humid climate of that area wore heavily upon his health. One Sunday morning, after preaching to a large outdoor crowd of Indians on the subject of the evils of their caste system, he evidently suffered a sun-stroke and died very suddenly. One year after his untimely death, a collection of his fifty-seven choice hymns was published by his widow and many friends. Most of these hymns are still in use today.

This hymn was written by Reginald Heber specifically for its liturgical use on Trinity Sunday, which occurs eight weeks after Easter. The emphasis of this Sunday's service is to reaffirm the doctrine of the triune Godhead. Though the word "trinity" is not found in the Scriptures, yet the truth of three Persons, equal and eternal with each other, is clearly taught throughout God's Word.

Reginald Heber is also the author of the hymn, "From Greenland's Icy Mountains" (No. 25).

The tune for this text has been named "Nicaea." It was named after the Council of Nicaea held in Asia Minor in 325 A.D., when the doctrine of the Trinity was examined and held to be a true and essential doctrine of the Christian faith. In 1861 this tune was composed specifically for these words by one of England's leading church musicians of the nineteenth century, Dr. John Bacchus Dykes. This popular composer has contributed more than 300 hymn tunes; most of them are still in use today.

Other hymns by John B. Dykes include "I Heard the Voice of Jesus Say" (No. 35), "Jesus, the Very Thought of Thee" (No. 49), and "Lead, Kindly Light" (No. 53).

129

32   How Firm a Foundation
FOUNDATION

"K" — in Rippon's *Selection of Hymns*, 1787

American melody
From Caldwell's *Union Harmony*, 1837

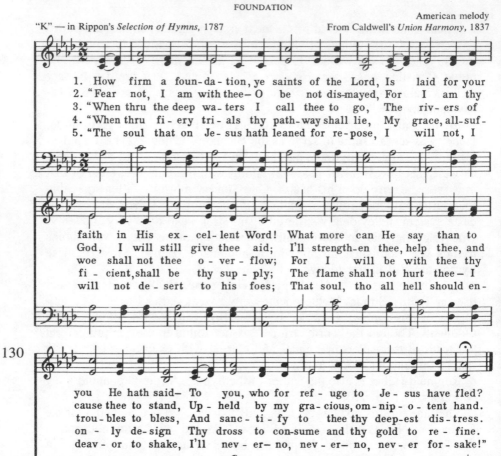

1. How firm a foun-da-tion, ye saints of the Lord, Is   laid for your
2. "Fear not, I am with thee— O   be   not dis-mayed, For   I   am thy
3. "When thru the deep wa-ters I   call thee to   go,   The   riv-ers of
4. "When thru fi-er-y tri-als thy path-way shall lie,   My   grace, all-suf-
5. "The soul that on Je-sus hath leaned for re-pose,   I   will not, I

faith   in His   ex-cel-lent Word! What more can He   say   than to
God,   I will still   give thee   aid;   I'll strength-en thee, help thee, and
woe shall not thee   o-ver-flow;   For   I   will be   with thee thy
fi-cient, shall be   thy sup-ply;   The flame shall not hurt thee— I
will   not de-sert   to his foes;   That soul, tho all hell should en-

130

you   He hath said— To   you, who for ref-uge to   Je-sus have fled?
cause thee to stand, Up-held by my gra-cious, om-nip-o-tent hand.
trou-bles to bless, And sanc-ti-fy to   thee thy deep-est dis-tress.
on-ly de-sign   Thy dross to con-sume and thy gold to   re-fine.
deav-or to shake, I'll   nev-er— no, nev-er— no, nev-er for-sake!"

Author—"K" in Rippon's *Selection of Hymns,* 1787
*Music—*An Early American Folk Melody from Caldwell's *Union Harmony,* 1837
Tune Name—"Foundation"
*Meter—*11 11. 11 11

So that we may boldly say, The Lord is my helper, and I will not fear what man shall
do unto me.   Hebrews 13:6

Throughout our country this hymn has been for many years one of the
stalwart hymns in evangelical churches, especially the Baptist Churches.

The authorship of the text has always been a mystery to hymnologists. Its first appearance was in 1787 in a hymnal, *Selection of Hymns,* published by Dr. John Rippon, pastor of the Carter's Lane Baptist Church, London, England. Dr. Rippon was pastor of this important church for sixty-three years and was considered to be one of the most popular and influential dissenting ministers of his time. The hymn appeared anonymously in his collection with the author indicated merely as "K-." Later reprints also gave "Kn," and one, "Keen." Since the music director in Dr. Rippon's church was named R. Keene, it has generally been thought that he was the author of the text.

Rippon's hymnal was exceedingly popular immediately: eleven editions were printed in England before the pastor's death in 1836, and an American edition was also printed by the Baptist Churches in Philadelphia in 1820. This hymnal has often been called the "unofficial hymn textbook for Baptist Churches." "How Firm a Foundation" became well-known throughout our Northern and Southern States during the time of the Civil War and was included in most American publications of that time.

The composer of this music is also unknown. It has been established that the tune is one of the sturdy folk tunes originating in the South. It first appeared in 1837 in William Caldwell's publication, *Union Harmony.*

131

Like many of our fine hymns this text is really a sermon in verse. In the first stanza the sure foundation of the Christian faith is established as being the Word of God. This challenging question is posed: what more can God do than provide His very Word as a completed revelation of Himself to man? The succeeding verses personalize the precious promises from His Word:

Verse Two–Isaiah 41:10– "Fear thou not, for I am with thee, be not dismayed, for I am thy God. . ."

Verse Three–Isaiah 43:2–"When thou passest through the waters, I will be with thee. . ."

Verse Four–2 Corinthians 12:9– "My grace is sufficient for thee; For my strength is made perfect in weakness. . ."

Verse Five–Hebrews 13:5– "I will never leave thee, nor forsake thee. . ."

"How Firm a Foundation" has been a favorite hymn and testimonial of many of God's children throughout the years. It was the favorite of such American leaders as Theodore Roosevelt, Andrew Jackson, who requested that it be sung at his bedside shortly before he died at the Hermitage, as well as Robert E. Lee, who also requested it for his funeral hymn "as an expression of his full trust in the ways of the Heavenly Father" (see page 38).

How Great Thou Art!

Stuart K. Hine, 1899-

Swedish melody
Arr. by Manna Music, Inc.

132

1. O Lord my God, when I in awe-some won-der Con-sid-er all the worlds Thy hands have made, I see the stars, I hear the roll-ing thun-der, Thy pow'r thru-out the un-i-verse dis-played!

2. When thru the woods and for-est glades I wan-der And hear the birds sing sweet-ly in the trees, When I look down from loft-y moun-tain gran-deur And hear the brook and feel the gen-tle breeze,

3. And when I think that God, His Son not spar-ing, Sent Him to die, I scarce can take it in— That on the cross, my bur-den glad-ly bear-ing, He bled and died to take a-way my sin!

4. When Christ shall come with shout of ac-cla-ma-tion And take me home, what joy shall fill my heart! Then I shall bow in hum-ble ad-o-ra-tion And there pro-claim, my God, how great Thou art!

REFRAIN

Then sings my soul, my Sav-ior God, to Thee; How great Thou art, how great Thou art! Then sings my soul, my Sav-ior God, to Thee; How great Thou art, how great Thou art!

* Translator's original words are "works" and "mighty."

How Great Thou Art

English Words by Stuart K. Hine 1899–
Music Arrangement by Stuart K. Hine and Manna Music of Swedish Folk
   Melody
Meter–11 10. 11 10 with Refrain

Great is the Lord, and greatly to be praised; and His greatness is unsearchable.
Psalm 145:3

This is a fine twentieth century hymn of praise that has become a favorite with God's people during the last three decades. Its popularity is due in large part to its wide use by favorite gospel singers, notably George Beverly Shea. Although introduced to American audiences when Mr. James Caldwell sang "How Great Thou Art" at Stony Brook Bible Conference on Long Island in 1951, it was not until Cliff Barrows and Bev Shea of the Billy Graham Evangelistic Team used it during the famed London Crusade in Harringay Arena that "How Great Thou Art" started to become universally well-known.

The original Swedish text was a poem entitled "O Store Gud," written by a Swedish pastor, the Reverend Carl Boberg, in 1886. In addition to being one of the leading evangelical preachers of his day, Boberg was also the successful editor of the periodical *Sanningsvittnet*. His inspiration for this text is said to have come from a visit to a beautiful country estate on the southeast coast of Sweden. He was suddenly caught in a midday thunderstorm with awe-inspiring moments of flashing violence, followed by a clear brilliant sun. Soon afterwards he heard the calm, sweet songs of the birds in nearby trees. The experience prompted the pastor to fall to his knees in humble adoration of his mighty God. He penned his exaltation in a nine-stanza poem beginning with the Swedish words "O Store Gud, nar jag den varld beskader."

Several years later Boberg was attending a meeting in the Province of Varmländ and was surprised to hear the congregation sing his poem to the tune of an old Swedish melody.

The subsequent history of this hymn is most interesting. It is thought that soon after Boberg's version, the text was translated into German by Manfred von Glehn and entitled "Wie gross bist Du." Later in 1925 the Reverend E. Gustav Johnson of North Park College, Chicago, Illinois, made the first literal English translation from the Swedish text. This translation is quite different from the text that we know today but may still be found in some hymnals. Johnson's literal translation of the Swedish text is entitled "O Mighty God, When I Behold the Wonder." In 1927 I. S. Prokhanoff came upon the German version and translated it into the Russian language.

133

SINGING WITH UNDERSTANDING

In 1923 the Reverend S. K. Hine and his wife, English missionaries, were ministering to the people of the Ukraine. It was there they learned the Russian translation of "O Store Gud" from a congregation of Ukrainians. They remember singing it as a duet in dark, unevangelized places and the telling effect it had on the unsaved. The thought of writing original English lyrics to this song did not then occur to them—that was to await their crossing into Sub-Carpathian Russia, where the mountain scenery was to play its part. The thoughts of the first three verses in English were born, line upon line, amid unforgettable experiences in the Carpathian mountains. (The fourth verse was written later in England.) Thus, inspired partially by the Russian words, partially by the awesome wonder at the sight of "all the works thy hand hath made," the thoughts of the first two verses sprang into life in English. As Reverend Hine and his wife continued their evangelizing in the Carpathian mountains and distribution of gospels in village after village, verse three came into being.

When war broke out in 1939, it was necessary for Reverend Hine and his wife to return to Britain; now armed with these three verses, the writer continued his gospel campaigns during the "Blitz years." The fourth verse did not come until after the war.

134
The tune for this hymn is an arrangement made of an old Swedish folk melody. It is typically characteristic of many other hymn tunes, i.e., "Day by Day" (No. 17) with its lilting, warm, singable simplicity. With his original English lyrics and his arrangement of the Swedish folk melody, Mr. Stuart K. Hine published what we know today as the hymn "How Great Thou Art." Assignments of copyrights and publication rights to an American publishing firm in 1954 helped spread the popularity of this hymn. In April of 1974 the *Christian Herald* magazine, in a poll presented to its readers, named "How Great Thou Art" the No. 1 hymn in America.

34   # I Gave My Life for Thee

KENOSIS

FRANCES R. HAVERGAL, 1836-1879   PHILIP P. BLISS, 1838-1876

135

1. I gave My life for thee, My pre-cious blood I shed,
2. My Fa-ther's house of light, My glo-ry-cir-cled throne
3. I suf-fered much for thee, More than thy tongue can tell,
4. And I have brought to thee, Down from My home a-bove,

That thou might'st ran-somed be, And quick-ened from the dead;
I left, for earth-ly night, For wan-d'rings sad and lone;
Of bit-t'rest ag-o-ny, To res-cue thee from hell;
Sal-va-tion full and free, My par-don and My love;

I gave, I gave My life for thee—What hast thou giv'n for Me?
I left, I left it all for thee—Hast thou left aught for Me?
I've borne, I've borne it all for thee—What hast thou borne for Me?
I bring, I bring rich gifts to thee—What hast thou brought to Me?

Author–Frances R. Havergal, 1836–1879
Composer–Philip P. Bliss, 1838–1876
Tune Name–"Kenosis"
Meter–66.66.86

> And that He died for all, that they which live should not henceforth live unto themselves, but unto Him which died for them, and rose again.   2 Corinthians 5:15

Frances Ridley Havergal, often referred to as "hymnody's sweetest voice," was born on December 14, 1836, at Astley, Worcestershire, England. She was the youngest child of the Rev. William Henry Havergal, a minister of the Church of England. He, too, was a noted poet and church musician. In addition to her natural talents, Miss Havergal had a thorough training in linguistics and music. Although she was highly educated and cultured, Miss Havergal always maintained a simple faith and confidence in her Lord. It is said that she never wrote a line without first praying over it. Her entire life was characterized by spiritual saintliness. In spite of being always frail in health, she lived an active and productive life until her early death at the age of forty-three.

As part of her education, Frances studied in Dusseldorf, Germany. In the art gallery of that city hangs the famous painting by Sternberg, "Ecce Homo," a vivid portrayal of Christ, wearing his crown of thorns, before Pilate and the Jewish mob. Beneath the picture are the words, "This have I done for thee; what hast thou done for Me?"

Upon visiting the museum and seeing the painting, Miss Havergal was profoundly moved. After gazing for a considerable time at the painting, she took a pencil and scrap paper and quickly drafted the stanzas for this hymn text. Later, when visiting her home in England, she again noted the text she had hurriedly scribbled, but she felt that the poetry was so poor that she tossed the paper into a stove. The paper, however, is said to have floated out of the flames and landed on the floor, where it was later found by her father. He encouraged her to keep the words and composed the first tune for the text.

Frances R. Havergal is also author of the hymn "Take My Life and Let It Be" (No. 87).

136

The present tune, "Kenosis," was composed for this text by the noted American gospel songwriter, Philip P. Bliss. It was dedicated to the Railroad Chapel Sunday School in Chicago, Illinois, and first appeared in Bliss's *Sunshine for Sunday Schools,* 1873.

Other hymns by Philip P. Bliss include "Hold the Fort" (No. 30), "It Is Well with My Soul" (No. 44), "Jesus Loves Even Me" (No. 46) and "My Redeemer" (No. 59).

35 I Heard the Voice of Jesus Say

VOX DILECTI

HORATIUS BONAR, 1808-1889

JOHN B. DYKES, 1823-1876

1. I heard the voice of Je - sus say, "Come un - to Me and rest;
2. I heard the voice of Je - sus say, "Be - hold, I free - ly give
3. I heard the voice of Je - sus say, "I am this dark world's Light;

Lay down, thou wea - ry one, lay down Thy head up - on My breast."
The liv - ing wa - ter— thirst - y one, Stoop down and drink, and live."
Look un - to Me— thy morn shall rise, And all thy day be bright."

137

I came to Je - sus as I was, Wea - ry and worn and sad;
I came to Je - sus, and I drank Of that life - giv - ing stream;
I looked to Je - sus, and I found In Him my Star, my Sun;

I found in Him a rest - ing-place, And He has made me glad.
My thirst was quenched, my soul re - vived, And now I live in Him.
And in that Light of life I'll walk, Till trav-'ling days are done.

SINGING WITH UNDERSTANDING

I Heard the Voice of Jesus Say

Author-Horatius Bonar, 1808-1889
Music-John B. Dykes, 1823-1876
Tune Name-"Vox Dilecti"
Meter-CM (86.86 Doubled)
Scripture References-Matthew 11:28; John 4:14; John 8:12

> And the Spirit and the bride say, Come. And let him that heareth say, Come. And let him that is athirst come. And whosoever will, let him take the water of life freely.
> Revelation 22:17

This hymn presents in a most meaningful way three of our Lord's pointed, personal invitations to mankind, which are followed in turn by the human responses and their spiritual results:
Stanza one-*Come Unto Me* (Matthew 11:28); I came, I found rest and gladness.
Stanza two-*Drink My Living Water* (John 4:10, 13-14); I came, drank, and life revived.
Stanza three-*Look Upon My Light* (John 8:12); I looked, and shall henceforth walk in that light.

138 The music for this fine text, written for the hymn in 1868 by John B. Dykes, noted English musician of the nineteenth century, relates the Lord's gracious invitations in the minor key, while the responses and the results are notated in the major mode. The hymn tune name, "Vox Dilecti," is Latin for "Voice of the Beloved." As is true of all of Dykes' fine tunes, this music is characterized by a warm, expressive quality, typical of nineteenth-century Romanticism at its finest.

Other hymns by John B. Dykes include "Holy, Holy, Holy" (No. 31), "Jesus, the Very Thought of Thee" (No. 49) and "Lead, Kindly Light" (No. 53).

Horatius Bonar is generally considered to be one of Scotland's most gifted and powerful evangelical ministers and hymn writers. He was born on December 19, 1808 in Edinburgh, Scotland. When the split occurred in the established Church of Scotland in 1843, Bonar became active in promoting the Free Church Movement. Throughout his ministry he was known as a man of boundless energy and ability. One of his tracts, "Believe and Live," had more than a million copies published. In addition to his widely-known reputation as an able Presbyterian preacher, earnest soul-winner, and avid student of the Scriptures, Bonar wrote approximately 600 hymns, 100 of which are still in general use.

"I Heard the Voice of Jesus Say" is generally considered to be the finest of all of Bonar's hymns. It first appeared in his collection *Hymns,*

Original and Selected in 1846 and later in his *Hymns of Faith and Hope* in 1862 with the title "The Voice from Galilee."

Bonar wrote this hymn while he was pastoring the Presbyterian Church at Kelso, Scotland. As he did most of his hymns, he wrote this one with children in mind. He was always concerned that boys and girls learn and sing the great truths concerning the person and work of Christ. Yet despite the simplicity of Bonar's writings, the spiritual depth and warmth of these expressions have ministered blessing to God's people of all ages for more than a century.

139

Horatius Bonar

I Love Thy Kingdom, Lord!

ST. THOMAS

TIMOTHY DWIGHT, 1752-1817   AARON WILLIAMS, 1731-1776

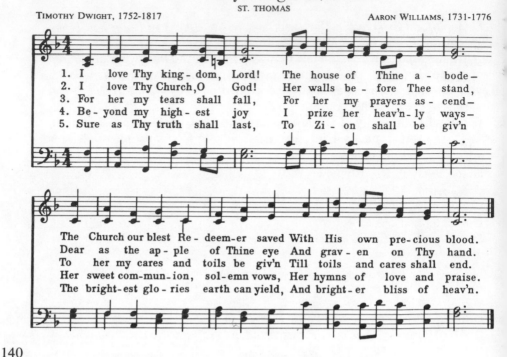

1. I love Thy king-dom, Lord! The house of Thine a - bode—
2. I love Thy Church, O God! Her walls be - fore Thee stand,
3. For her my tears shall fall, For her my prayers as - cend—
4. Be - yond my high - est joy I prize her heav'n - ly ways—
5. Sure as Thy truth shall last, To Zi - on shall be giv'n

The Church our blest Re - deem-er saved With His own pre-cious blood.
Dear as the ap - ple of Thine eye And grav - en on Thy hand.
To her my cares and toils be giv'n Till toils and cares shall end.
Her sweet com-mun-ion, sol-emn vows, Her hymns of love and praise.
The bright-est glo - ries earth can yield, And bright - er bliss of heav'n.

140

Author-Timothy Dwight, 1752–1817
Composer-Aaron Williams, 1731–1776
Tune Name-"St. Thomas"
Meter-SM (66.86)
Scripture Reference-Psalm 137:5,6

Let us consider one another to provoke unto love and to good works: Not forsaking the
assembling of ourselves together. . .   Hebrews 10:24–25

This is the only American hymn written from the time of the Pilgrim
Fathers until the beginning of the nineteenth century that is still in general
use today. It has been termed "one of the imperishable lyrics of the Christian Church."

Timothy Dwight is truly one of the illustrious names in early American
history. He was born in Northampton, Massachusetts, on May 14, 1752.
His mother was the daughter of evangelist Jonathan Edwards. Young
Timothy was graduated from Yale College at the age of seventeen. The
adult career of this man is amazing. He served for a time as chaplain with
George Washington in the American Revolutionary War. Upon his return
from service he became a Congregational minister, a successful farmer, a
representative in the Connecticut State Legislature, a faculty member at
Yale and President of that institution in 1795.

His work at Yale was outstanding. Not only did he raise the academic standards, but he brought a spiritual emphasis to the campus that was startling. Prior to his administration most of the students at Yale had been infected with the "free thought" of Thomas Paine, Rousseau and the French Revolution. It is estimated that there were no more than five professing Christians on campus when Dwight assumed the presidency. His dynamic leadership ignited a spiritual revival which soon spread to other New England campuses as well.

In 1797 Timothy Dwight revised Isaac Watts's *Psalms and Hymns* and added thirty-three of his own hymn texts, including "I Love Thy Kingdom, Lord." This collection was so successful that it was used almost exclusively in Congregational and Presbyterian Churches throughout the New England States for the next thirty years. Other literary works by Dwight include five volumes of sermons under the title, *Theology Explained and Defended.* He also authored an important book entitled *The Triumph of Infidelity,* a satire against the leading sceptics of his day. His most valuable historical secular work, since it depicted social and economic conditions in New England at the time, were his four volumes entitled *Travels in New England and New York.*

All of Timothy Dwight's accomplishments seem more amazing when it is realized that for the last forty years of his life he was unable to read consecutively for more than fifteen minutes a day. His defective eyesight had been caused by a case of small-pox, and the pain in his eyes is said to have been agonizing and constant.

141

The tune for this hymn text, "St. Thomas," first appeared in Aaron Williams's collection of tunes of 1763. It is also often used with Isaac Watts's text, "Come, We That Love the Lord." Since Williams never claimed authorship of this tune, many believe that it was not Williams's original melody but rather an adaptation from a work by George F. Handel, composer of the oratorio, *The Messiah.* Aaron Williams was a music director and clerk of a Scottish Presbyterian Church in London, England.

37　I Love to Tell the Story

A. Catherine Hankey, 1834-1911　　　　　　　　　　　　　William G. Fischer, 1835-1912

1. I love to tell the sto - ry Of un - seen things a - bove, Of
2. I love to tell the sto - ry— More won - der - ful it seems Than
3. I love to tell the sto - ry—'Tis pleas - ant to re - peat What
4. I love to tell the sto - ry, For those who know it best Seem

Je - sus and His glo - ry, Of Je - sus and His love; I love to
all the gold - en fan - cies Of all our gold - en dreams; I love to
seems, each time I tell it, More won - der - ful - ly sweet; I love to
hun - ger - ing and thirst - ing To hear it like the rest; And when in

142

tell the sto - ry Be - cause I know 'tis true, It sat - is - fies my
tell the sto - ry— It did so much for me, And that is just the
tell the sto - ry For some have nev - er heard The mes - sage of sal -
scenes of glo - ry I sing the new, new song, 'Twill be the old, old

REFRAIN

long - ings As noth - ing else can do.
rea - son I tell it now to thee.　　　I love to tell the sto - ry! 'Twill
va - tion From God's own ho - ly Word.
sto - ry That I have loved so long.

be my theme in glo - ry— To tell the old, old sto - ry Of Je - sus and His love.

I Love to Tell the Story

Author–A. Katherine Hankey, 1834–1911
Composer–William G. Fischer, 1835–1912
Meter–13 7 6. 13 7 6. with Refrain

The fruit of the righteous is a tree of life; and he that winneth souls is wise.
Proverbs 11:30

The evangelical emphasis or movement really began in England during the mid-eighteenth century with the ministries of such leaders as George Whitefield and John and Charles Wesley. The movement in its earliest days reached mainly the lower and middle classes of society with the upper classes remaining quite aloof from its influence. During the nineteenth century, however, the evangelical movement began to have considerable influence upon the upper classes as well. One such influential group was known as the Clapham Sect because the activities of this group centered in the elite suburb of Clapham in Southwest London. These men were wealthy evangelical philanthropists, students of the Bible, and men of prayer. They gave freely of their time, talents, and money to spread the gospel. Though these individuals generally maintained their membership within the Anglican Church, their emphasis was always on the necessity of personal conversion and guidance by the Holy Spirit rather than on a mere reliance upon the sacraments and rituals of the Church. There are numerous examples of the zealous ministries carried on by these influential Christian laymen, including a number of members of Parliament, who exercised great compassion upon the masses of impoverished people throughout the United Kingdom. A noted historian says of this Clapham Sect, "Never in the history of Anglicanism had any group exercised so profound an influence."

143

Katherine Hankey was born in 1834, the daughter of a wealthy English banker. Though the members of her family were prominent members of the Anglican Church, they were always associated with its more evangelical faction. Her father was one of the influential members of the Clapham Sect. Early in life Katherine, or Kate, as she was affectionately known, caught this same evangelical concern from her father. She began organizing Sunday School classes for rich and poor throughout London. These classes had a profound influence throughout the city with a large number of the young students in turn becoming zealous Christian workers. Kate also did considerable writing, including such works as *Bible Class Teachings,* a booklet on confirmation, as well as a number of books of verse. All of the royalties received from these publications were always directed to some foreign missions project.

When Katherine was only thirty years of age, she experienced a serious illness. During a long period of recovery she wrote a lengthy poem on the life of Christ. The poem consisted of two main sections, each containing fifty verses. The first section of the poem was entitled "The Story Wanted." It was from this part of her poem that she later adapted the words for another of her familiar hymn texts, "Tell Me the Old, Old Story." This hymn has since become another of the church's classic children's hymns.

Later that same year while still recovering from her illness, Kate Hankey completed the second part of her poem on the life of Christ. This sequel to the first section was entitled "The Story Told." From these verses came the text for "I Love to Tell the Story," written in the same meter but with a different accent than her other familiar hymn text.

Being musically inclined, Kate also composed her own tunes for these two texts. Her hymns received little notice, however, when used with this music. The following year, 1867, a large international YMCA convention was held in Montreal, Canada. One of the speakers at the convention, Major General Russell from England, closed his emotionally charged message to the delegates by quoting the verses from Miss Hankey's two hymn texts. In the audience that day was a noted American gospel musician, William H. Doane, composer of more than 2,000 gospel songs. Mr. Doane was greatly moved by these lines and promptly composed musical settings for both texts.

144

Later a new musical setting, which replaced Doane's music for "I Love to Tell the Story," was composed by William G. Fischer, a Philadelphia musician and piano dealer. Fischer also added the refrain for the hymn, "I love to tell the story! 'Twill be my theme in glory–to tell the old, old story of Jesus and His love." In 1875 the hymn appeared in its present form in Bliss and Sankey's collection, *Gospel Hymns and Sacred Songs,* which brought "I Love to Tell the Story" to the attention of evangelical congregations everywhere. Both of Katherine Hankey's hymns are still widely used today.

38

I Sing the Mighty Power of God

ELLACOMBE

Isaac Watts, 1674-1748 — alt.

From *Gesangbuch der Herzogl,*
Württemberg, 1784

1. I sing the might-y pow'r of God That made the moun-tains rise,
2. I sing the good-ness of the Lord That filled the earth with food;
3. There's not a plant or flow'r be - low But makes Thy glo - ries known;

That spread the flow-ing seas a - broad And built the loft - y skies.
He formed the crea-tures with His word And then pro-nounced them good.
And clouds a - rise and tem-pests blow By or - der from Thy throne;

I sing the wis - dom that or-dained The sun to rule the day;
Lord, how Thy won-ders are dis-played Wher-e'er I turn my eye:
While all that bor-rows life from Thee Is ev - er in Thy care,

145

The moon shines full at His com-mand, And all the stars o - bey.
If I sur - vey the ground I tread Or gaze up - on the sky!
And ev - 'ry-where that man can be, Thou, God, art pres - ent there.

Author–Isaac Watts, 1674–1748, with alterations by others
Music–From *Gesangbuch der Herzogl,* Württemberg, 1784
Tune Name–"Ellacombe"
Meter–CMD (86.86 Doubled)

He shall have dominion also from sea to sea, and from the rivers unto the ends of the earth.
Psalm 72:8

Isaac Watts, the father of English hymnody, was frail in health during
much of his life. For the last thirty years of his life he was more or less an

invalid at the home of his friend, Sir Thomas Abney, where Watts devoted himself in comfortable and happy surroundings to the writing of many of the fine hymns still used today. Watts's ambition, according to his own words, was as follows: "My design was not to exalt myself to the rank and glory of poets, but I was ambitious to be a servant to the churches, and a helper to the joy of the meanest Christian."

Although frail in health and grotesque in appearance, described as five feet tall with a big head and a long-hooked nose, Watts was a scholarly genius in many different fields. His writings included essays, discussions of psychology, three volumes of sermons, catechisms, twenty-nine treatises on theology, textbooks on logic, and a variety of other works.

Though he never married, Isaac Watts always loved children and wrote much for them. In 1715 he wrote a book of songs especially for young people, *Divine Songs for Children,* which has recently been republished by the Oxford University Press. This hymnal was the first hymnal ever written exclusively for children. His unusual love and concern for children is commemorated on his fine statue located at Southampton, England.

The text for this hymn is from Watts's hymnal of 1715. In the preface to this hymnal Watts wrote, ". . . children of high and low degree, of the
146   Church of England or dissenters, baptized in infancy or not, may all join together in these songs. And as I have endeavored to sink the language to the level of a child's understanding, and yet to keep it, if possible, above contempt, so I have designed to profit all, if possible, and offend none."

It is interesting to realize that this great scholar and literary genius was also capable of writing for children such tender expressions as these:

> Hush, my dear, be still and slumber
> Holy angels guard thy bed;
> Heavenly blessings without number
> Gently falling on thy head.

Other hymns by Isaac Watts include "Jesus Shall Reign" (No. 48), "O God, Our Help in Ages Past" (No. 66) and "When I Survey the Wondrous Cross" (No. 100).

The music for this text was first found in a collection published in 1784. It was originally intended for use in the Roman Catholic Chapel of the Duke of Württemberg. Interestingly, of the fifty-five hymns in this collection, the majority were written by German Protestant hymn writers. The tune, "Ellacombe," first appeared in England in 1868 in the Appendix to *Hymns Ancient and Modern,* a widely published Anglican hymnal of the nineteenth century. The tune was named for a village in Devonshire, England.

39 I Will Sing the Wondrous Story

FRANCIS H. ROWLEY, 1854-1952

PETER P. BILHORN, 1865-1936

1. I will sing the won-drous sto - ry Of the Christ who died for me—
2. I was lost but Je-sus found me— Found the sheep that went a - stray,
3. I was bruised but Je-sus healed me— Faint was I from man-y a fall;
4. Days of dark-ness still come o'er me, Sor-row's paths I oft - en tread;
5. He will keep me till the riv - er Rolls its wa - ters at my feet;

How He left His home in glo - ry For the cross of Cal - va - ry.
Threw His lov- ing arms a - round me, Drew me back in - to His way.
Sight was gone and fears pos-sessed me, But He freed me from them all.
But the Sav - ior still is with me— By His hand I'm safe - ly led.
Then He'll bear me safe - ly o - ver, Where the loved ones I shall meet.

CHORUS

Yes, I'll sing the wondrous sto - ry Of the Christ
Yes, I'll sing the wondrous sto-ry Of the Christ

who died for me, Sing it with the saints in
who died for me, Sing it with

glo - ry, Gath-ered by the crys-tal sea.
the saints in glo-ry, Gath-ered by the crys-tal sea, the crys-tal sea.

147

SINGING WITH UNDERSTANDING

I Will Sing the Wondrous Story

Author-Francis H. Rowley, 1854-1952
Composer-Peter P. Bilhorn, 1865-1936
Meter-87. 87. with Chorus

> I will sing of the mercies of the Lord forever; with my mouth will I make known Thy faithfulness to all generations. Psalm 89:1

Francis H. Rowley was born in Hilton, New York, on July 25, 1854. Later he became a Baptist minister and served churches in Massachusetts, Pennsylvania and Illinois. He has given the following account for the writing of this hymn:

> I was minister of the First Baptist Church of North Adams, Massachusetts in 1886. The church and community were experiencing a period of unusual interest in religious matters, and I was assisted by a remarkable young Swiss musician by the name of Peter Bilhorn. One Sunday following the evening service he said, "Why don't you write a hymn for me to set to music?" During the night these verses came to me. The original poem began "Can't You Sing the Wondrous Story?" However, when the song was first published by Ira Sankey in 1887, the phrase was changed to "I Will Sing...."

148

Peter P. Bilhorn was born in Mendota, Illinois, in 1865. With the death of his father, Peter was forced to leave school at eight years of age to help support his mother and family. At the age of fifteen he moved with his family to Chicago, where his voice became a great attraction in concert halls and among his worldly comrades. When he was twenty he was converted to Christ at one of the meetings conducted by Dr. Pentecost and musician George Stebbins. Following his conversion, he was used greatly of God in various forms of Christian service.

The organ he used in services was a small folding organ bearing his name. Feeling the need of a small portable organ for use in street meetings, he had designed a folding organ weighing only sixteen pounds and had started its manufacture in 1887. This venture proved most successful, and the organs were widely used around the world.

It is estimated that he wrote approximately 2,000 gospel songs. This particular hymn is one of his finest compositions. His evangelistic ministry carried him into all the states of the union, to Great Britain, and to other foreign countries. He preceded Homer Rodeheaver as Billy Sunday's song leader prior to 1908.

P. P. Bilhorn was not only a skillful songwriter and leader but also an earnest soul-winner. One night, while conducting revival meetings in

Reedsburg, Wisconsin, he retired to his room but later felt strangely compelled to dress, take his folding organ, and start walking down the street, even though the weather was bitterly cold. Seeing a gleam of light from a basement window, he knocked and was admitted. He found a group of men gambling. Bilhorn began to sing to the men "Where is My Wandering Boy Tonight?" Six of these men made their peace with God that night.

"I Will Sing the Wondrous Story" was presented by Rowley and Bilhorn to Ira D. Sankey as a gift. Sankey was so impressed with the merit and usefulness of this hymn that he published it in the 1887 edition of *Gospel Hymns and Sacred Songs and Solos*. It soon became one of the most popular songs in the entire collection.

40   I'll Stand By Until the Morning

Daniel W. Whittle, 1840-1901   James McGranahan, 1840-1907

150

1. Fierce and wild the storm is rag - ing Round a help - less bark,
2. Wea - ry, help-less, hope-less sea - men, Faint - ing on the deck,
3. On a wild and storm-y o - cean, Sink - ing 'neath the wave,
4. Dar - ing death thy soul to res - cue, He in love has come;

On to doom 'tis swift - ly driv - ing, O'er the wa - ters dark!
With what joy they hail their Sav - ior, As He hails their wreck!
Souls that per - ish heed the mes - sage— Christ has come to save!
Leave the wreck and, in Him trust - ing, Thou shalt reach thy home!

CHORUS

Joy! be-hold the Sav - ior! Joy! the mes-sage
Joy, O joy! be - hold the Sav - ior! Joy, O joy! the

hear: "I'll stand by un - til the morn - ing— I've
mes - sage hear:

come to save you, do not fear; Yes, I'll stand by un - til the

morn - ing— I've come to save you, do not fear."
(do not fear.")

I'll Stand by Until the Morning

Author–Daniel W. Whittle, 1840–1901
Composer–James McGranahan, 1840–1907
Meter–8 5. 8 5 with Chorus

Let the redeemed of the Lord say so, whom He hath redeemed from the hand of the enemy.   Psalm 107:2

Daniel W. Whittle was born in Chicopee Falls, Massachusetts, on November 22, 1840. At the age of twenty-one he joined the 72nd Illinois Infantry, enlisting in Company B as a Second Lieutenant. Later he rose to the rank of Major on General O. O. Howard's staff. He was with General Sherman on his march to the sea and was later wounded at the battle of Vicksburg. Upon his recovery and return home, he met the noted evangelist, D. L. Moody. His relationship with Moody changed the course of Whittle's life. After a rather brief time in business with the Elgin Watch Company, whose treasurer he became, he was persuaded by Moody to enter full-time evangelistic work. Soon he became known as one of the leading evangelists of his day.

Whittle always worked with a gospel singer and song leader. His first such associate was Philip P. Bliss, whose tragic death at the Ashtabula, Ohio, train wreck in 1876 ended a most happy relationship. James McGranahan succeeded Bliss as Major Whittle's singing companion. The greater number of Whittle's more than two hundred hymn texts were set to music by McGranahan. Most of Whittle's hymns bore the pseudonym "El Nathan." Moody once said, "I think Major Whittle has written some of the best hymns of this century." Together Whittle and McGranahan made several trips to Great Britain for evangelistic crusades and traveled extensively in this country until about 1890, when McGranahan's health began to fail.

At Northfield, Massachusetts, on March 4, 1901, at the age of sixty-one, Major Daniel W. Whittle completed his colorful and fruitful pilgrimage and went to be with the Lord he loved and served so faithfully.

James McGranahan was born on July 4, 1840 near Adamsville, Pennsylvania, of Scotch-Irish descent. From his earliest years his rare tenor voice had been the delight of all who heard it. Many encouraged him to enter the operatic field, a career in which, it was felt, he would certainly achieve success. For some time Philip Bliss had encouraged McGranahan to devote his total life to an evangelistic ministry. Upon hearing of Bliss's tragic accident at Ashtabula, Ohio, on December 29, 1876, McGranahan went immediately to the site, seeking to identify the body and to locate some remembrance of his beloved friend. (Neither the body of Bliss nor his wife was ever found.) Moving about in the large

151

crowd gathered at the site of the accident, McGranahan recognized Major Whittle, although they had never before met. The Major, too, had heard previous accounts from Bliss about the talented James McGranahan and how this man should be in full-time Christian service. The Major immediately challenged McGranahan to be the gospel musician God could use to replace Philip Bliss. Before leaving the site of the accident together, they found Bliss's trunk undamaged, containing the text for "My Redeemer" (No. 59), which Bliss had evidently been working on during the trip. McGranahan immediately began composing the music for this text; and at their next service in Chicago, he introduced the song, where it made a great spiritual impact upon the congregation. Thus was begun between these two men a fruitful evangelistic ministry as well as a productive output of the many fine gospel songs on which they collaborated.

After many years of constant labor in the evangelistic field, McGranahan was compelled by failing health to retire to private life; but his remaining years, even to the last, were spent in composing hymns for use in the Master's service. He died on July 9, 1907, at the age of sixty-seven, resting upon his favorite Scripture verse–John 6:47.

James McGranahan is also the composer of the hymn, "My Redeemer" (No. 59).

41 In Christ There Is No East or West

ST. PETER

JOHN OXENHAM, 1852-1941
ALEXANDER R. REINAGLE, 1799-1877

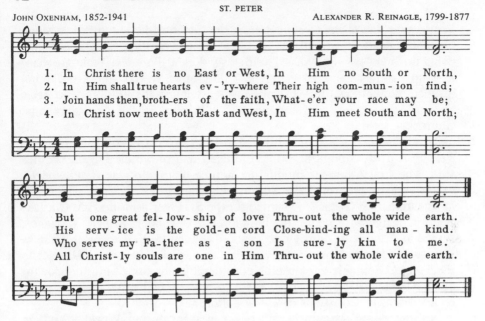

1. In Christ there is no East or West, In Him no South or North,
2. In Him shall true hearts ev-'ry-where Their high com-mun-ion find;
3. Join hands then, broth-ers of the faith, What-e'er your race may be;
4. In Christ now meet both East and West, In Him meet South and North;

But one great fel-low-ship of love Thru-out the whole wide earth.
His serv-ice is the gold-en cord Close-bind-ing all man - kind.
Who serves my Fa-ther as a son Is sure-ly kin to me.
All Christ-ly souls are one in Him Thru-out the whole wide earth.

Words from "Bees in Amber" by John Oxenham.

153

Author–John Oxenham, 1852–1941
Composer–Alexander R. Reinagle, 1799–1877
Tune Name–"St. Peter"
Meter–CM (86.86)

> There is neither Jew nor Greek, there is neither bond nor free, there is neither male nor female: For ye are all one in Christ Jesus.   Galatians 3:28

This hymn was part of a script written in 1908 by John Oxenham for a giant missionary exhibit sponsored by the London Missionary Society's exhibition, The Orient in London. It is estimated that over a quarter of a million people viewed this work. It was presented for a series of years both in England and in the United States from 1908–14. Oxenham wrote the entire text for this presentation.

John Oxenham was born in Manchester, England, on November 12, 1852. His real name was William Arthur Dunkerley. As Mr. Dunkerley he ran a successful wholesale grocery company with branches in Europe and the United States. As Julian Ross he wrote fictional serial stories in a newspaper. As John Oxenham, a pseudonym borrowed from *Western Ho!*, a book given him by his Sunday School teacher, he wrote many best-selling poems and hymns. It is said that he published more than forty novels and twenty other volumes of verse and prose. During the First

World War, his *Hymns for the Men at the Front* sold eight million copies. Upon his death it was discovered that he had written sixty-two books using different pseudonyms. The British *Who's Who* says that Oxenham took up writing as an "alleviative and alternative from business and found it much more enjoyable." Despite his busy financial and literary interests he was known as a devout and active layman in the Congregational Churches.

This hymn text was first published in 1913 in one of Oxenham's works, *Bees in Amber,* a book he printed himself and of which 285,000 copies sold. The first American hymnal to include the hymn was *Hymns of the Living Age* by H. Augustine Smith, published in 1925.

The tune, "St. Peter," is named for the St. Peter's-in-the-East Church, Oxford, England, where its composer, Alexander Robert Reinagle, served as organist for thirty-one years. The tune first appeared in 1836 in Reinagle's *Psalm Tunes for the Voice and Pianoforte,* originally set to Psalm 118. Reinagle composed a considerable amount of music throughout his career. All of his tunes seem to have a distinctive quality which endear them to Christians of every culture.

154 An interesting account is told of an incident during World War II in which there were two ships anchored together, one containing Japanese aliens and the other American aliens, waiting to be repatriated. For one day they lined the rails, glaring at each other. Suddenly, someone began to sing "In Christ There is No East or West." Then another, on the opposite ship, joined in. Soon there was an extraordinary chorus of former enemies praising God together.

*   *   *

"Music is the universal language of mankind."

Longfellow

42 In the Cross of Christ I Glory

RATHBUN

JOHN BOWRING, 1792-1872   ITHAMAR CONKEY, 1815-1867

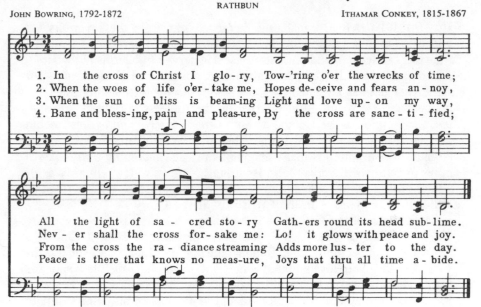

1. In the cross of Christ I glo-ry, Tow-'ring o'er the wrecks of time;
2. When the woes of life o'er-take me, Hopes de-ceive and fears an-noy,
3. When the sun of bliss is beam-ing Light and love up-on my way,
4. Bane and bless-ing, pain and pleas-ure, By the cross are sanc-ti-fied;

All the light of sa-cred sto-ry Gath-ers round its head sub-lime.
Nev-er shall the cross for-sake me: Lo! it glows with peace and joy.
From the cross the ra-diance streaming Adds more lus-ter to the day.
Peace is there that knows no meas-ure, Joys that thru all time a-bide.

155

Author–John Bowring, 1792–1872
Composer–Ithamar Conkey, 1815–1867
Tune Name–"Rathbun"
Meter–87.87
Scripture Reference–Galatians 6:14

For the preaching of the cross is to them that perish foolishness; but unto us which are
saved it is the power of God.   I Corinthians 1:18

It is claimed by some writers that Sir John Bowring had visited Macao,
on the South Chinese coast, and was much impressed by the sight of a
bronze cross towering on the summit of the massive wall of what had
formerly been a great cathedral. This cathedral, originally built by the
early Portuguese colonists, overlooked the harbor and had been destroyed
by a typhoon and left crumbled in its wake–except for one wall topped by
the huge metal cross. This scene is said to have so impressed Bowring
that it eventually served as the inspiration for this beloved hymn.

John Bowring was born at Exeter in Devon, England, on October 17,
1792. He was considered to be one of the most remarkable men of his day
as well as one of the greatest linguists who ever lived. He was a member
of nearly every learned society in Europe. Before he was sixteen years of
age he had mastered five languages without the aid of a teacher. It is said
that he could converse in over 100 different languages before his death.

He also did much in translating literary works from these various languages. Throughout his life he was noted as a biographer, naturalist, financier, statesman and philanthropist. He served two terms in the House of Commons and in 1854 was appointed governor of Hong Kong. This same year he was knighted by Queen Victoria for outstanding service to his country. He was a prolific writer on the subjects of politics, economics, and religion as well as the author of many poems and hymns, including the rather familiar missionary hymn, "Watchman, Tell Us of the Night." Yet despite his many accomplishments, including thirty-six volumes of published works, John Bowring is known today primarily as the author of this simply stated hymn text. On his tombstone are inscribed the words of this hymn, "In the Cross of Christ I Glory."

The writing of the tune in 1851 by Ithamar Conkey is also interesting. He was the organist and choir master at the Central Baptist Church of Norwich, Connecticut. One Sunday during the Lenten season of that year, Conkey was disappointed when only one choir member appeared for the morning service, a faithful soprano by the name of Mrs. Beriah S. Rathbun. Conkey was so displeased and irritated with his choir's unfaithfulness that he left the service in disgust immediately after playing the prelude. That afternoon he thought with remorse of the service that he had left and recalled one of the hymns to have been used, John Bowring's text, "In the Cross of Christ I Glory," sung to a dull and obsolete tune. Before the evening service Conkey composed a new tune for this text and named it after his one faithful choir member, Mrs. Rathbun. He confessed later that "the inspiration that came to me at that moment was a vivid contrast to my feelings at the morning service."

The cross has been the most significant symbol of the Christian faith throughout church history. It is said that as many as 400 different forms or designs of it have been used–the usual Latin Cross, the Greek Cross (all parts of the cross of equal length), the Budded Cross (each arm with three buds representing the Trinity), etc. Regardless of design, the symbol of the cross should always remind us of the price that was paid by the eternal God for man's redemption.

156

43

In the Garden

C. Austin Miles, 1868-1946   C. Austin Miles, 1868-1946

1. I come to the gar-den a - lone, While the dew is
2. He speaks, and the sound of His voice Is so sweet the
3. I'd stay in the gar-den with Him Tho the night a -

still on the ros - es; And the voice I hear, fall-ing on my ear,
birds hush their sing - ing; And the mel - o - dy that He gave to me
round me be fall - ing; But He bids me go— thru the voice of woe,

REFRAIN

The Son of God dis - clos - es.
With - in my heart is ring - ing. And He walks with me, and He
His voice to me is call - ing.

157

talks with me, And He tells me I am His own, And the joy we

share as we tar - ry there, None oth-er has ev - er known.

In the Garden

Author–C. Austin Miles, 1868–1946
Composer–C. Austin Miles, 1868–1946
Meter–Irregular
Scripture Reference–John 20

> Mary Magdalene came and told the disciples that she had seen the Lord, and that He had spoken these things unto her.   John 20:18

It was in 1912 that music publisher Dr. Adam Geibel (No. 85) asked C. Austin Miles to write a hymn text that would be "sympathetic in tone, breathing tenderness in every line; one that would bring hope to the hopeless, rest for the weary, and downy pillows to dying beds."

In George W. Sanville's book, *Forty Gospel Hymn Stories,* Miles has left the following account of the writing of this hymn:

158

> One day in March, 1912, I was seated in the dark room, where I kept my photographic equipment and organ. I drew my Bible toward me; it opened at my favorite chapter, John 20–whether by chance or inspiration let each reader decide. That meeting of Jesus and Mary had lost none of its power to charm.
>
> As I read it that day, I seemed to be part of the scene. I became a silent witness to that dramatic moment in Mary's life, when she knelt before her Lord, and cried, "Rabboni!"
>
> My hands were resting on the Bible while I stared at the light blue wall. As the light faded, I seemed to be standing at the entrance of a garden, looking down a gently winding path, shaded by olive branches. A woman in white, with head bowed, hand clasping her throat, as if to choke back her sobs, walked slowly into the shadows. It was Mary. As she came to the tomb, upon which she placed her hand, she bent over to look in, and hurried away.
>
> John, in flowing robe, appeared, looking at the tomb; then came Peter, who entered the tomb, followed slowly by John.
>
> As they departed, Mary reappeared; leaning her head upon her arm at the tomb, she wept. Turning herself, she saw Jesus standing, so did I. I knew it was He. She knelt before Him, with arms outstretched and looking into His face cried "Rabboni!"
>
> I awakened in full light, gripping the Bible, with muscles tense and nerves vibrating. Under the inspiration of this vision I wrote as quickly as the words could be formed the poem exactly as it has since appeared. That same evening I wrote the music.

Next to "The Old Rugged Cross" (No. 92), this hymn has been one of the most popular gospel hymns ever written, beginning with the days when Homer Rodeheaver led singing for the great Billy Sunday campaigns and used the hymn extensively.

A typical scene at one of the Billy Sunday-Homer Rodeheaver tabernacle services

159

44   It Is Well with My Soul

HORATIO G. SPAFFORD, 1828-1888   PHILIP P. BLISS, 1838-1876

1. When peace, like a river, attendeth my way, When sorrows like
2. Tho Satan should buffet, tho trials should come, Let this blest as-
3. My sin— O the bliss of this glorious tho't— My sin, not in
4. And, Lord, haste the day when my faith shall be sight, The clouds be rolled

sea-billows roll— Whatever my lot, Thou hast taught me to say,
sur-ance control, That Christ hath regarded my helpless estate,
part, but the whole, Is nailed to the cross, and I bear it no more:
back as a scroll: The trump shall resound and the Lord shall descend,

160

CHORUS

It is well, it is well with my soul.
And hath shed His own blood for my soul. It is well
Praise the Lord, praise the Lord, O my soul!   It is well
"Even so"— it is well with my soul.

with my soul,   It is well, it is well with my soul.
with my soul,

It is Well with My Soul

Author-Horatio G. Spafford, 1828–1888
Music-Philip P. Bliss, 1838–1876
Meter-11 8 11 9 with Chorus

God is our refuge and strength, a very present help in trouble.   Psalm 46:1

This beloved gospel song was written by a Chicago Presbyterian layman, Horatio G. Spafford, born in North Troy, New York, on October 20, 1828. As a young man Spafford had established a most successful legal practice in Chicago. Despite his financial success, he always maintained a keen interest in Christian activities. He enjoyed a close and active relationship with D. L. Moody and the other evangelical leaders of that era. He was described by George Stebbins, a noted gospel musician, as a "man of unusual intelligence and refinement, deeply spiritual, and a devoted student of the Scriptures."

Some months prior to the Chicago Fire of 1871, Spafford had invested heavily in real estate on the shore of Lake Michigan, and his holdings were wiped out by this disaster. Just before this he had experienced the death of his son. Desiring a rest for his wife and four daughters as well as wishing to join and assist Moody and Sankey in one of their campaigns in Great Britain, Spafford planned a European trip for his family in 1873. In November of that year, due to unexpected last minute business developments, he had to remain in Chicago; but he sent his wife and four daughters on ahead as scheduled on the *S.S. Ville du Havre*. He expected to follow in a few days. On November 22 the ship was struck by the *Lochearn,* an English vessel, and sank in twelve minutes. Several days later the survivors were finally landed at Cardiff, Wales, and Mrs. Spafford cabled her husband, "Saved alone." Shortly afterward Spafford left by ship to join his bereaved wife. It is speculated that on the sea near the area where it was thought his four daughters had drowned, Spafford penned this text with words so significantly describing his own personal grief-"When sorrows like sea billows roll..." It is noteworthy, however, that Spafford does not dwell on the theme of life's sorrows and trials but focuses attention in the third stanza on the redemptive work of Christ and in the fourth verse anticipates His glorious second coming. Humanly speaking, it is amazing that one could experience such personal tragedies and sorrows as did Horatio Spafford and still be able to say with such convincing clarity, "It is well with my soul."

In his late life Spafford experienced a mental disturbance which prompted him to go to Jerusalem under the strange delusion that he was the second Messiah. He died there in 1888 at the age of sixty.

161

Philip P. Bliss was so impressed with the experience and expression of Spafford's text that he shortly wrote the music for it, first published in one of the Sankey-Bliss Hymnals, *Gospel Hymns No. Two,* in 1876. Bliss was a prolific writer of gospel songs throughout his brief lifetime. In most cases he wrote both the words and music for his hymns. His songs, like most early gospel hymnody, are strong in emotional appeal with tunes that are easily learned and sung (see page 42).

Other hymns by Philip P. Bliss include "Hold the Fort" (No. 30), "I Gave My Life for Thee" (No. 34), "Jesus Loves Even Me" (No. 46) and "My Redeemer" (No. 59).

162

Philip Paul Bliss

Jesus, Lover of My Soul

CHARLES WESLEY, 1707-1788
MARTYN
SIMEON B. MARSH, 1798-1875

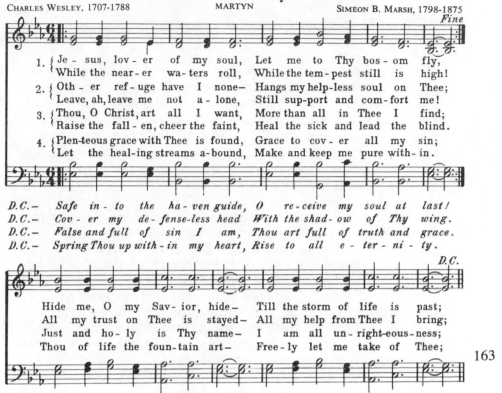

Fine

1. { Je - sus, lov - er of my soul, Let me to Thy bos - om fly,
   { While the near - er wa - ters roll, While the tem - pest still is high!
2. { Oth - er ref - uge have I none— Hangs my help-less soul on Thee;
   { Leave, ah, leave me not a - lone, Still sup-port and com-fort me!
3. { Thou, O Christ, art all I want, More than all in Thee I find;
   { Raise the fall - en, cheer the faint, Heal the sick and lead the blind.
4. { Plen-teous grace with Thee is found, Grace to cov - er all my sin;
   { Let the heal-ing streams a-bound, Make and keep me pure with- in.

D.C.— Safe in - to the ha - ven guide, O re - ceive my soul at last!
D.C.— Cov - er my de - fense-less head With the shad - ow of Thy wing.
D.C.— False and full of sin I am, Thou art full of truth and grace.
D.C.— Spring Thou up with - in my heart, Rise to all e - ter - ni - ty.

D.C.

Hide me, O my Sav- ior, hide— Till the storm of life is past;
All my trust on Thee is stayed— All my help from Thee I bring;
Just and ho- ly is Thy name— I am all un- right-eous-ness;
Thou of life the foun-tain art— Free- ly let me take of Thee;

163

Author–Charles Wesley, 1707–1788
Composer–Simeon B. Marsh, 1798–1875
Tune Name–"Martyn"
Meter–77.77 Doubled

The Lord is good, a strong hold in the day of trouble; and He knoweth them that trust in Him.   Nahum 1:7

Of the 6500 hymns written by Charles Wesley, this is generally considered to be his finest. It is still found in nearly every published hymnal and has been translated into almost every known language. It is interesting to note, however, that when Charles first presented this text to his brother, John, for approval, it was rejected as being too sentimental. It was not until after the author's death that the song came into general use. It was first published in 1740 in a collection of 139 hymns known as *Hymns and Sacred Poems*.

Many authorities have acclaimed the greatness of this hymn. The late Dr. Bodine said, "It is the finest heart-hymn in the English language."

Henry Ward Beecher, noted American preacher of the past century, once wrote,

> I would rather have written that hymn of Wesley's than to have the fame of all the kings that ever sat on earth; it is more glorious, it has more power in it. I would rather be the author of that hymn than to hold the wealth of the richest man in New York. He will die after a little while, pass out of men's thoughts, what will there be to speak of him? But people will go on singing that hymn until the last trump brings forth the angel band; and then I think it will mount upon some lips to the very presence of God.

There are various stories concerning the experiences that prompted Charles Wesley to pen these words, though none has ever been completely authenticated. Several of these stories are described as follows: On his return to England in the fall of 1736, following his brief and disappointing experience in the United States, Charles Wesley was caught in a very frightening storm at sea when it appeared for certain that all would be lost. Finally on December 3 the ship reached land. Wesley wrote in his journal for that date "I knelt down and blessed the Hand that had conducted me through such inextricable mazes." Some writers state that during this storm experience a frightened bird flew into Wesley's cabin and sheltered itself in his bosom for comfort and safety. Another account says that Wesley wrote this text while lying under a hedge, having been beaten up by an angry mob opposing his ministry. Still others see this text as a picture of Wesley's own life as a young man as he struggled to find his peace with God before his dramatic Aldersgate conversion experience on May 21, 1738.

164

A hymn of this quality, however, really doesn't need any popular account of its origin to give it added greatness. The meaningful simplicity of the text is sufficient. It should be noted that 156 simple one-syllable words appear among the 188 words of the text. Christ is presented as a "lover," "healer," "refuge," "fountain," "wing," and "pilot"–the all-sufficient One. Truly each believer can say with Wesley, "Thou, O Christ, art all I want, more than all in Thee I find. . . ."

Many different tunes have been used with this text, including several fine anthem and classical settings. The best-known of these tunes in America is "Martyn," composed by Simeon B. Marsh, who was born in Sherborne, New York, in 1798. He was an organist, choir director and itinerant singing-school teacher. He was also known as a devout Presbyterian Christian layman. One day in the fall of 1834 he wrote out this tune and called it "Martyn." No reason has been given for the significance of this name. It was originally intended as a new setting for one of John Newton's lesser known hymns, "Mary at Her Savior's Tomb." Because of this association, the melody is sometimes listed as the "Resurrection Tune." Thirty years later Thomas Hastings, a leading American musician of sacred music, discovered that the "Martyn" tune was well-suited for Wesley's text and began using it with great response in his new publications.

This is a hymn that never loses its appeal for it speaks to the basic need of every human heart, a personal dependence upon the infinite God.

Other hymns by Charles Wesley include "Christ the Lord Is Risen Today" (No. 13) and "O For a Thousand Tongues" (No. 65).

165

Charles Wesley

46 Jesus Loves Even Me

PHILIP P. BLISS, 1838-1876

PHILIP P. BLISS, 1838-1876

1. I am so glad that our Father in heav'n Tells of His love in the Book He has giv'n; Won-der-ful things in the Bi-ble I see— This is the dear-est, that Je-sus loves me.

2. Tho I for-get Him and wan-der a-way, Still He doth love me wher-ev-er I stray; Back to His dear lov-ing arms would I flee When I re-mem-ber that Je-sus loves me.

3. O if there's on-ly one song I can sing When in His beau-ty I see the great King, This shall my song in e-ter-ni-ty be: "O what a won-der that Je-sus loves me!"

CHORUS

I am so glad that Je-sus loves me, Je-sus loves me, Je-sus loves me; I am so glad that Je-sus loves me, Je-sus loves e-ven me.

Jesus Loves Even Me

Author–Philip P. Bliss, 1838–1876
Composer–Philip P. Bliss, 1838–1876
Meter–10 10. 10 10 with Chorus

As the Father hath loved me, so have I loved you: Continue ye in my love. John 15:9

No one can deny that one of the all-important contributions to the ministry of evangelical Christianity during our country's history has been the role of the Sunday School. This concern for reaching children and teaching them the gospel had not always been present throughout church history, however. For years the church's main goal was merely the catechetical indoctrination of its children in the practices and responsibilities of good churchmanship. There was little desire for establishing personal life-changing relations with God and not much genuine interest in the social and moral welfare of the masses of children in society.

One of the important names in the history of the modern Sunday School movement is the name of Robert Raikes, 1736–1811, often called the "founder of the modern Sunday School." Raikes was born in Gloucester, England, of respected, middle-class parents. Though he himself enjoyed a prosperous and good life early in his career as the town's newspaper editor, Raikes became intensely concerned with the spiritual and social condition of the great masses of poor, illiterate children. Except for the wealthy there was no education for four out of five children. Child labor was shamefully exploited. The child that reached adolescence with normal health was almost an exception. The great masses of people were poor, wretched moral degenerates while the respected church people remained politely detached from them. In the midst of these conditions Raikes began taking children off the street and teaching them Biblical truths as well as the ability to read and write.

167

Later the followers of John and Charles Wesley, the Methodists, began establishing Sunday Schools, first in England and then in this country after the Revolutionary War. Still later the Sunday School movement was encouraged further by the founding of the American Sunday School Union in 1824. As this concern for children developed, it became apparent to Christian leaders that music is a natural means for working with children, since most children respond readily to musical activities. Such gospel musicians as Philip Bliss, Ira Sankey, George Root, Charles Gabriel and Fanny Crosby began writing a great wealth of simple types of songs that children could enjoy. This desire to reach and teach children for Christ through appropriate songs was one of the important factors that led to the rise of the gospel song movement during the latter part of the nineteenth century.

Philip P. Bliss was born in Clearfield County, Pennsylvania, on July 9, 1838. His youthful days were spent on a farm in a lumber camp. He described his childhood as one of abject poverty. He was known as a large, awkward, overgrown boy. In 1850 he accepted Christ as his Savior and shortly thereafter joined the Cherry Flats Baptist Church of Tioga County, Pennsylvania. Early in life Bliss showed unusual talent for music. After a brief period of training, he moved to Chicago, where he became involved with Dr. George Root, conducting musical institutes and conventions throughout the West for nearly ten years. In 1874 Bliss was approached and challenged by evangelists D. L. Moody and Major Daniel W. Whittle to enter full-time evangelistic work with them. From this time until his untimely death two years later, Bliss's personal singing and song leadership were always outstanding features of any service in which he was engaged. His early home-going occurred when the train on which he and his wife were traveling from Pennsylvania to Chicago during the Christmas season overturned and plunged into a ravine, sixty feet below, killing 100 passengers.

In addition to being known as a man with a commanding stature and an impressive public personality, Bliss was also highly regarded by his fellow music colleagues. George C. Stebbins, also a noted gospel hymn writer of that era, wrote as follows:

168

> There has been no writer of verse since his time who has shown such a grasp of the fundamental truths of the gospel, or such a gift for putting them into a poetic and singable form.

This hymn, "Jesus Loves Even Me," was written and composed by Bliss after attending a meeting where the hymn "O How I Love Jesus" was repeated frequently. The thought occurred to Bliss, "Have I not been singing enough about my poor love for Jesus and shall I not rather sing of His great love for me?" Under the impulse of this thought Philip Bliss composed this hymn, later to become one of the all-time favorite children's hymns. It became popular immediately in Great Britain as well as in this country. The hymn was first published in Bliss's *The Charm for Sunday Schools,* 1871.

Other hymns by Philip P. Bliss include "Hold the Fort" (No. 30), "I Gave My Life for Thee" (No. 34), "It Is Well with My Soul" (No. 44) and "My Redeemer" (No. 59).

Jesus Loves Me

ANNA B. WARNER, 1820-1915

WILLIAM B. BRADBURY, 1816-1868

1. Je-sus loves me! this I know, For the Bi-ble tells me so; Lit-tle
2. Je-sus loves me! He who died Heav-en's gate to o-pen wide; He will
3. Je-sus loves me! He will stay Close be-side me all the way; Thou hast

ones to Him be-long, They are weak but He is strong.
wash a-way my sin, Let His lit-tle child come in.
bled and died for me, I will hence-forth live for Thee.

CHORUS

Yes, Je-sus loves me!

Yes, Je-sus loves me! Yes, Je-sus loves me! The Bi-ble tells me so.

169

Author–Anna B. Warner, 1820–1915
Composer–William B. Bradbury, 1816–1868
Meter–77.77 with Chorus

And He took them up in His arms, put His hands upon them, and blessed them.
Mark 10:16

Without doubt the hymn that has influenced children for Christ more than any other is this simply stated one, written in 1860 by Anna Bartlett Warner. Miss Warner wrote this text in collaboration with her sister Susan as a part of one of the best-selling novels of that day, a novel written by Susan entitled *Say and Seal*. Today few remember the plot of that novel, which stirred the hearts of many readers. But the simple poem spoken by one of the characters, Mr. Linden, as he comforts Johnny Fax, a dying child, still remains the favorite hymn of children around the world to this day.

Anna and Susan Warner were highly educated and deeply devoted Christian young women who lived all of their lives along the Hudson

River in New York, in a lovely but secluded area apart from the busy world. Their home was near the U.S. Military Academy at West Point, and for a number of years these two sisters conducted Sunday School classes for the young cadets. Their home, Good Crag, was willed to the Academy and made into a national shrine. Both sisters were buried with military honors in recognition of their spiritual contributions to the lives of the young military officers.

After the death of their widower father, a well-known New York lawyer, the Warner sisters were left with a meager income and of necessity turned to serious literary writing. Susan became especially noted for several of her works, including a popular book, *The Wide, Wide World*, considered at that time to be the best seller after *Uncle Tom's Cabin*. Although not as well-known as Susan for her literary fame, Anna wrote a number of novels under the pseudonym "Amy Lothrop" and published two collections of verse, *Hymns of the Church Militant*, 1858, and *Wayfaring Hymns, Original and Translated*, 1869.

The popularity of "Jesus Loves Me" soon spread quickly beyond the boundaries of our own land. Numerous stories are told by missionaries of the universal appeal this hymn text has had with children in every culture. It is often one of the first hymns taught to new converts in foreign lands. The hymn has even been appropriated by other religious sects; missionaries have reported that they have heard groups in Buddhist Temples singing, "Yes, Buddha loves me, Yes, Buddha loves me..."

170

Dr. William B. Bradbury, the composer of the music for the text, was one of the important contributors to the development of early gospel hymnody in this country. He was born in York, Maine, on October 6, 1816. As a young man he moved to Boston, Massachusetts, where he became associated with Lowell Mason, often called the father of American public school and church music. Bradbury served as choir director and organist in several large Baptist churches in the East, where he became especially noted for his work with children. Among the highlights of his career were his annual Musical Festivals, where more than one thousand children would gather, all dressed alike, and sing many of his own compositions. Soon Bradbury gave himself exclusively to the teaching, writing and publishing of a great volume of music. From 1841 until his death in 1868, he was involved with the publishing of fifty-nine collections of sacred and secular music. Bradbury composed the music for "Jesus Loves Me" in 1861 especially for Anna Warner's text and personally added the chorus to the four stanzas. It appeared in its present form in 1862 in his hymnal publication, *The Golden Shower*.

Other hymns by William B. Bradbury include "He Leadeth Me" (No. 28) and "Just As I Am" (No. 52).

48 Jesus Shall Reign

DUKE STREET

ISAAC WATTS, 1674-1748

JOHN HATTON, c. 1710-1793

1. Je - sus shall reign wher-e'er the sun Does his suc-ces-sive jour-neys run,
2. From north to south the princ-es meet To pay their hom-age at His feet,
3. To Him shall end-less prayer be made And end-less prais-es crown His head;
4. Peo-ple and realms of ev-'ry tongue Dwell on His love with sweet-est song,

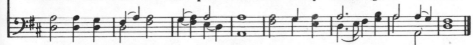

His king-dom spread from shore to shore Till moons shall wax and wane no more.
While western em - pires own their Lord And sav-age tribes at-tend His word.
His name like sweet per-fume shall rise With ev-'ry morn-ing sac - ri - fice.
And in-fant voic-es shall pro-claim Their ear-ly bless-ings on His name.

171

Author–Isaac Watts, 1674–1748
Composer–John Hatton, c. 1710–1793
Tune Name–"Duke Street"
Meter–LM (88.88)
Scripture Reference–Psalm 72

The mighty God, even the Lord, hath spoken, and called the earth from the rising of the sun unto the going down thereof. Psalm 50:1

One of the earliest hymns written with a missionary emphasis, this is another of the more than 600 hymns by Isaac Watts, often called the father of English hymnody. When this text was written in 1719, the evangelical missionary movement had scarcely begun. It was not until 1779 that William Carey began to stir Christians with their responsibility of fulfilling the Great Commission to the heathen. Even then, an Anglican bishop expressed the attitude of his Church to missions in his reply to Carey, "Young man, if God wants to save the heathen, He will do so without any help from you."

This is still considered one of the finest missionary hymns ever written and one of the most widely used. The text, one of the newer metrical versions of the psalms by Watts, is a paraphrase of Psalm 72. It has been sung by countless missionaries in numerous tongues. The story is told of an event in the South Sea Islands in 1862 when 5,000 natives sang this hymn as their native king replaced a pagan constitution with a Christian one.

Other hymns by Isaac Watts include "I Sing the Mighty Power of God" (No. 38), "O God, Our Help in Ages Past" (No. 66) and "When I Survey the Wondrous Cross" (No. 100).

The tune, "Duke Street," was composed for this text by John Hatton in 1793. Nothing much is known of Hatton except that he was born in Warrington, England, and that he was killed in a stagecoach accident shortly after composing this tune. The tune is thought to be named after the street on which he lived in the village of St. Helens, England. The tune first appeared in Henry Boyd's *A Select Collection of Psalm and Hymn Tunes* in 1793. It was originally intended for use with Addison's setting of Psalm 19.

172

Isaac Watts

49   Jesus, the Very Thought of Thee

ST. AGNES

Attr. to Bernard of Clairvaux, 1091-1153
Trans. by Edward Caswall, 1814-1878

JOHN B. DYKES, 1823-1876

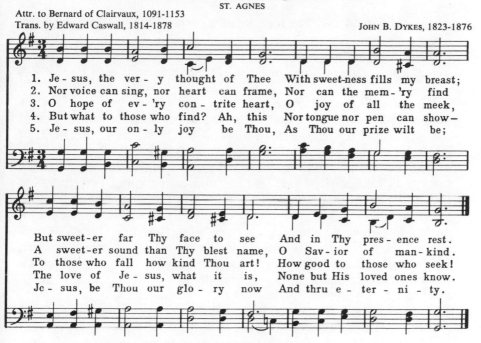

1. Je - sus, the ver - y thought of Thee   With sweet-ness fills my breast;
2. Nor voice can sing, nor heart can frame,   Nor can the mem - 'ry find
3. O hope of ev - 'ry con - trite heart,   O joy of all the meek,
4. But what to those who find? Ah, this   Nor tongue nor pen can show—
5. Je - sus, our on - ly joy be Thou,   As Thou our prize wilt be;

But sweet-er far Thy face to see   And in Thy pres - ence rest.
A sweet-er sound than Thy blest name,   O Sav-ior of man-kind.
To those who fall how kind Thou art!   How good to those who seek!
The love of Je - sus, what it is,   None but His loved ones know.
Je - sus, be Thou our glo - ry now   And thru e - ter - ni - ty.

173

Author-Attributed to Bernard of Clairvaux, 1091–1153
English Translation-Edward Caswall, 1814–1878
Composer-John B. Dykes, 1823–1876
Name of Tune-"St. Agnes"
Meter-CM (86.86)

> As the hart panteth after the water brooks, so panteth my soul after Thee, O God. My soul thirsteth for God, for the living God: When shall I come and appear before God?   Psalm 42:1,2

This hymn comes from the height of the Middle Ages, a period of history often scornfully called "The Dark Ages." The spiritual and moral darkness of the Church reached a new blackness. The institution founded by Christ some 1,000 years prior was for the most part degenerate and corrupt. The moral standards of many of its prominent leaders were characterized by utter disgrace and shame.

Bernard was born to a noble family at Fontaine in Burgundy, France; his father was a knight and his mother a person of radiant goodness. At an early age young Bernard showed a bent for piety and scholarship. With his natural charms and talents Bernard had many opportunities open to him for a successful secular life. However, while still in his early twenties, he chose the life of a monk at the monastery of Citeaux. Within three years his forceful personality, talents and leadership qualities were recognized, and he was asked to form other branches of this order throughout Europe. Within Bernard's lifetime 162 other such monasteries were founded. One of these new monasteries was at Clairvaux, France, where Bernard was made its abbot or head. Here he remained until his death in 1153.

It is generally agreed that Bernard of Clairvaux was the greatest of the medieval leaders of this period. He is said to have represented the best of monastic life of his time. In the sixteenth century Martin Luther wrote of Bernard that "he was the best monk that ever lived, whom I admire beyond all the rest put together." Bernard's influence was soon felt throughout Europe. It is said that he commanded kings, emperors, and prelates, and they obeyed him. In 1146 he was commissioned by the pope to lead a second preaching crusade against the Moslems. With his eloquence and strong preaching, great crowds followed him. One of the conditions for those joining the Crusade was a personal conversion experience. It is recorded that multitudes of vicious men were changed through his preaching and carried a cross unashamedly as a symbol of their commitment to Christ and this Crusade.

Bernard wrote a number of books, chiefly on such subjects as church government, monasticism, and other church-related topics. It is generally thought that he wrote a long 192 line poem entitled "Dulcis Jesu Memorial" ("Joyful Rhythm on the Name of Jesus"). From this poem Edward Caswall in the nineteenth century translated portions of the lines for this hymn text. It has since been translated into more languages than any other hymn with the exception of Luther's "A Mighty Fortress is Our God" (No. 1).

174

Edward Caswall is considered to be one of the important nineteenth-century English translators of ancient hymnody. He was born in Yately, Hampshire, England, on July 15, 1814. Though ordained to the Anglican Church, he became strongly involved in the Oxford Movement that began in England in the 1830's. Finally, in 1847, Caswall resigned his Anglican pastorate at Stratford and was received into the fellowship of the Roman Catholic Church. Following the death of his wife in 1849, he was ordained as a Catholic Priest. His most significant publication was *Lyra Catholic,* 1849, which contained 197 translations of Latin hymns from the Roman Breviary and other sources. This translation was part of that collection.

Caswall is also the translator of the well-known German hymn, "May Jesus Christ be Praised" (No. 57).

The tune, "St. Agnes," was composed by John B. Dykes, one of the important names in English church music during the nineteenth century. He wrote more than 300 hymn tunes, most of them still in use today.

Other hymns by John B. Dykes include "Holy, Holy, Holy" (No. 31), "I Heard the Voice of Jesus Say" (No. 35) and "Lead, Kindly Light" (No. 53).

50   Jesus, Thy Blood and Righteousness

GERMANY

NICOLAUS L. VON ZINZENDORF, 1700-1760

Trans. by John Wesley, 1703-1791

From Gardiner's *Sacred Melodies*, 1815

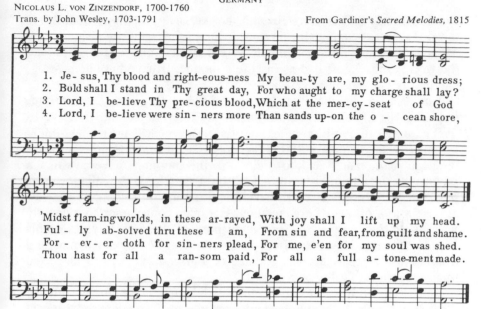

1. Je - sus, Thy blood and right-eous-ness My beau-ty are, my glo - rious dress;
2. Bold shall I stand in Thy great day, For who aught to my charge shall lay?
3. Lord, I be-lieve Thy pre-cious blood, Which at the mer-cy-seat of God
4. Lord, I be-lieve were sin-ners more Than sands up-on the o - cean shore,

'Midst flam-ing worlds, in these ar-rayed, With joy shall I lift up my head.
Ful - ly ab-solved thru these I am, From sin and fear, from guilt and shame.
For - ev - er doth for sin-ners plead, For me, e'en for my soul was shed.
Thou hast for all a ran-som paid, For all a full a - tone-ment made.

175

Author–Nicolaus L. von Zinzendorf, 1700–1760
Translated–John Wesley, 1703–1791
Music–From Gardiner's "Sacred Melodies," 1815
Tune Name–"Germany"
Meter–88.88

Not by works of righteousness which we have done, but according to His mercy He saved us, by the washing of regeneration, and renewing of the Holy Spirit. Titus 3:5

Count von Zinzendorf was born at Dresden, Germany, into one of the most noble and wealthy families in all of Saxony, Germany. He was educated at the Universities of Hale and Wittenberg and was known as a man of high culture and yet sincere piety. Later he became Counselor of the State at the Court of Saxony. Desiring to preach, however, he received his preaching license from the Theological Faculty of the University of Tubingen in 1734. He associated himself with the Church of the Moravian Brethren, a group long known for its missionary zeal and its love for church music. In 1737 he was made Bishop of the Moravian Brethren Churches in Berlin, Germany, and continued to be a real promoter of the evangelical cause. He was always concerned about personal religion, or as he called it, "Christianity of the heart." Zinzendorf used his funds to support the church as well as to support on his estate at Herrnhut a settlement of Moravian refugees which became widely known as a flourishing colony of evangelical believers. The Count was an ardent lover of music and is credited with the authorship of more than 2,000 texts. He was continually involved in editing and publishing new Moravian hymnals. These hymnals were translated into languages around the world. Zinzendorf had as his life's motto, "I have but one passion, and that is He and only He."

John Wesley was born on June 17, 1703 at Epworth, Lincolnshire, England. His life and accomplishments are truly incredible. He traveled over a quarter of a million miles, mostly on horseback, preaching 40,000 sermons, with more than 100,000 professions of faith. He was an indefatigable man, rising at 4:00 o'clock in the morning, never wasting a moment of the day until he retired at 10:00 PM. He wrote voluminously, publishing 233 original works besides editing and translating many others. He was a master of organization. His main contribution to hymnody was his editing, organizing and publishing of the 6,500 hymns of his brother Charles. However, John did contribute 27 original hymns and translations. He was a great admirer of Zinzendorf's hymns and used them extensively in his own ministry.

Both John and Charles lived and died in full communion with the Church of England, though their ministry was exclusively to independent congregations. Methodism was never established as a separate, organized dissenting group until 1808, following the deaths of both Wesleys.

176

Today, the city of Bethlehem, Pennsylvania, is one of the leading centers of the Moravian Church in America. Their festivals of sacred music at Lehigh University have gained national recognition.

The music for this hymn is taken from William Gardiner's collection, *Sacred Melodies,* published in 1815. William Gardiner was born in Leicester, England, on March 15, 1770. During his lifetime he traveled extensively, making the acquaintance of as many great musicians throughout Europe as he could, including Mozart, Haydn and Beethoven.

One of Gardiner's major contributions to the elevation of sacred music in his day was his publication of a six-volume work entitled *Sacred Melodies* in which he sought to acquaint the people of England with the great master composers of that time. The appropriation of classic melodies for hymn texts became a popular practice both in England and the United States during the nineteenth century.

51

Joyful, Joyful, We Adore Thee

HYMN TO JOY

HENRY VAN DYKE, 1852-1933

Melody from *Ninth Symphony*
LUDWIG VAN BEETHOVEN, 1770-1827

1. Joy - ful, joy - ful, we a - dore Thee, God of glo - ry, Lord of love;
2. All Thy works with joy sur-round Thee, Earth and heav'n re - flect Thy rays,
3. Thou art giv - ing and for - giv - ing, Ev - er bless - ing, ev - er blest,
4. Mor-tals, join the might-y cho - rus Which the morn - ing stars be-gan;

Hearts un - fold like flow'rs be-fore Thee, Hail Thee as the sun a-bove.
Stars and an - gels sing a - round Thee, Cen - ter of un - bro - ken praise;
Well - spring of the joy of liv - ing, O - cean-depth of hap - py rest!
Fa - ther love is reign - ing o'er us, Broth-er love binds man to man.

177

Melt the clouds of sin and sad - ness, Drive the dark of doubt a - way;
Field and for - est, vale and moun-tain, Bloss-'ming mea-dow, flash-ing sea,
Thou the Fa - ther, Christ our Broth-er— All who live in love are Thine:
Ev - er sing - ing, march we on - ward, Vic - tors in the midst of strife;

Giv - er of im - mor - tal glad-ness, Fill us with the light of day!
Chant-ing bird and flow-ing foun-tain Call us to re - joice in Thee.
Teach us how to love each oth - er, Lift us to the joy di - vine.
Joy - ful mu - sic lifts us sun-ward In the tri-umph song of life.

Joyful, Joyful, We Adore Thee

Author-Henry van Dyke, 1852–1933
Music-Ludwig van Beethoven, 1770–1827
Tune Name-"Hymn to Joy"
Meter-87.87 Doubled

But the fruit of the Spirit is love, JOY. . . .   Galatians 5:22

This hymn is generally considered by hymnologists to be one of the most joyous expressions of hymn lyrics in the English language. Its author, Henry van Dyke, was born at Germantown, Pennsylvania, on November 10, 1852. During his lifetime he was recognized as one of the ablest Presbyterian preachers and leading liturgy figures in this country. In addition to achieving fame as a preacher, he served as a professor of literature at Princeton University from 1900–1923, was the moderator of his denomination, became a Navy chaplain during World War I, and represented his country as an ambassador to Holland and Luxembourg under an appointment by President Wilson. He was a prolific writer of devotional material with many of his books being best sellers.

This is the best-known of van Dyke's hymns. He stated his purpose in writing it as follows:

178

These verses are simple expressions of common Christian feelings and desires in this present time, hymns of today that may be sung together by people who know the thought of the age, and are not afraid that any truth of science will destroy their religion or that any revolution on earth will overthrow the kingdom of heaven. Therefore these are hymns of trust and hope.

"Joyful, Joyful, We Adore Thee" portrays a joyful interplay between God's created world and the manifestation of this same creative spirit in the life of a believer. Such interesting similes as "hearts unfold like flow'rs before Thee. . ." illustrate this interesting technique. The second verse reminds us that all of God's creation speaks of His glory and, in doing so, directs our worship to the Creator Himself. The fourth stanza concludes with an invitation for all of God's children to join the mighty chorus of joy begun at creation's dawn (Job 38:7) and, in so doing, to find the encouragement needed for any circumstance of life.

The text for this hymn was written while van Dyke was a guest preacher at Williams College, Williamstown, Massachusetts. It is said that one morning van Dyke handed the manuscript to the college president, saying, "Here is a hymn for you. Your mountains (the Berkshires) were my inspiration. It must be sung to the music of Beethoven's "Hymn of Joy.'" It was first included in van Dyke's *Book of Poems,* third edition, published in 1911.

The tune, "Hymn of Joy," comes out of the final movement of Beethoven's Ninth Symphony, composed from 1817–23, and published in 1826. Although Beethoven never wrote a tune specifically for a hymn text, a number have been adapted from his many famous works. This is the most widely used of these adopted hymn tunes. It was first adapted for a hymnal by Edward Hodges, an English organist who served the Trinity Church in New York City.

The Ninth or "Choral" Symphony was Beethoven's last symphony and is generally considered to be his greatest. It took him six years to complete the writing of this work. It was his supreme desire to complete one great symphony that would combine both instruments and voices in one majestic expression of sound. He was inspired for this work by a poem written by his German poet friend, Friedrich Schiller, a work entitled "Ode to Joy." It has always been a mystery to musicians to comprehend how Beethoven could conceive this work, as well as all of his great music that was composed after he was thirty years old, since at that age he became stone deaf. The account is given that when the Ninth Symphony was initially heard in Vienna, Austria, in 1824, the soloists had to come down from the stage and turn Beethoven around so that he could recognize the thunderous applause he was being given.

179

It is well said that the Bible contains very little humor, but it does have much to say about the importance of genuine joy in the life of each believer.

*   *   *

"Music is God's gift to man, the only art of heaven given to earth, the only art of earth we take to heaven."

Walter Savage Landor

52

Just As I Am

WOODWORTH

CHARLOTTE ELLIOTT, 1789-1871

WILLIAM B. BRADBURY, 1816-1868

1. Just as I am, with-out one plea But that Thy blood was shed for me,
2. Just as I am, and wait-ing not To rid my soul of one dark blot,
3. Just as I am, tho tossed a-bout With man-y a con-flict, man-y a doubt,
4. Just as I am, poor, wretch-ed, blind— Sight, rich-es, heal-ing of the mind,
5. Just as I am, Thou wilt re-ceive, Wilt wel-come, par-don, cleanse, re-lieve;

And that Thou bidd'st me come to Thee, O Lamb of God, I come! I come!
To Thee whose blood can cleanse each spot, O Lamb of God, I come! I come!
Fight-ings and fears with-in, with-out, O Lamb of God, I come! I come!
Yea, all I need in Thee to find— O Lamb of God, I come! I come!
Be - cause Thy prom-ise I be-lieve, O Lamb of God, I come! I come!

180

Author–Charlotte Elliott, 1789–1871
Composer–William B. Bradbury, 1816–1868
Tune Name–"Woodworth"
Meter–LM (88.88)

> And Jesus said unto them, I am the bread of life: he that cometh to me shall never hunger; and he that believeth on Me shall never thirst. All that the Father giveth me shall come to me; and him that cometh to me I will in no wise cast out. John 6:35, 37

Without question, this hymn has touched more hearts and influenced more people for Christ than any other song ever written. The text was born within the soul of an invalid woman who wrote these words out of intense feelings of uselessness and despair.

Charlotte Elliott was born in Clapham, England, on March 18, 1789. As a young person she lived a carefree life, gaining popularity as a portrait artist and writer of humorous verse. By the time she was thirty, however, her health began to fail rapidly, and soon she became a bed-ridden invalid for the remaining years of her life. With her failing health came great feelings of despondency. In 1822 a noted Swiss evangelist, Dr. Caesar Malan, visited the Elliott home in Brighton, England. His visit proved to be a turning point in Charlotte's life. In counselling Miss Elliott about her spiritual and emotional problems, Dr. Malan impressed upon her this truth, "You must come just as you are, a sinner, to the Lamb of God that taketh away the sin of the world." Throughout the remainder of her life, Miss Elliott celebrated every year the day on which her Swiss friend had led her to a personal relationship with Christ, for she considered it to be her spiritual birthday. Although she did not write her text for this hymn until 1836, fourteen years after her conversion experience, it is apparent that she never forgot the words of her friend, for they form the very essence of this hymn.

Though Charlotte Elliott lived to be eighty-two years of age, she never regained normal health, and she often endured seasons of great physical suffering. Of her own afflictions she once wrote, "He knows, and He alone, what it is, day after day, hour after hour, to fight against bodily feelings of almost overpowering weakness, languor and exhaustion, to resolve not to yield to slothfulness, depression and instability, such as the body causes me to long to indulge, but to rise every morning determined to take for my motto, 'If a man will come after Me, let him deny himself, take up his cross daily, and follow Me.'" Another time she wrote, "God sees, God guides, God guards me. His grace surrounds me, and His voice continually bids me to be happy and holy in His service just where I am."

Miss Elliott wrote the text for "Just As I Am" in 1836. It was published that same year in the second edition of *The Invalid's Hymn Book,* a collection which contained 115 of her original works. She wrote this hymn with the desire that it might aid financially in building a school for the children of poor clergymen that her own pastor brother was trying to build in Brighton, England. Miss Elliott felt so helpless in her desire to aid the parishioners in this worthy project. Interestingly enough, this one hymn from the pen of the clergyman's invalid sister brought in more funds than all of his bazaars and projects combined. The brother himself has left these words, "In the course of a long ministry, I hope to have been permitted to see some fruit of my labors; but I feel more has been done by a single hymn of my sister's."

181

In all, Charlotte Elliott wrote approximately 150 hymns. She is generally regarded as one of the finest of all English women hymnwriters. It is said that after her death more than a thousand letters were found among her papers from individuals around the world, expressing testimonials for what this one hymn had meant in their lives.

The tune, "Woodworth," composed by the well-known American gospel musician, William B. Bradbury, was not originally intended for this text. It first appeared in 1849 as a musical setting for the hymn, "The God of Love Will Soon Indulge." Several years later another prominent American gospel song writer, Thomas Hastings, wedded Bradbury's tune with Miss Elliott's text.

Other hymns by William B. Bradbury include "He Leadeth Me" (No. 28) and "Jesus Loves Me" (No. 47).

Only eternity will reveal the vast number of individuals whose lives have been dramatically changed through the use of this one hymn from the pen of an invalid woman. It is a hymn that can and should be used more frequently than merely an invitational number at the close of a service. Its message is one that we as believers need to be reminded of frequently–that our eternal standing and peace with God depend solely on Christ's merits and not our own.

182

Charlotte Elliott

53 Lead, Kindly Light

LUX BENIGNA

JOHN H. NEWMAN, 1821–1890

JOHN B. DYKES, 1823–1876

1. Lead, kind-ly Light, a-mid th' en-cir-cling gloom, Lead Thou me on;
2. I was not ev - er thus, nor prayed that Thou Shouldst lead me on;
3. So long Thy power hath blest me, sure it still Will lead me on,

The night is dark, and I am far from home; Lead Thou me on:
I loved to choose and see my path; but now Lead Thou me on.
O'er moor and fen, o'er crag and tor - rent, till The night is gone;

183

Keep Thou my feet; I do not ask to see
I loved the gar - ish day, and, spite of fears,
And with the morn those an - gel fa - ces smile,

The dis - tant scene—one step e - nough for me.
Pride ruled my will: re - mem - ber not past years.
Which I have loved long since, and lost a - while. A - men.

SINGING WITH UNDERSTANDING

Lead, Kindly Light

Author-John Henry Newman, 1801–1890
Composer-John B. Dykes, 1823–1876
Tune Name-"Lux Benigna" ("kindly light")
Meter-10.4.10.4.10.10.
Scripture Reference-Exodus 13:21–22

> I will instruct thee and teach thee in the way which thou shalt go: I will guide thee with mine eye.
> Psalm 32:8

Just as John and Charles Wesley were the main influences in the religious life of England during the eighteenth century, so John Henry Newman was one of the leading figures of the nineteenth century. Both the Wesleys and Newman were sincerely concerned about the moral and spiritual conditions of their native land and the ineptness of the Anglican Church in meeting these needs. The Wesleys' approach was to take the Gospel to the masses with a message of personal salvation and forgiveness. Newman, however, became increasingly opposed to this evangelical emphasis, expressing concern that it lacked appropriate dignity and reverence. He claimed that a true religious experience could only be attained through proper church forms and rituals.

184

The son of a banker, John Henry Newman was born in London, England, on February 21, 1801. He was converted at the age of fifteen and from that time became an ardent student of the Bible and church doctrine. He was graduated from Oxford University at the age of nineteen and four years later was ordained by the Church of England. His eloquent preaching attracted large crowds wherever he spoke. He was known as a man of rare ability and magnetic personality who influenced his listeners mightily. In his early ministry he was a staunch evangelical, strongly opposed to the Roman Catholic Church, even holding the view that the Pope was the Anti-Christ. Gradually, however, he changed in the direction of those who promoted the idea of a high, liturgical church.

When Newman was thirty-two years of age, his busy life and spiritual struggles began taking their toll upon him physically and emotionally. He was forced to spend several months recuperating. During this time he travelled to Italy, and while in Rome he consulted with leaders of the Catholic Church about his own personal spiritual struggles as well as his desire to see the Anglican Church revitalized. Then while travelling further throughout Italy he had a frightening and all but fatal experience. The weather became unbearably hot and he contracted Sicilian fever. He felt that he must get back to England immediately, but no transportation was available. Finally, a boat carrying a load of oranges was found ready to sail for France. The voyage was lonely and tedious. On the way because of the lack of wind and a heavy fog the ship was anchored for a considerable time off the straits of Bonifazio between Corsica and Sardinia, Italy. On June 16, 1833, while aboard this ship and experiencing great physical, emotional and spiritual despair, Newman penned these words pleading for God's divine guidance. He titled his poem "The Pillar of the Cloud," an allusion to God's guidance of the Israelites through their wilderness journey (Exodus 13:21–22).

The first stanza is, no doubt, a depiction of Newman's spiritual and emotional struggles, likening his own personal feelings to the experience of being aboard a ship that appeared to be going nowhere. The second verse is a personal confession, perhaps of a spirit of rebelliousness that characterized his early life. The final two lines of the third stanza have long been questioned as to intended meaning. Some interpret "angel faces" as being loved ones lost in death, and consequently this hymn is often used as a funeral hymn. Other writers feel that this refers to actual visions of angels that Newman is said to have had in his youth, the loss of which greatly grieved him in later years. Still others feel that this is merely a reference to the prospect of seeing familiar, friendly faces upon his arrival in England.

Upon his return to England Newman became the dynamic leader of the High Church emphasis known as the Oxford or Tractarian Movement. Through the writing and distribution of tracts on various phases of church doctrine, these leaders sought to stimulate a deeper allegiance to a strong State Church by such teachings as Apostolic Succession, continuing revelation of truth through this Apostolic Church, and the administering of the sacraments by the Church as the sole means of grace and salvation. Twelve years after writing this hymn text Newman broke completely with the Anglican Church and became a leader in the Roman Catholic Church. His brilliance and organizational ability were quickly recognized, and in 1879 his career was climaxed when he was made a Cardinal by Pope Leo XIII. He spent the last years of his life as an administrator of a large Catholic establishment, including a school for boys, in Birmingham, England, where he died in his 89th year on August 11, 1890. He was eulogized widely as "a great Englishman and a great saint." Yet today John Henry Newman is best remembered for this one fine hymn written during a time of great personal anguish and despair in the early years of his ministry.

185

In 1867 this tune was composed specifically for these words by one of England's leading church musicians of the nineteenth century, Dr. John Bacchus Dykes. This popular composer has contributed more than 300 hymn tunes, with most of them still in use today.

Other hymns by John B. Dykes include "Holy, Holy, Holy" (No. 31), "I Heard the Voice of Jesus Say" (No. 35) and "Jesus, the Very Thought of Thee" (No. 49).

54 Lead On, O King Eternal

LANCASHIRE

ERNEST W. SHURTLEFF, 1862-1917

HENRY SMART, 1813-1879
Arr. by Jon Drevits, 1928-

1. Lead on, O King E - ter - nal, The day of march has come!
2. Lead on, O King E - ter - nal, Till sin's fierce war shall cease
3. Lead on, O King E - ter - nal, We fol - low— not with fears!

Hence-forth in fields of con - quest Thy tents shall be our home;
And ho - li - ness shall whis - per The sweet A - men of peace;
For glad-ness breaks like morn - ing Wher-e'er Thy face ap - pears;

Thru days of prep - a - ra - tion Thy grace has made us strong,
For not with swords loud clash - ing Nor roll of stir - ring drums—
Thy cross is lift - ed o'er us— We jour-ney in its light:

And now, O King E - ter - nal, We lift our bat - tle song.
With deeds of love and mer - cy The heav'n-ly king-dom comes.
The crown a - waits the con - quest—Lead on, O God of might.

186

Author–Ernest W. Shurtleff, 1862–1917
Composer–Henry Smart, 1813–1879
Tune Name–"Lancashire"
Meter–76.76 Doubled

> I have fought a good fight, I have finished my course, I have kept the faith: Henceforth there is laid up for me a crown of righteousness, which the Lord, the righteous judge, shall give me at that day: And not to me only, but unto all them also that love His appearing.   II Timothy 4:7,8

This hymn was written by a young graduating seminarian, Ernest W. Shurtleff, in 1887. Shurtleff was born in Boston, Massachusetts, on April 4, 1862. His classmates at Andover Theological Seminary, recognizing the poetic ability of their colleague, asked him to write a hymn which they might all sing together for their commencement service. Shurtleff responded with this excellent text. At the time of his graduation he had already published two volumes of verse and throughout his later ministry wrote a number of additional hymns. This is his one hymn text, however, which has endured the passing of time.

Following his graduation from seminary, Shurtleff served with distinction Congregational Churches in California, Massachusetts and Minnesota. During this time he was awarded the Doctor of Divinity Degree from Ripon College, Wisconsin. In 1905 he and his family went to Europe, where he organized the American Church in Frankfort, Germany. Later, in Paris, Shurtleff carried on a ministry with students and did relief work among the poor and needy. It was said that his entire life was truly the epitome of the hymn text he had written many years earlier for his own graduation service.

Although the metaphors and imagery used in this text were intended for their original purpose, the graduation, we can apply these truths to our personal lives and ministries today:

187

Verse One– "days of preparation"–the time needed to prepare for the graduation hour from Seminary.
"fields of conquest"–the specific responsibilities: pastorates to be assumed by these prospective ministers.
"Thy tents..." speaks of the fact that the Christian minister is not called to a permanent abode but must be willing to move and live wherever God places him.

Verse Two– Here is a summary of the whole purpose of the Christian ministry–warfare against sin, but always accomplished "with deeds of love and mercy."

Verse Three–This is the motivation for Christian service–the sense of God's abiding presence throughout this life and the promised reward that awaits the faithful servant when his earthly task is complete.

The well-suited martial music for this text was borrowed by Shurtleff from a tune written fifty-two years earlier by an English organist and composer, Henry Smart. Smart originally composed this tune for the text "From Greenland's Icy Mountains" (No. 25) to be used at a musical festival at Blackburn, England on October 4, 1835, observing the three-hundredth anniversary of the Reformation in England. "Lancashire," the name of this tune, is the county location of Blackburn, where Smart was organist at the time of this composition. Henry Smart became well-known throughout England as a nineteenth-century composer, conductor and compiler of sacred music, even though he spent the last fifteen years of his life in total blindness. Despite this affliction he continued his work as organist at St. Pancras Church, London, until his death in 1879. Another of his favorite tunes is used for the familiar Christmas carol, "Angels From the Realms of Glory" (No. 7).

*   *   *

"O for a faith that will not shrink
    Though pressed by ev'ry foe,
That will not tremble on the brink
    Of any earthly woe.

188

"That will not murmur nor complain
    Beneath the chast'ning rod,
But in the hour of grief or pain
    Will lean upon its God.

"A faith that shines more bright and clean
    When tempests rage without,
That, when in danger, knows no fear,
    In darkness feels no doubt.

"Lord, give me such a faith as this,
    And then, whate'er may come,
I'll taste e'en now the hallowed bliss
    Of an eternal home."

William H. Bathurst, 1796–1877

55   Look, Ye Saints! the Sight Is Glorious

CORONAE

THOMAS KELLY, 1769-1854   WILLIAM H. MONK, 1823-1889

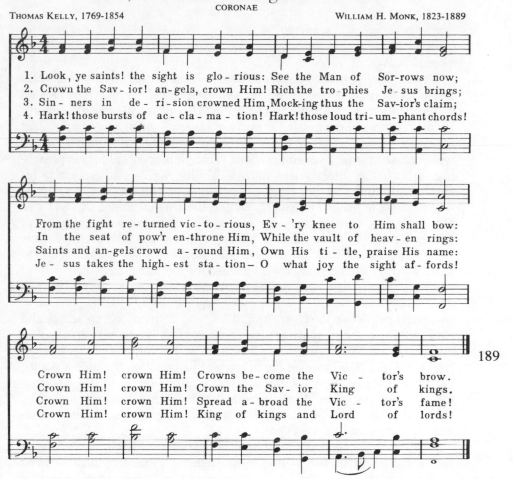

1. Look, ye saints! the sight is glo-rious: See the Man of Sor-rows now;
2. Crown the Sav-ior! an-gels, crown Him! Rich the tro-phies Je-sus brings;
3. Sin-ners in de-ri-sion crowned Him, Mock-ing thus the Sav-ior's claim;
4. Hark! those bursts of ac-cla-ma-tion! Hark! those loud tri-um-phant chords!

From the fight re-turned vic-to-rious, Ev-'ry knee to Him shall bow:
In the seat of pow'r en-throne Him, While the vault of heav-en rings:
Saints and an-gels crowd a-round Him, Own His ti-tle, praise His name:
Je-sus takes the high-est sta-tion— O what joy the sight af-fords!

189

Crown Him! crown Him! Crowns be-come the Vic-tor's brow.
Crown Him! crown Him! Crown the Sav-ior King of kings.
Crown Him! crown Him! Spread a-broad the Vic-tor's fame!
Crown Him! crown Him! King of kings and Lord of lords!

Author-Thomas Kelly, 1769-1854
Composer-William H. Monk, 1823-1889
Tune Name-"Coronae"
Meter-87.87.47

> ... Great and marvelous are Thy works, Lord God Almighty; just and true are Thy ways, Thou King of saints. Who shall not fear Thee, O Lord, and glorify Thy name? For Thou only art holy: For all nations shall come and worship before Thee; for Thy judgments are made manifest.   Revelation 15:3,4

Ascension Day, forty days after Easter, never falls on a Sunday, but the Sunday following Ascension Day is designated as Ascension Sunday. This hymn is generally regarded as one of the finest Ascension Hymns in the English language, one that is worthy of much greater use than it normally receives. It was first included by Thomas Kelly in his *Hymns on Various Passages of Scripture*, 1806. It was originally entitled "The Second Advent."

Thomas Kelly wrote 765 hymn texts over a period of fifty-one years and is recognized as one of Ireland's finest evangelical preachers as well as one of its most distinguished spiritual poets of the nineteenth century. He also composed the music for many of his texts, being an accomplished musician as well as poet. Kelly authored a number of hymnals, all of which passed through several editions. Though recognized for his preaching, scholarship, literary and musical ability, Kelly was especially respected and loved for his gracious, generous spirit, always giving liberally to those in need. Particularly during the Dublin famine of 1847 was his benevolence appreciated. Typical of the relationship he had with his people is the story told of a poor Irish man in that city who comforted his wife by saying, "Hold up, Bridget! Bedad, there's always Mr. Kelly to pull us out of the bog, after we've sunk for the last time."

Thomas Kelly was born in Dublin, Ireland, on July 13, 1769, the son of an Irish jurist. He entered Trinity College, Dublin, with the purpose of studying law. While in school he had a strong conversion experience and eventually decided to study for the ministry. In 1792 he was ordained to the priesthood by the Anglican Church. His forceful evangelical preaching, however, especially on the subject of justification by faith–a doctrinal taboo by the High Church–led to his dismissal from the Anglican Church. He associated himself with the dissenting Congregationalists, where his reputation was established as a magnetic preacher, warmhearted pastor and an excellent scholar.

190

William H. Monk, born in London, England, on March 16, 1823, was the music editor of the well-known Anglican Church hymnal, *Hymns Ancient and Modern*. This well-suited tune was composed by Monk in 1871 especially for Thomas Kelly's text. It must always be sung in a spirited, vibrant manner.

William H. Monk has also supplied the music for the hymn, "Abide with Me" (No. 2).

> "Praise the Savior, ye who know Him!
> Who can tell how much we owe Him?
> Gladly let us render to Him
> All we are and have.
>
> "Jesus is the name that charms us;
> He for conflict fits and arms us
> Nothing moves and nothing harms us
> While we trust in Him."

> Written by Thomas Kelly in 1806

56   Majestic Sweetness Sits Enthroned

ORTONVILLE

SAMUEL STENNETT, 1727-1795

THOMAS HASTINGS, 1784-1872

1. Ma - jes - tic sweet - ness sits en - throned Up - on the Sav - ior's brow; His head with ra - diant glo - ries crowned, His lips with grace o'er - flow, His lips with grace o'er - flow.

2. No mor - tal can with Him com - pare A - mong the sons of men; Fair - er is He than all the fair Who fill the heav'n - ly train, Who fill the heav'n - ly train.

3. He saw me plunged in deep dis - tress And flew to my re - lief; For me He bore the shame - ful cross And car - ried all my grief, And car - ried all my grief.

4. To Him I owe my life and breath And all the joys I have; He makes me tri - umph o - ver death And saves me from the grave, And saves me from the grave.

191

Author–Samuel Stennett, 1727–1795
Composer–Thomas Hastings, 1784–1872
Tune Name–"Ortonville"
Meter–CM (86.86)
Scripture Reference–Song of Solomon 5:10–16

> But we see Jesus, who was made a little lower than the angels for the suffering of death, crowned with glory and honor; that He by the grace of God should taste death for every man.   Hebrews 2:9

This is one of the finest communion hymns found in evangelical hymnals. The dominant theme of this beautifully expressed text is the adoration of the person of Christ and the work He did in our behalf, based on the passage from the Song of Solomon 5:10–16. The hymn originally had nine stanzas and was entitled "The Chief Among Ten Thousand" or "The Excellencies of Christ."

Samuel Stennett was born in Exeter, England, in 1727. His father, Dr. Joseph Stennett, was a well-known Baptist pastor of the Little Wild Street Church in London. In 1748 Samuel became an assistant to his father and ten years later succeeded him in the pastorate of that church. Stennett remained at this church for the next thirty-seven years, where he became known as one of the outstanding evangelical preachers of his day. It is said that he was a confidant to many of the most distinguished statesmen of that time, and even King George III was one of his most ardent admirers. In 1763 the University of Aberdeen conferred the Doctor of Divinity Degree upon him in recognition of his many accomplishments. Samuel Stennett died in London on August 24, 1795. He had served as a faithful pastor of one church for thirty-seven years.

Dr. Stennett was also an influential writer on numerous theological subjects as well as the author of thirty-nine hymns. Most of these hymns were contributed to Rippon's famous Baptist collection, *A Selection of Hymns from the Best of Authors,* published in 1787. "Majestic Sweetness Sits Enthroned" first appeared in that collection. It became Stennett's best-known hymn and is still widely used today.

192 The popularity of this hymn text has been enhanced by the moving tune composed for it in 1837 by the talented American church musician, Thomas Hastings. Hastings is credited with being one of the most influential church musicians of the nineteenth century in raising the standards of sacred music in this country. Despite a serious eye affliction, he composed more than 1,000 hymn tunes as well as more than 600 hymn texts.

Other hymns by Thomas Hastings include "From Every Stormy Wind That Blows" (No. 24) and "Rock of Ages" (No. 78).

57

May Jesus Christ Be Praised

LAUDES DOMINI

German hymn, c. 1800
Trans. by Edward Caswall, 1814-1878

JOSEPH BARNBY, 1838-1896

1. When morn-ing gilds the skies, My heart a-wak-ing cries:
2. Does sad-ness fill my mind? A sol-ace here I find:
3. In heav'n's e-ter-nal bliss The love-liest strain is this:
4. Be this, while life is mine, My can-ti-cle di-vine:

May Je-sus Christ be praised! A-like at work and prayer
May Je-sus Christ be praised! Or fades my earth-ly bliss?
May Je-sus Christ be praised! The pow'rs of dark-ness fear
May Je-sus Christ be praised! Be this th'e-ter-nal song

To Je-sus I re-pair: May Je-sus Christ be praised!
My com-fort still is this: May Je-sus Christ be praised!
When this sweet chant they hear: May Je-sus Christ be praised!
Thru all the a-ges long: May Je-sus Christ be praised!

193

Author-German Hymn from the 18th century
English Translation-Edward Caswall, 1814-1878
Composer-Joseph Barnby, 1838-1896
Tune Name-"Laudes Domini"
Meter-666. Doubled

I will bless the Lord at all times; His praise shall continually be in my mouth.
Psalm 34:1

One of the important sources of English hymnody is the wealth of
worthy hymns translated from earlier Greek, Latin and German sources
during the mid-nineteenth century. This particular interest by many English writers in the hymns from these other cultures was largely a part of a
movement within the Anglican Church known as the Oxford Movement.

The rediscovery of the writings of the Middle Ages became especially important during this time. Another important emphasis of this movement was an attempt by these leaders to rejuvenate the Anglican Church by making it more "high church" and to re-establish the concept of the church as the true Apostolic Church ordained by Christ Himself. Much of this concern was a reaction to what was felt to be a looseness within the church that was caused by the Evangelical influence with its emphasis upon the individual and his need for a personal conversion experience.

The Oxford Movement began in 1833 with a sermon by John Keble (author of "Sun of My Soul" [No. 85]) entitled "National Apostasy." For several years this movement tenaciously directed religious England. During this time many of the leading Anglicans actually seceded to the Roman Church in their obsession with having a more liturgical and authoritative church.

One of these leaders was Edward Caswall, one of the best-known scholars and translators of the earlier writings. He was born in Edgbaston, Birmingham, England in 1814. Later he graduated from the distinguished Oxford College and was ordained by the Anglican Church at the age of twenty-six. While at Oxford Caswall became deeply interested and involved in the Oxford Movement. After pastoring a parish church at Stratford for seven years, he resigned that charge and with his wife traveled to Rome, where they were both received into the full communion of the Roman Church. Three years later his wife died, and soon he became an ordained priest in the Roman Catholic Church. From this time until his death in 1878 Caswall made it his life's mission to faithfully translate the early hymns for the services of the Catholic Church. Another well-known hymn translated from the Latin is "Jesus, the Very Thought of Thee" (No. 49).

194

Nothing is known of the original writer of this text other than the fact that he was a German. The hymn first appeared in a German hymnal in 1828. Other writers also attempted English translations of this text, but Caswall's work in 1853 became the most widely used both in England and in the United States. Throughout his life Caswall kept adding new verses to this work until eventually this hymn included twenty-eight stanzas.

The tune, entitled "Laudes Domini" ("Praises of the Lord"), was composed for this text in 1868 by one of England's noted composers of that era, Joseph Barnby. Barnby was born on August 12, 1838, in London, England. In addition to many other musical accomplishments, he edited five important hymnals. He was later knighted by Queen Victoria in 1892 in recognition of his many musical feats. Joseph Barnby is also the composer for the hymn, "Now the Day is Over" (No. 63).

58

My Country, 'Tis of Thee

AMERICA

SAMUEL FRANCIS SMITH, 1808-1895

Source unknown
From *Thesaurus Musicus*, 1744

195

1. My coun-try, 'tis of thee, Sweet land of lib-er-ty,
2. My na-tive coun-try, thee, Land of the no-ble free,
3. Let mu-sic swell the breeze, And ring from all the trees
4. Our fa-thers' God, to Thee, Au-thor of lib-er-ty,

Of thee I sing: Land where my fa-thers died, Land of the
Thy name I love: I love thy rocks and rills, Thy woods and
Sweet free-dom's song: Let mor-tal tongues a-wake, Let all that
To Thee we sing: Long may our land be bright With free-dom's

pil-grims' pride, From ev-'ry moun-tain side Let free-dom ring!
tem-pled hills; My heart with rap-ture thrills Like that a-bove.
breathe par-take; Let rocks their si-lence break, The sound pro-long.
ho-ly light; Pro-tect us by Thy might, Great God, our King!

Author–Samuel Francis Smith, 1808–1895
Music–Source Unknown. From *Thesaurus Musicus,* 1744
Tune Name–"America"
Meter–664.6664

Blessed is the nation whose God is the Lord; and the people whom He hath chosen for
His own inheritance.   Psalm 33:12

Music has always been closely allied with the emotions of national
patriotism and loyalty. Every country has nationalistic music that is dis-
tinctly its own. For a number of years, however, our country lacked such
patriotic songs. Even our present national anthem, "The Star-Spangled

Banner,'' was not officially adopted as such until March 3rd, 1931. Concern for a worthy hymn to represent our young nation was fulfilled in part by a twenty-four year old Baptist theological student in 1832 with the writing of this patriotic expression, which many have since called our "unofficial national anthem.''

Samuel Francis Smith was one of the outstanding Baptist preachers and patriots of the past century. He was born in Boston, Massachusetts, on October 21, 1808. He was graduated from Harvard in 1829 and then studied for the ministry at Andover Theological Seminary, finishing in the same year that he wrote this hymn. He served with distinction several large Baptist churches throughout the East. In 1843 in cooperation with Barton Stow, Smith compiled a hymnal, *The Psalmist,* which became the most widely used Baptist hymnal in its day. Samuel Smith himself composed 150 hymns during his lifetime. He was also editor of a missionary magazine, through which he exerted a strong influence in promoting the cause of missions. Later he became the Secretary of the Baptist Missionary Union and spent considerable time visiting various foreign fields. Smith was also recognized as an accomplished linguist in fifteen different languages, even beginning the study of the Russian language at the age of eighty-six, just one year before his death.

196

One day the noted American music educator, Lowell Mason, gave to Smith for his perusal and interest a copy of a German patriotic poem, which was translated as "God Bless our Native Land.'' Samuel Smith, then only twenty-four years of age, was so moved by the thought that our young nation needed a similar stirring bit of verse that under an inspirational impulse he began writing this text on a scrap of waste paper. Within half an hour he finished what is generally considered to be our best-loved patriotic hymn. The present four stanzas have remained intact exactly as they were written on that original piece of paper. On the following July 4th Lowell Mason's children's choir from the Park Street Congregational Church of Boston sang this hymn for the first time at a Sunday School celebration in a nearby public park. It had an immediate response and soon became popular nationally. One of our eminent leaders of that era once paid this tribute to the hymn:

Strong in simplicity and deep in its trust in God, children and philosophers can repeat the hymn together. Every crisis will hear it above the storm.

Though the text of the hymn is distinctively American, the tune is an international one. It is the official or semi-official national melody of about twenty nations, notably that of England where "God Save the King/Queen'' has been sung for more than 200 years. The origin of the tune seems to go back deeply into the singing traditions of Europe. Traces of the tune have been found in Swiss music as early as the seventeenth century. It has also been found in the musical heritages of Germany, Sweden and Russia. Its first known publication was in a hymnal entitled "Thesaurus Musicus" in 1740. In 1841 one of the world's master composers, Ludwig Beethoven, wrote several interesting piano variations on this tune.

Samuel Smith's text originally contained five stanzas. One of these verses was soon dropped, however, because of its strong anti-British sentiment. The existing four verses have since remained in common usage.

197

Samuel Francis Smith

59 My Redeemer

PHILIP P. BLISS, 1838-1876

JAMES McGRANAHAN, 1840-1907

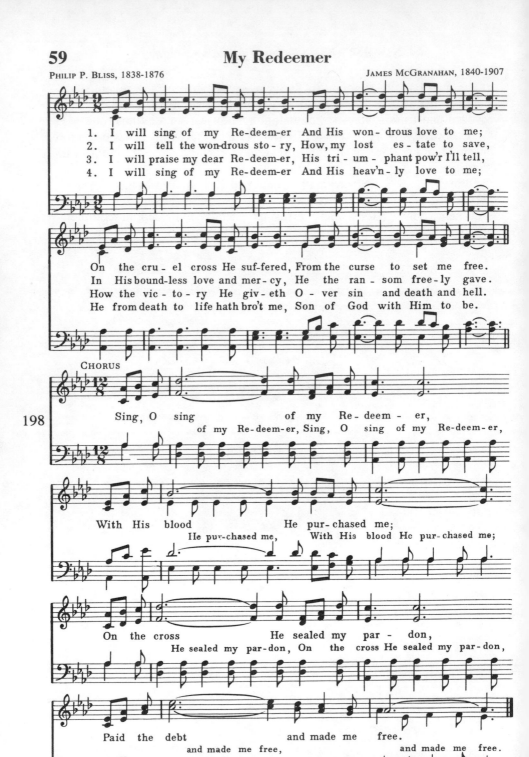

1. I will sing of my Re-deem-er And His won-drous love to me;
2. I will tell the won-drous sto-ry, How, my lost es-tate to save,
3. I will praise my dear Re-deem-er, His tri-um-phant pow'r I'll tell,
4. I will sing of my Re-deem-er And His heav'n-ly love to me;

On the cru-el cross He suf-fered, From the curse to set me free.
In His bound-less love and mer-cy, He the ran-som free-ly gave.
How the vic-to-ry He giv-eth O-ver sin and death and hell.
He from death to life hath bro't me, Son of God with Him to be.

CHORUS

198

Sing, O sing of my Re-deem-er,
of my Re-deem-er, Sing, O sing of my Re-deem-er,

With His blood He pur-chased me;
He pur-chased me, With His blood He pur-chased me;

On the cross He sealed my par-don,
He sealed my par-don, On the cross He sealed my par-don,

Paid the debt and made me free.
and made me free, and made me free.

UNDERSTANDING the Hymnal's Contents

My Redeemer

Author–Philip P. Bliss, 1838–1876
Composer–James McGranahan, 1840–1907
Meter–87.87 with Chorus

> Who gave Himself for us, that He might redeem us from all iniquity, and purify unto Himself a peculiar people, zealous of good works. Titus 2:14

A shocking train accident caused the untimely death of Philip P. Bliss when he was only thirty-eight years of age. He had visited his old childhood home in Rome, Pennsylvania, at Christmas time in 1876, and was returning to Chicago in company with his wife when a railroad bridge near Ashtabula, Ohio, collapsed. The train plunged into a ravine, sixty feet below, where it caught fire, and one hundred passengers perished miserably. Bliss survived the fall and escaped through a window. However, he returned to the wreckage in an attempt to rescue his wife and in so doing perished with her in the fire.

This hymn text by P. P. Bliss was found in his trunk, which had escaped damage in the accident. The tune was composed by James McGranahan shortly after Bliss's death, while McGranahan was in Chicago considering Major Whittle's invitation to replace Bliss as Whittle's song leader in his future evangelistic endeavors. The hymn had a great spiritual impact when it was first introduced to a large tabernacle audience in Chicago as Major Whittle related how the text had been found among Bliss's belongings. He told how James McGranahan had composed the music for this text and how that this musician would now continue the work begun by Bliss.

The hymn first appeared in print in 1877 in *Welcome Tidings,* a new collection for Sunday schools, compiled by Robert Lowry, Wm. H. Doane, and Ira D. Sankey.

Other hymns by Philip P. Bliss include 'Hold the Fort" (No. 30), "I Gave my Life for Thee" (No. 34), "It Is Well with My Soul" (No. 44) and "Jesus Loves Even Me" (No. 46).

James McGranahan is also the composer of the hymn, "I'll Stand By Until the Morning" (No. 40).

My Savior First of All

FANNY J. CROSBY, 1820-1915

JOHN R. SWENEY, 1837-1899

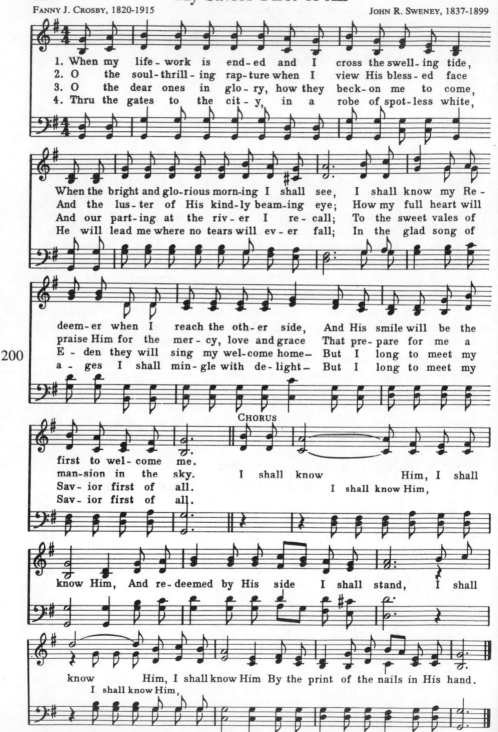

200

My Savior First of All

Author–Fanny J. Crosby, 1820–1915
Composer–John R. Sweney, 1837–1899
Meter–14 11. 14 11. with Chorus

> Thou wilt show me the path of life: In Thy presence is fulness of joy; at Thy right hand there are pleasures for evermore.   Psalm 16:11

This is another of the more than 8,000 gospel hymns written by the blind American poetess, Fanny Crosby. Although she wrote on a great variety of subjects, the themes of heaven and the Lord's return seem to have been her favorites. The anticipation of seeing her Savior undoubtedly had great personal meaning to this blind believer.

Early in life Fanny Crosby showed an unusual poetic talent. At the age of eight she wrote these words:

> Oh, what a happy soul am I!
> Although I cannot see,
> I am resolved that in this world
> Contented I will be.

201

> How many blessings I enjoy
> That other people don't;
> To weep and sigh because I'm blind,
> I cannot, and I won't.

This same strong spirit characterized her entire life. Once a well-intentioned Scotch minister remarked to her, "I think it is a great pity that the Master, when He showered so many gifts upon you, did not give you sight."

Her rebuke came quickly, "Do you know that if at birth I had been able to make one petition to my Creator, it would have been that I should be born blind?"

"Why?" asked the surprised clergyman.

"Because, when I get to heaven, the first face that shall ever gladden my sight will be that of my Savior."

The hymn first appeared in *Songs of Love and Praise,* compiled by Sweney, W. J. Kirkpatrick and Henry L. Gilmour, 1894.

Other hymns by Fanny J. Crosby include "All the Way My Savior Leads Me" (No. 5), "Blessed Assurance" (No. 11) and "Rescue the Perishing" (No. 76).

John R. Sweney was born in West Chester, Pennsylvania, on December 31, 1837. He was a successful music teacher in various schools and colleges around the country. He was considered to be one of the most successful song leaders of his day. For twenty-five years, Sweney served as Professor of Music at the Pennsylvania Military Academy. In 1886 the Doctor of Music Degree was conferred upon him by that institution. John Sweney personally wrote or composed over 1,000 sacred songs as well as editing or being associated with the publication of more than sixty hymnbooks.

202

Fanny Crosby

61

Nearer, My God, to Thee

BETHANY

SARAH F. ADAMS, 1805-1848

LOWELL MASON, 1792-1872

1. Near - er, my God, to Thee, Near - er to Thee! E'en tho it
2. Tho like the wan - der - er, The sun gone down, Dark - ness be
3. There let the way ap - pear, Steps un - to heav'n; All that Thou
4. Then with my wak-ing thoughts, Bright with Thy praise, Out of my
5. Or if on joy - ful wing, Cleav - ing the sky, Sun, moon, and

be a cross That rais - eth me; Still all my song shall be,
o - ver me, My rest a stone, Yet in my dreams I'd be
send - est me, In mer - cy giv'n— An - gels to beck - on me
ston - y griefs, Beth - el I raise; So by my woes to be
stars for - got, Up - ward I fly, Still all my song shall be,

Near-er, my God, to Thee, Near-er, my God, to Thee, Near - er to Thee!

203

Author–Sarah F. Adams, 1805–1848
Composer–Lowell Mason, 1792–1872
Tune Name–"Bethany"
Meter–64.64.6664
Scripture Reference–Genesis 28:10–22

Draw nigh to God, and He will draw nigh to you.   James 4:8

"Nearer, My God, to Thee" is generally considered by students of hymnology to be the finest hymn ever written by any woman hymnwriter. Sarah Flower Adams was born at Harlow, England, on February 22, 1805. She died at the early age of forty-three. In this brief lifetime, however, Sarah Adams lived a full and productive life. She was active for a time on the stage, playing the part of Lady MacBeth in London. She was also widely known for her many literary accomplishments, though her delicate health was always a handicap for her many ambitions. In 1834 she married a prominent inventor and civil engineer, John Brydges Adams, and, until Sarah's death fourteen years later, this distinguished couple continued to make their home in London. Sarah's talent, beauty, charm and exalted character always made a deep impression upon all who knew her.

Sarah's sister, Eliza, was also a talented lady. Being an accomplished musician, she wrote the music for many of Sarah's hymn texts. One day their Unitarian pastor, the Rev. Wm. Johnson Fox, asked these two exceptional sisters if they would aid him in the preparation of a new hymnal he was compiling for the congregation. The two sisters soon became busily involved and committed to this project. Together, they contributed thirteen texts and sixty-two new tunes.

The text for this hymn is based on the dream that Jacob had in the desert when he was fleeing as a fugitive from his home and his brother Esau. Upon awakening from his dream and seeing the ascending and descending angels, Jacob called the place "Bethel"–"The House of God." One day the two sisters were busily involved with their pastor in completing the final details for the new hymnal soon to be published. The pastor remarked that he wished he could find a hymn to conclude a sermon he was preparing on the account of Jacob and Esau as recorded in Genesis 28:10–22. Sister Eliza interrupted enthusiastically, "Sarah, now there's an excellent idea for a new hymn for our hymnal. Why don't you write your own hymn about Jacob's dream?"

204

"Splendid!" replied the pleased pastor. Later that day, after spending much time in studying the Genesis account, absorbing the atmosphere and feeling the dramatic movement of this Old Testament narrative, Sarah began to write. Soon she had versified the complete Biblical story in these five stanzas still in use today.

The hymn has sometimes been criticized since there is no reference to the person or work of Christ throughout the text. During most of Sarah Adam's life she attended the Unitarian Church. This association no doubt accounts for the lack of evangelical fervor in her text. Interestingly enough, however, the hymn is found in nearly every published hymnal and has won its way into the hearts of believers around the world with its many translations into other languages. There is evidence from some of her last writings that shortly before the close of her life, Sarah Adams had a conversion experience and became associated with a congregation of Baptist believers in London.

"Nearer, my God, to Thee" was one of the hymns included in that new hymnal published in 1841. It was known as *Hymns and Anthems* and was geared especially for Fox's Unitarian Congregation in London. The hymn was introduced in America three years later in 1844. But it did not gain real popularity for twelve years until it was wedded with the present tune,

"Bethany," composed especially for the text by Lowell Mason, often known as the father of American church and school music. Other hymns by Lowell Mason include "From Greenland's Icy Mountains" (No. 25) and "When I Survey the Wondrous Cross" (No. 100).

Many very interesting incidents have been associated with the use of this hymn. In 1871 three eminent theologians, Professors Hitchcock, Smith and Park, were traveling in Palestine when they heard the strains of this hymn being sung. Drawing near, they saw, to their amazement, fifty Syrian students standing under some trees in a circle, singing in the Arabic language "Nearer, My God, to Thee." Professor Hitchcock, speaking afterward of the event, said that the singing of that Christian hymn by those Syrian youths moved him to tears and affected him more than any singing he had ever heard before.

During the Johnstown City Flood of May 21, 1889, a railroad train rushed into the swirling waters. One car was turned on end, and in it was imprisoned, beyond the hope of rescue, a woman on her way to be a missionary in the far East. The young lady spoke calmly to the awe-stricken multitude gazing helplessly at the tragedy. Then she prayed and finally sang the hymn "Nearer, my God to Thee," in which she was joined by the sorrowing, sympathizing throng. As she sang, she was ushered into the presence of the God she loved and desired to serve.

This hymn has also been the favorite hymn of many of the world's great leaders. Our own martyred President, William McKinley, claimed this as his favorite hymn, and it is said that he was heard to whisper its words as he drew his last breath. The hymn was widely sung and played at his funeral and at memorial services held throughout our land in 1901. There is also the well-known account of the sinking of the ill-fated ship, *The Titanic,* as it plunged into the icy waters of the Atlantic in 1912, sending 1500 people into eternity while the ship's band played the strains of this hymn.

Despite the Unitarian affiliation of the hymn writer, one would have to conclude that this hymn has been greatly used of God to bring spiritual comfort and blessing to many of His people everywhere. It expresses so aptly the common yearning in the hearts of men to know God and to experience His nearness and victory.

62

Now Thank We All Our God

NUN DANKET

Martin Rinkart, 1586-1649
Trans. by Catherine Winkworth, 1827-1878

Johann Crüger, 1598-1662
Arr. by Eldon Burkwall, 1928-

1. Now thank we all our God With hearts and hands and voic - es,
2. O may this boun-teous God Thru all our life be near us,
3. All praise and thanks to God The Fa - ther now be giv - en,

Who won-drous things hath done, In whom His world re - joic - es;
With ev - er joy - ful hearts And bless - ed peace to cheer us;
The Son and Him who reigns With Them in high-est heav - en—

206

Who from our moth-ers' arms Hath blessed us on our way
And keep us in His grace, And guide us when per - plexed,
The one e - ter - nal God Whom earth and heav'n a - dore—

With count - less gifts of love, And still is ours to - day.
And free us from all ills In this world and the next.
For thus it was, is now, And shall be ev - er - more.

UNDERSTANDING the Hymnal's Contents

Now Thank We All Our God

Author–Martin Rinkart, 1586–1649
English Translation–Catherine Winkworth, 1827–1878
Music–Johann Crüger, 1598–1662
Tune Name–"Nun Danket"
Meter–67.67.66.66
Scripture Reference–Psalm 147

> Who shall separate us from the love of Christ? Shall tribulation, or distress, or persecution, or famine, or nakedness, or peril, or sword? Nay, in all these things we are more than conquerors through Him that loved us. Romans 8:35, 37

Upon hearing the hymn, one would never realize that this paean of praise was forged during times of tragic experiences. From some of the most severe human hardships imaginable during the Thirty Years' War (1618–1648) came this stately hymn, often called the national "Te Deum" of Germany because it has been sung on many occasions of national rejoicing.

Martin Rinkart, born on April 23, 1586, in Eilenberg, Saxony, Germany, was the son of a poor coppersmith. He was for a time a boy chorister in the famous St. Thomas Church of Leipzig, Germany, where J. S. Bach was later musical director. There Rinkart worked his way through the University of Leipzig and was ordained to the ministry of the Lutheran Church. At the age of thirty-one he was called to be the pastor in his native town of Eilenberg. He arrived there just when the dreadful bloodshed was starting. Because Eilenberg was a walled city, it became a frightfully overcrowded refuge for political and military fugitives from far and near. Throughout these war years several waves of deadly pestilence and famine swept the city as the various armies marched through the town, leaving death and destruction in their wake. The Rinkart home served as a refuge for the afflicted victims, even though it is said that Martin Rinkart often had difficulty in providing food and clothing for his own family. The plague of 1637 was particularly severe. At its height Rinkart was the only remaining minister, often conducting as many as forty to fifty funeral services daily. Yet, amazingly enough, he was a prolific writer of seven different dramatic productions on the events of the Reformation as well as a total of sixty-six hymns.

During the closing years of the war Eilenberg was overrun by invading armies on three different occasions, once by the Austrian army and twice by the Swedish army. During one of the occupations by the Swedish army, there came the demand that a large tribute payment be made by these already impoverished people. Rinkart interceded with the leaders of the army with such purpose, supported by the prayers of his people, that

207

the tribute demand was finally reduced to a much smaller amount. It is said that when the Swedish commander would not at first consider Rinkart's request for a lowering of the levy, the pastor turned to his humble parishioners and said, "Come, my children, we can find no mercy with man; let us take refuge with God." On his knèes Rinkart led his parishioners in prayer and in the singing of a familiar hymn. This demonstration of spiritual fervency so moved the Swedish commander that he reconsidered and finally lowered the demands of the tribute payment.

Germany is the home of Protestant church music, and no hymn, with the exception of Luther's "A Mighty Fortress is Our God" (No. 1), has been used more widely in German churches than has this hymn. The fine English translation by Catherine Winkworth in 1858 has aided its popularity in the English-speaking countries as well as in Germany. This gifted English woman is also the translator of another well-known German hymn, "Praise Ye the Lord, the Almighty" (No. 75).

The majestic tune for this text was written by one of Germany's finest and most prolific composers, Johann Crüger, whose hymnal, *Praxix Pietatis Melica,* published in 1644, was the outstanding German hymnal of the seventeenth century. It had forty-four editions from 1644–1731. This tune with Rinkart's text first appeared in the 1647 edition of that publication.

208

The first stanza of this hymn is a general expression of gratitude to God for His "countless gifts of Love." The second verse is a petition for God's continued care and keeping, with perhaps just a suggested hint of Rinkart's own personal hardships, "Guide us when perplexed, and free us from all ills. . . . " The final stanza is a grand doxology of praise to the Father, Son and Holy Spirit–"the one eternal God."

63

Now the Day Is Over

MERRIAL

SABINE BARING-GOULD, 1834-1924   JOSEPH BARNBY, 1838-1896

1. Now the day is o - ver, Night is draw-ing nigh;
2. Je - sus, give the wea - ry Calm and sweet re - pose;
3. Grant to lit - tle chil - dren Vi - sions bright of Thee;
4. Thru the long night-watch - es May Thine an - gels spread
5. When the morn - ing wak - ens, Then may I a - rise

Shad - ows of the eve - ning Steal a - cross the sky.
With Thy ten-d'rest bless - ing May our eye - lids close.
Guard the sail - ors toss - ing On the deep blue sea.
Their white wings a - bove me, Watch - ing round my bed.
Pure and fresh and sin - less In Thy ho - ly eyes.

1. eve-ning Steal a - cross the sky.

209

Author–Sabine Baring-Gould, 1834–1924
Composer–Joseph Barnby, 1838–1896
Tune Name–"Merrial"
Meter–65.65
Scripture Reference–Proverbs 3:24

I will both lay me down in peace, and sleep: For Thou, Lord, only makest me to dwell
in safety.   Psalm 4:8

Sabine Baring-Gould was born in Exeter, England on January 28,
1834. A member of an aristocratic family, he spent most of his early life
traveling and gaining an education in Germany and France. Later he
became known as one of England's most prolific writers, contributing
books on history, biographies, poetry, fiction and pioneering in the field
of English folk songs. The catalog of the British Museum lists more titles
by this man than by any other author of his time.

Baring-Gould wrote this text especially for the children of his parish at
Hornbury Bridge, near Wakefield, England. It was based on the text,
Proverbs 3:24, "When thou liest down, thou shalt not be afraid: Yea,
thou shalt lie down, and thy sleep shall be sweet." The hymn first
appeared in the *Church Times* on February 16, 1865.

Sabine Baring-Gould is also the author of the well-known children's hymn, "Onward, Christian Soldiers" (No. 73).

Joseph Barnby was known as one of England's most famous choral conductors during his time and was knighted for his many musical achievements. He is credited with composing 246 hymn tunes. This tune was composed in 1868 and was first published in Barnby's *Original Tunes to Popular Hymns* in 1869. It was first used in the United States by Charles S. Robinson in his *Spiritual Songs for Social Worship,* 1878. Dr. Robinson was especially fond of this tune and named it "Merrial" after one of his daughters.

Joseph Barnby is also the composer of the hymn tune for "May Jesus Christ Be Praised" (No. 57).

*   *   *

210

"Now the darkness gathers,
    Stars begin to peep,
Birds and beasts and flowers
    Soon will be asleep.

"Comfort every sufferer
    Watching late in pain,
Those who plan some evil
    From their sin restrain.

"Glory to the Father,
    Glory to the Son,
And to thee, blest Spirit,
    Whilst all ages run. Amen."

Additional verses written by Sabine Baring-Gould in 1865

O Come, O Come, Emmanuel

VENI EMMANUEL

Latin hymn, 12th century
Trans. by John M. Neale, 1818-1866 — alt.

Plainsong, 13th century
Arr. by Eldon Burkwall, 1928-

Unison

1. O come, O come, Em-man - u - el, And ran-som cap-tive
2. O come, O come, Thou Lord of might, Who to Thy tribes, on
3. O come, Thou Rod of Jes - se, free Thine own from Sa-tan's
4. O come, Thou Day-spring, come and cheer Our spir-its by Thine
5. O come, Thou Key of Da - vid, come And o - pen wide our

Is - ra - el, That mourns in lone-ly ex - ile here
Si - nai's height, In an-cient times didst give the law
tyr - an - ny; From depths of hell Thy peo - ple save
ad - vent here; O drive a-way the shades of night
heav'n - ly home Where all Thy saints with Thee shall dwell—

211

REFRAIN
Parts

Un - til the Son of God ap - pear.
In cloud and maj - es - ty and awe.
And give them vic-t'ry o'er the grave. Re - joice! re - joice!
And pierce the clouds and bring us light.
O come, O come, Em-man - u - el!

Em - man - u - el Shall come to thee, O Is - ra - el.

O Come, O Come, Emmanuel

Author–Latin origin from c. 12th century
Translated into English–John M. Neale, 1818–1866
Music–A Plainsong/chant from c. 13th century
Name of Tune–"Veni Emmanuel" ("Come God With Us")
Meter–LM (88.88) with Refrain
Scripture References–Isaiah 7:14, Zechariah 9:9, Matthew 1:23

> The Lord God shall give unto Him the throne of His father David.   Luke 1:32

The hymnal is truly an amazing collection of expressions regarding spiritual truths. It represents the experiences and feelings of people from many different religious backgrounds throughout various cultures and periods of history. This hymn, for example, finds its origin in the medieval Roman Church of the twelfth century and possibly even earlier. It began as a series of Antiphons–short statements sung at the beginning of the Psalm or of the Magnificat at Vespers during the Advent season. Each of the Antiphons greets the Savior with one of the many titles ascribed to Him in the Scriptures: Emmanuel, Lord of Might, Rod of Jesse, Day-Spring, Key of David. The hauntingly catchy modal melody for this text was originally a Plainsong or Chant, the earliest form of singing in the Church.

212

During the nineteenth century there were a number of Anglican ministers and scholars, such as John M. Neale, who developed a keen interest in rediscovering and translating into English many of the ancient Greek, Latin and German hymns. John Neale, born in London, England, on January 24, 1818, undoubtedly did more than any other person to make available the rich heritage of Greek and Latin hymns.

John M. Neale is also the translator of the hymn, "The Day of Resurrection" (No. 89).

Advent, beginning four Sundays before Christmas, is the season of the church year that emphasizes the anticipation of the first coming of Christ to this earth. His coming as the Messiah was first prophesied in the sixth century B.C. when the Jews were captive in Babylon. For centuries thereafter faithful Hebrews looked for their Messiah with great longing and expectation, echoing the prayer that He would "ransom captive Israel." The tragedy of tragedies, however, is the Biblical and historical fact that He did come "unto His own" to establish a spiritual kingdom of both redeemed Jew and Gentile, "but His own received Him not. . . ."

Today most hymnbooks use just five of the original statements addressed to the anticipated Messiah.

Verse One– "Emmanuel"–Deliverer. (Pronounced Em-manuel, not E-manuel.) God's people now separated from heaven are here compared to Israel, during its Babylonian exile, being separated from God's holy temple in Jerusalem.

Verse Two– "Lord of Might." This is addressed to Almighty Jehovah, the One who first gave the Law at Mount Sinai to the awesome accompaniment of lightning and thunder (Exodus 19:16).

Verse Three–"Rod of Jesse." This is a reference to Isaiah 11:1: "and there shall come forth a rod out of the stem of Jesse, and a Branch shall grow out of his roots." This prophecy was perfectly fulfilled with the birth of Christ, who came from the kingly line of David, the son of Jesse.

Verse Four– "Day-Spring." This address to the Messiah means literally "sun-rising." This prophetic reference was re-echoed by the priest Zacharias in these words upon hearing of Christ's birth: "The day-spring from on high has visited us, to give light to them that sit in darkness and in the shadow of death" (Luke 1:78b, 79a).

Verse Five– "Thou Key of David." This expression is first recorded in Isaiah 22:22: "And the key of the house of David will I lay upon His shoulder." The well-known verse from Isaiah 9:6 also confirms this royal authority of Christ: "and the government shall be upon His shoulder..."

213

Truly our hearts can rejoice with God's people of all ages when we realize that Christ the Messiah did come two thousand years ago and accomplished a perfect redemption for Adam's hopeless race. Yet we wait with the same urgent expectancy, as did the Israelites of old, for the piercing of the clouds–His second advent, when victory over sin and death will be final.

65   O for a Thousand Tongues

AZMON

CHARLES WESLEY, 1707-1788   CARL G. GLÄSER, 1784-1829

Arr. by Lowell Mason, 1792-1872

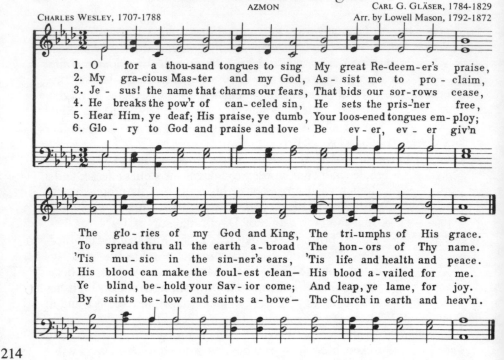

1. O   for   a   thou-sand tongues to sing   My   great Re-deem-er's   praise,
2. My   gra-cious Mas-ter   and my God,   As-sist me   to   pro-claim,
3. Je - sus! the name that charms our fears,   That bids our sor-rows   cease,
4. He   breaks the pow'r of   can-celed sin,   He   sets the pris-'ner   free,
5. Hear Him, ye deaf; His praise, ye dumb,   Your loos-ened tongues em-ploy;
6. Glo - ry to God and praise and love   Be   ev-er, ev-er   giv'n

The   glo-ries of   my God and King,   The   tri-umphs of   His   grace.
To   spread thru all the earth a-broad   The   hon-ors of   Thy   name.
'Tis   mu-sic in   the sin-ner's ears,   'Tis   life and health and   peace.
His   blood can make the foul-est clean—   His blood a-vailed for   me.
Ye   blind, be-hold your Sav-ior come;   And leap, ye lame, for   joy.
By   saints be-low and saints a-bove—   The Church in earth and heav'n.

214

Author–Charles Wesley, 1707–1788
Composer–Carl G. Glaser, 1784–1829
Tune Name–"Azmon"
Meter–CM (86.86)

> Let every thing that hath breath praise the Lord. Praise ye the Lord.   Psalm 150:6

It is generally agreed that Isaac Watts and Charles Wesley have been the two most influential writers of English hymnody to date. Following the new metrical psalmody introduced by Watts, the eighteenth-century Christian church was ready for the more warm, experiential hymns of Charles Wesley. God providentially raised Charles Wesley up to take the harp of Watts when the older poet laid it down and thus kept the church's song vibrant.

John and Charles Wesley, while students at Oxford University, formed a religious "Holy Club" because of their dissatisfaction with the spiritual lethargy at the school. As a result of their methodical habits of living and studying, they were jokingly called "methodists" by their fellow students. Upon graduation these young brothers were sent to America by the Anglican Church to help stabilize the religious climate of the Georgia Colonies and to evangelize the Indians.

UNDERSTANDING the Hymnal's Contents

On board ship as they crossed the Atlantic, the Wesley brothers came into contact with a group of German Moravians, a small evangelical group long characterized by missionary concern and enthusiastic hymn singing. The spiritual depth of these believers soon became evident during a raging storm. The following account is taken from Wesley's journal, January 25, 1736:

> In the midst of the Psalm wherewith their service began, the sea broke over, split the main sail in pieces, covered the ship and poured in between the decks. . . . A terrible screaming began among the English. The Moravians looked up, and without intermission calmly sang on. I asked one of them afterwards, "Were you not afraid?" He answered, "Thank God, no!"

John Wesley was so impressed with these people that he eventually made a detailed study of the hymnal used in their home church in Herrnhut, Germany. Soon he introduced a number of English translations of these Moravian hymns into the Anglican services. Between 1737 and 1786 the Wesleys published between them sixty-three hymnals, with many hymns of Moravian background.

Following a short and unsuccessful ministry in America, the disillusioned Wesleys returned to England, where once again they came under the influence of a group of devout Moravian believers meeting in Aldersgate, London. In May, 1738, both of these brothers had a spiritual heart-warming experience, realizing that though they had been zealous in the Church's ministry, neither had ever personally accepted Christ as Savior nor had known the joy of their religious faith as did their Moravian friends. From that time the Wesleys' ministry took on a new dimension and power.

215

Both John and Charles were endued with an indefatigable spirit, usually working fifteen to eighteen hours each day. It is estimated that they traveled a quarter of a million miles throughout Great Britain, mostly on horseback, while conducting more than 40,000 public services. Charles alone wrote no less than 6,500 hymn texts, with hardly a day or an experience passing without its crystallization into verse.

"O For a Thousand Tongues" was written in 1749 on the occasion of Charles's eleventh anniversary of his own Aldersgate conversion experience. It is thought to have been inspired by a chance remark by Peter Bohler, an influential Moravian leader, who exclaimed, "Had I a thousand tongues, I would praise Christ Jesus with all of them." The hymn originally had nineteen stanzas and when published was entitled, "For the Anniversary Day of One's Conversion." Most of the verses, no longer used, dealt in a very personal way with Wesley's own conversion experience. For example,

I felt my Lord's atoning blood close to my soul applied
Me, me He loved—the Son of God—for me, for me He died.

Charles Wesley died on March 29, 1788, having spent over fifty years in the service of the Lord he loved so intimately and served so effectively. Even as he lay on his death bed, it is said that he dictated a final hymn of praise to his wife.

Other hymns by Charles Wesley include "Christ the Lord Is Risen Today" (No. 13) and "Jesus, Lover of My Soul" (No. 45).

216

John Wesley

66   O God, Our Help in Ages Past

ST. ANNE

From Psalm 90
ISAAC WATTS, 1674-1748

Attr. to William Croft, 1678-1727

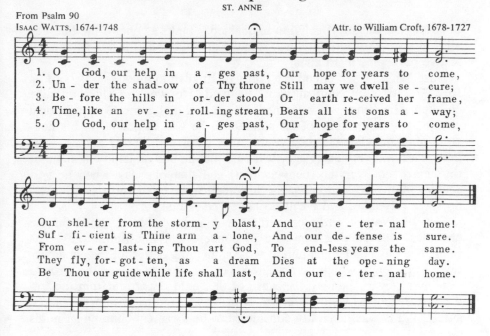

1. O God, our help in a - ges past, Our hope for years to come,
2. Un - der the shad-ow of Thy throne Still may we dwell se - cure;
3. Be - fore the hills in or - der stood Or earth re-ceived her frame,
4. Time, like an ev - er - roll-ing stream, Bears all its sons a - way;
5. O God, our help in a - ges past, Our hope for years to come,

Our shel-ter from the storm-y blast, And our e - ter - nal home!
Suf - fi - cient is Thine arm a - lone, And our de - fense is sure.
From ev - er - last-ing Thou art God, To end-less years the same.
They fly, for - got - ten, as a dream Dies at the ope - ning day.
Be Thou our guide while life shall last, And our e - ter - nal home.

217

Author–Isaac Watts, 1674–1748
Composer–Attributed to William Croft, 1678–1727
Tune Name–"St. Anne"
Meter–CM (86.86)
Scripture Reference–Psalm 90

> Lord, Thou hast been our dwelling place in all generations. Before the mountains were brought forth, or ever Thou hadst formed the earth and the world, even from everlasting to everlasting, Thou art God.   Psalm 90:1, 2

This hymn, considered to be one of the grandest in the whole realm of English hymnody, is a paraphrase of Psalm 90, a psalm of Moses. It is more than a metrical version of this Psalm; it is a grand commentary on the whole subject of time, which is the theme of the Psalm. It originally consisted of nine stanzas. In present usage, however, the hymn is usually limited to stanzas one, two, three, five and nine. In 1738 John Wesley in his hymnal, *Psalms and Hymns,* changed the first line of the text from "Our God" to "O God." The hymn was originally part of *The Psalms of David Imitated in the Language of the New Testament,* published by Watts in 1719. In this book he paraphrased in Christian verse the entire psalter with the exception of twelve Psalms which he felt were unsuited for Christian usage. This hymn undoubtedly ranks as one of the finest of all Watts's 600 or more hymns. It is the one hymn that is still sung at all festive occasions in England.

Isaac Watts, often called the father of English hymnody, was born on July 17, 1674, in Southampton, England. He was the eldest of nine children. His father was a learned deacon in a dissenting Congregational church, and at the time of his son's birth he was in prison for his non-conformist beliefs. As a boy young Isaac displayed literary genius, writing verses at a very early age. It is said that he had an annoying habit of rhyming even everyday conversation, and that one day when he was scolded by his irritated father for this practice, he cried out, "Oh, Father, do some pity take, and I will no more verses make."

One of Watts's early concerns was the low ebb of music in the churches. The singing consisted of ponderous hymn-psalms only. His father one day challenged him to write something better for the congregation, a challenge which he accepted. For the next two years he wrote a new hymn every Sunday. Because of this bold departure from the traditional Psalms as well as the use of his new "hymns of human composure," Watts was generally considered to be a radical churchman in his day.

218 Although Isaac Watts was frail in health during much of his life, he was a scholarly genius in many different fields. His writings include essays, discussions of psychology, three volumes of sermons, catechisms, twenty-nine treatises on theology, textbooks on logic, and a variety of other works. All of these works had a powerful influence upon the thinking of the late seventeenth and early eighteenth centuries.

Isaac Watts died in 1748 at the age of seventy-four. His monument was placed in Westminster Abbey, the highest honor that any Englishman can have.

Other hymns by Isaac Watts include "I Sing the Mighty Power of God" (No. 38), "Jesus Shall Reign" (No. 48) and "When I Survey the Wondrous Cross" (No. 100).

A great hymn text deserves majestic music. No one has ever disputed the musical worth of the tune for this hymn, "St. Anne," composed by William Croft in 1708. Croft was a well-trained church musician, having earned his Doctorate in Music at Oxford University. He was known as one of the finest English musicians of his time. He was the organist at the Church of St. Anne in Soho, London, during the reign of Queen Anne. This tune first appeared anonymously in the *Supplement to the New Version of the Psalms, 6th edition* in 1708. It was originally intended to be used with a version of Psalm 62. It was not until sometime later when set to Watts's text that the tune gained recognition.

As evidence of the musical worth of this tune, master composers such as George F. Handel and J. S. Bach have borrowed it for their own works. For example, Handel used the tune in an anthem entitled "O Praise the Lord," while Bach made use of it in his great Fugue in E-Flat Major, often called "St. Anne's Fugue."

Watts's grave at the Bunhill Cemetery in London where many 17th and 18th century Dissenting Preachers were buried.

67 O Little Town of Bethlehem

ST. LOUIS

Phillips Brooks, 1835-1893

Lewis H. Redner, 1831-1908

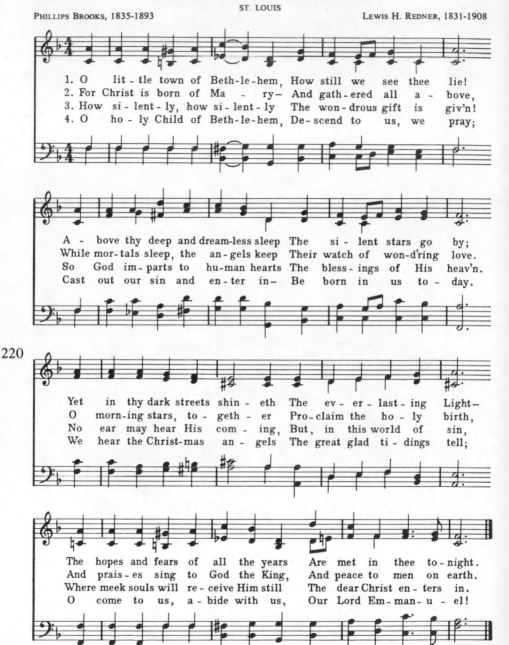

1. O little town of Beth-le-hem, How still we see thee lie!
2. For Christ is born of Ma - ry— And gath-ered all a - bove,
3. How si - lent - ly, how si - lent - ly The won - drous gift is giv'n!
4. O ho - ly Child of Beth-le-hem, De-scend to us, we pray;

A - bove thy deep and dream-less sleep The si - lent stars go by;
While mor-tals sleep, the an-gels keep Their watch of won-d'ring love.
So God im-parts to hu-man hearts The bless-ings of His heav'n.
Cast out our sin and en-ter in— Be born in us to - day.

220

Yet in thy dark streets shin - eth The ev - er - last - ing Light—
O morn-ing stars, to - geth - er Pro-claim the ho - ly birth,
No ear may hear His com - ing, But, in this world of sin,
We hear the Christ-mas an - gels The great glad ti - dings tell;

The hopes and fears of all the years Are met in thee to - night.
And prais - es sing to God the King, And peace to men on earth.
Where meek souls will re - ceive Him still The dear Christ en - ters in.
O come to us, a - bide with us, Our Lord Em - man - u - el!

O Little Town of Bethlehem

Author-Phillips Brooks, 1835-1893
Composer-Lewis H. Redner, 1831-1908
Tune Name-"St. Louis"
Meter-86.86.76.86

> And Joseph also went up from Galilee, out of the city of Nazareth, into Judaea, unto the city of David, which is called Bethlehem.... Luke 2:4

This beloved Christmas carol is from the pen of one of America's outstanding preachers of the past century, Phillips Brooks. In his day he was often referred to as the "Prince of the Pulpit." His many published volumes of sermons have since become classics of American literature. He is said to have won the hearts of people with his preaching and writing as few clergymen have ever done.

"O Little Town of Bethlehem" was written in 1868, several years after Brooks had returned from a trip to the Holy Land. The experience of spending Christmas Eve in Bethlehem and worshipping in the Church of the Nativity, thought to be the place of Christ's birth, made an indelible impression upon the young preacher. Three years later, while pastor at the Holy Trinity Church, Philadelphia, Pennsylvania, he was searching for a new carol for his children to sing in their Sunday School Christmas program. The still vivid memory of his Holy Land visit inspired Brooks to write this text.

Brooks gave a copy of the newly written carol to his organist and Sunday School superintendent, Lewis H. Redner, and asked him to compose a simple melody that children could sing easily. Redner was known throughout the Philadelphia area as a devoted Christian leader in Sunday School work as well as one deeply interested in church music. He struggled for a considerable time to contrive just the right tune for his pastor's text. On the evening before the program was to be given, he suddenly awakened from his sleep and quickly composed the present melody. Redner always insisted that the tune was a gift from heaven. The carol was an immediate favorite with the children, as it has been with children and adults around the world to the present time. It was first published in 1874. Although Brooks wrote a number of other Christmas and Easter carols especially for children, this is the only one to survive the test of time.

Phillips Brooks was born in Boston, Massachusetts, in 1835. After graduation from Harvard and the Episcopal Theological Seminary in Virginia in 1859, he began a long and distinguished career in the ministry, serving as pastor in Philadelphia from 1859-69 and at the Trinity

Church in Boston from 1869–91. He was appointed Bishop of all of the Episcopal churches in the Massachusetts area shortly before his untimely death in 1893.

Brooks was known as an impressive and gifted man, a giant in body (6'6") as well as in mind and heart. His forceful, yet eloquent evangelical preaching, estimated to have been delivered at the rate of 250 words per minute, did much to stem the tide of the Unitarian movement especially rampant in the New England area during that time. Even sedate Harvard University, which had been virtually taken over by the Unitarians, was stirred by Brooks' preaching.

Though a bachelor, Brooks was especially fond of children. It is said that he kept a supply of toys, dolls and other objects of interest for children in his study so that youngsters would be encouraged to stop in and chat with him. A familiar sight was this important man of the pulpit sitting on the floor of his study sharing a fun time with a group of youngsters. His sudden death was greatly mourned by everyone who knew him. The story is told of a five-year-old girl who was upset because she hadn't seen her preacher friend for several days. When told by her mother that Bishop Brooks had gone to heaven, the child exclaimed, "Oh, Mama, how happy the angels will be."

68   O Love That Wilt Not Let Me Go

ST. MARGARET

GEORGE MATHESON, 1842-1906   ALBERT L. PEACE, 1844-1912

1. O Love that wilt not let me go,   I rest my wea-ry soul in Thee; I give Thee back the life I owe, That in Thine o-cean depths its flow May rich-er, full-er be.
2. O Light that fol-l'west all my way,   I yield my flick-'ring torch to Thee; My heart re-stores its bor-rowed ray, That in Thy sun-shine's blaze its day May bright-er, fair-er be.
3. O Joy that seek-est me thru pain,   I can-not close my heart to Thee; I trace the rain-bow thru the rain, And feel the prom-ise is not vain That morn shall tear-less be.
4. O Cross that lift-est up my head,   I dare not ask to fly from Thee; I lay in dust life's glo-ry dead, And from the ground there blos-soms red Life that shall end-less be.

223

Author–George Matheson, 1842–1906
Composer–Albert L. Peace, 1844–1912
Tune Name–"St. Margaret"
Meter–88.886

I have loved thee with an everlasting love.   Jeremiah 31:3

This hymn is generally considered to be one of the best-loved hymns written during the latter part of the nineteenth century. The writing of this thoughtful and artistically constructed text is even more remarkable when it is remembered that it was authored by one who was totally blind and who describes the writing as the "fruit of much mental suffering."

Born in Glasgow, Scotland, March 27, 1842, George Matheson had only partial vision as a boy. After he entered Glasgow University, his sight failed rapidly and he became totally blind at the age of eighteen. Despite this handicap he was a brilliant scholar and finished the University and the Seminary of the Church of Scotland with high honors. In 1886 he became pastor of the 2,000 member St. Bernard's Parish Church in Edinburgh. He went on to become known as one of Scotland's outstanding preachers and pastors, greatly esteemed in Edinburgh, where his eloquent preaching consistently attracted large crowds. Matheson never married, but throughout his fruitful ministry he was aided by a devoted sister, who herself learned Greek, Latin, and Hebrew in order to aid him in his theological studies. She was his faithful co-worker and helper throughout his life, assisting in his calling and other pastoral duties.

Many conjectures have been made regarding the cause of the mental distress which prompted the author to write this text. A very popular account, although never substantiated, is that this text was an outgrowth of Matheson's fiancee's leaving him just before their marriage when she learned of his impending total blindness. Although this story cannot be documented, there are many significant hints in this hymn reflecting a saddened heart, such as the "flickering torch" and the "borrowed ray" in the second stanza, the tracing of the "rainbow through the rain" in the third stanza, as well as the "cross" in the last verse. Fortunately, Dr. Matheson did leave an account of his writing of this hymn:

224

My hymn was composed in the manse of Innellan on the evening of the 6th of June, 1882. I was at that time alone. It was the day of my sister's marriage, and the rest of the family were staying overnight in Glasgow. Something happened to me, which was known only to myself, and which caused me the most severe mental suffering. The hymn was the fruit of that suffering. It was the quickest bit of work I ever did in my life. I had the impression rather of having it dictated to me by some inward voice than of working it out myself. I am quite sure that the whole work was completed in five minutes, and equally sure it never received at my hands any retouching or correction. I have no natural gift of rhythm. All the other verses I have ever written are manufactured articles; this came like a dayspring from on high. I have never been able to gain once more the same fervor in verse.

The hymn first appeared in the Church of Scotland monthly magazine, *Life and Work,* in January, 1883. The tune was composed one year later by a prominent Scotch organist of his day, Albert L. Peace, who was requested by the Scottish Hymnal Committee to write a tune especially for Matheson's text. Peace's own account of the writing of this fine tune is as follows, "After reading it over carefully, I wrote the music straight off, and may say that the ink of the first note was hardly dry when I had finished the tune."

The significance of the tune name, "St. Margaret," is unknown except that it is a name greatly revered in Scotland, no doubt because of the beloved Queen Margaret, who was canonized in 1251.

The later years of Matheson's life were spent in writing some of the finest devotional literature in the English language, including *Moments on the Mount, Voice of the Spirit,* and *Rests by the River.* Although this is his only hymn found in most evangelical hymnals, Matheson did write a number of other fine hymns, including a thoughtful text entitled "Make Me a Captive Lord, and Then I Shall Be Free."

The four key words or symbols of "O Love, That Wilt Not Let Me Go" are Love, Light, Joy, Cross. These words have been described as the total fulfillment for any believer whose life is totally committed to the will of God. One could probe for considerable time the depth and personal significance of these four expressions.

Inset: Dr. George Matheson. *Innellan Manse*

The birthplace of "O Love that wilt not let me go."

69

O Master, Let Me Walk with Thee
MARYTON

WASHINGTON GLADDEN, 1836-1918   H. PERCY SMITH, 1825-1898

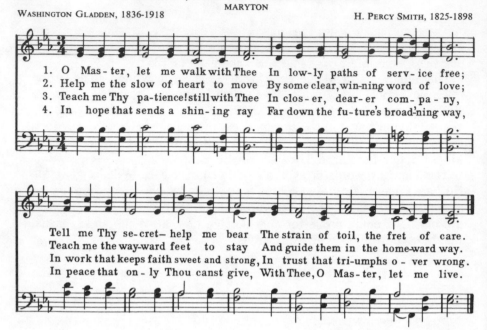

1. O Mas-ter, let me walk with Thee In low-ly paths of serv-ice free;
2. Help me the slow of heart to move By some clear, win-ning word of love;
3. Teach me Thy pa-tience! still with Thee In clos-er, dear-er com-pa-ny,
4. In hope that sends a shin-ing ray Far down the fu-ture's broad'ning way,

Tell me Thy se-cret— help me bear The strain of toil, the fret of care.
Teach me the way-ward feet to stay And guide them in the home-ward way.
In work that keeps faith sweet and strong, In trust that tri-umphs o-ver wrong.
In peace that on-ly Thou canst give, With Thee, O Mas-ter, let me live.

226

Author-Washington Gladden, 1836–1918
Composer-H. Percy Smith, 1825–1898
Tune Name-"Maryton"
Meter-LM (88.88)
Scripture Reference-Matthew 25:31–46

> He hath showed thee, O man, what is good; and what doth the Lord require of thee, but to do justly, and to love mercy, and to walk humbly with thy God.   Micah 6:8

This hymn, published in 1879, comes from a period of religious history in this country when there was much emphasis given to the social implications of the Gospel. The Civil War had ended and our country was in the throes of a great industrial revolution. As is often true in such times, the individual is exploited for the cause of economic progress. Many of our country's more liberal clergymen became enthusiastic champions for the cause of social justice. One of the recognized leaders of the social gospel movement was Washington Gladden, known until his death as one of America's most distinguished liberal clergymen.

Washington Gladden was born on a farm in Potts Grove, Pennsylvania, on February 11, 1836. Following graduation from Williams College in 1859, he was ordained to the Congregational Churches' ministry. While ministering in pulpits in the East for eleven years, Gladden spent much time fighting such political groups as the corrupt Tweed Ring, and it was largely through Gladden's personal efforts that the Tammany boss himself was eventually put behind prison bars for fifteen years. In 1882 Gladden was called to the First Congregational Church in Columbus, Ohio, where he remained for the next thirty-two years. There he became known as one of the most powerful pulpit voices in America as he continued to apply "the gospel to the social, political and economic life of America and the world." Gladden was known not only for his influential pulpiteering and writing, but also for his negotiations in various national disputes and strikes. In 1883 he arbitrated the Telegraphers' strike and the following year the Hocking Valley Coal Strike. It was always his conviction that it was the duty of the Christian Church to "elevate the masses not only spiritually and morally, but to be concerned about their social and economic welfare as well."

Throughout his life Gladden was the object of bitter criticism from many leaders of the business world as well as from the conservative factions of the church. Even his own denomination turned against him when he attacked John D. Rockefeller, Sr., for his gift of $100,000 to the Congregational Church Foreign Missions Board, a gift which Gladden termed "tainted money" because of Rockefeller's monopolistic practices with Standard Oil. Washington Gladden's views on Biblical criticism were also strongly denounced by conservative churchmen when he preached that the Bible was not inerrant science and history but merely a book of religion. Two interesting original stanzas of this hymn no longer included in church hymnals reflect Gladden's feelings toward those he felt were his oppressors:

O Master let me walk with Thee before the taunting Pharisee;
Help me to bear the sting of spite, the hate of men who hide Thy light.

The sore distrust of souls sincere who cannot read Thy judgments clear,
The dullness of the multitude who dimly guess that Thou art good.

The tune, "Maryton," was originally composed by an Anglican minister, H. Percy Smith, for John Keble's hymn, "Sun of My Soul" (No. 85). It first appeared in *Church Hymns with Tunes* published in 1874. "O Master, Let Me Walk with Thee" was not meant to be used as a hymn text but merely as a devotional meditation. It first appeared as a poem in a publication called *Sunday Afternoon,* of which Gladden was editor, under the caption, "Walking with God." When it was eventually suggested that the poem be used as a hymn, the "Maryton" tune was the choice of Dr. Gladden for his text. Although Washington Gladden was widely known in his day for his influential preaching and writings, he is best remembered today for this one fine hymn.

70

O That Will Be Glory

CHARLES H. GABRIEL, 1856-1932   CHARLES H. GABRIEL, 1856-1932

228

1. When all my la-bors and tri-als are o'er And I am safe on that
2. When, by the gift of His in-fi-nite grace, I am ac-cord-ed in
3. Friends will be there I have loved long a-go, Joy like a riv-er a-

beau-ti-ful shore, Just to be near the dear Lord I a-dore
heav-en a place, Just to be there and to look on His face
round me will flow; Yet, just a smile from my Sav-ior, I know,

Will thru the a-ges be glo-ry for me.

CHORUS

O that will be glo-ry for me, Glo-ry for me, glo-ry for me; When by His grace
O that will be glo-ry for me, Glo-ry for me, glo-ry for me;

I shall look on His face, That will be glo-ry, be glo-ry for me!

O That Will be Glory

Author-Charles H. Gabriel, 1856-1932
Composer-Charles H. Gabriel, 1856-1932
Meter-10 10. 10 10 with Chorus

> And God shall wipe away all tears from their eyes; and there shall be no more death, neither sorrow, nor crying, neither shall there be any more pain; For the former things are passed away.   Revelation 21:4

Charles H. Gabriel, one of this country's most influential and prolific gospel songwriters of the early twentieth century, was born in a prairie shanty on August 18, 1856, at Wilton, Iowa. The settlers in that area often gathered in the Gabriel home for singing sessions and fellowship, with Charles's father generally serving as the leader. At an early age Charles developed a love for music and soon gave evidence of a gift for composing. One day he told his mother that it was his supreme desire to write a song that would become famous. She wisely replied, "My boy, I would rather have you write a song that will help somebody than see you President of the United States." Two years later Charles began teaching singing schools in the surrounding area without ever having the benefit of a single formal music lesson. He began writing and selling many of his songs during those early days but never received more than two and one half dollars for any of his works.

229

In all Mr. Gabriel edited thirty-five different gospel songbooks, eight Sunday School songbooks, seven books for male choruses, six for ladies' voices, ten children's songbooks, nineteen collections of anthems, twenty-three choir cantatas, forty-one Christmas cantatas, ten children's cantatas, and numerous books on musical instruction. From 1912 until his death in 1932 he was associated with the Homer Rodeheaver Publishing Company. His fame as a successful composer became widely known, especially with the use of his songs by Rodeheaver in the large Billy Sunday evangelistic campaigns. Like many of the early gospel song musicians, Gabriel usually wrote both the texts and music for his songs. Some of his hymn texts are shown with his pseudonym, Charlotte G. Homer.

"O That Will be Glory" first appeared in a publication entitled *Make His Praise Glorious,* compiled and published in 1900 by a fellow gospel musician, E. O. Excell. The text was inspired by Mr. Gabriel's good friend, Ed Card, Superintendent of the Sunshine Rescue Mission of St. Louis, Missouri. Ed was a radiant believer who always seemed to be bubbling over with the joy of the Lord. During a sermon or prayer he would often explode with the expression, "Glory!" His smiling face earned him the nickname "Old Glory Face." It was his custom to close his own praying with a reference to heaven, ending with the phrase "and that will be glory for me!" It is said that Card had the joy of singing this hymn just before his home-going with the pleasure of knowing that his Christian life had been its inspiration. This hymn has since been translated into many different languages and dialects with an estimated publication of over 100 million copies.

* * *

"In loving kindness Jesus came
My soul in mercy to reclaim
And from the depths of sin and shame
Through grace He lifted me.

"He called me long before I heard,
Before my sinful heart was stirred,
But when I took Him at His word,
Forgiv'n He lifted me.

"His brow was pierced with many a thorn,
His hands by cruel nails were torn,
When from my guilt and grief, forlorn,
In love He lifted me.

"Now on a higher plane I dwell,
And with my soul I know 'tis well;
Yet how or why, I cannot tell,
He should have lifted me.

"From sinking sand He lifted me,
With tender hand He lifted me,
From shades of night to plains of light,
O praise His name, He lifted me!"

Written and composed by Charles H. Gabriel in 1905

230

71　O Word of God Incarnate

MUNICH

WILLIAM W. HOW, 1823-1897

From *Meiningen Gesangbuch*, 1693
Har. by Felix Mendelssohn, 1809-1847

1. O Word of God in-car-nate, O Wis-dom from on high,
2. The Church from her dear Mas-ter Re-ceived the gift di-vine,
3. It float-eth like a ban-ner Be-fore God's host un-furled;
4. O make Thy Church, dear Sav-ior, A lamp of pur-est gold,

O Truth un-changed, un-chang-ing, O Light of our dark sky:
And still that light she lift-eth O'er all the earth to shine.
It shin-eth like a bea-con A-bove the dark-ling world.
To bear be-fore the na-tions Thy true light, as of old.

We praise Thee for the ra-diance That from the hal-lowed page,
It is the gold-en cas-ket Where gems of truth are stored;
It is the chart and com-pass That o'er life's surg-ing sea,
O teach Thy wan-d'ring pil-grims By this their path to trace,

A lan-tern to our foot-steps, Shines on from age to age.
It is the heav'n-drawn pic-ture Of Christ, the liv-ing Word.
'Mid mists and rocks and quick-sands, Still guides, O Christ, to Thee.
Till, clouds and dark-ness end-ed, They see Thee face to face.

231

SINGING WITH UNDERSTANDING

O Word of God Incarnate

Author-William W. How, 1823–1897
Music-From the Meiningen Gesangbuch, 1693 and Harmonized by Felix Mendelssohn, 1809–1847
Tune Name-"Munich"
Meter-76.76 Doubled
Scripture Reference-Psalm 119:105

> All Scripture is given by inspiration of God, and is profitable for doctrine, for reproof, for correction, for instruction in righteousness: That the man of God may be perfect, thoroughly furnished unto all good works.   2 Timothy 3:16,17

William W. How, born in Shrewsbury, England, on December 13, 1823, is considered to be one of the last of the outstanding English hymnists of the nineteenth century. In addition to composing his sixty hymns, of which twenty-five are still in use, he served as an Anglican Bishop for the eastern section of London, the slum district of that city. In this capacity he was affectionately known as the poor man's bishop for his tireless efforts in alleviating the dire social conditions in that poverty stricken area. He was also called the omnibus bishop because, unlike the typical bishop who lived in a palace and rode in a private coach, How always used public transportation and lived and worked with his people. Throughout his busy life the good bishop always maintained a keen interest in the hymns of the church. With his friend, Sir Arthur Sullivan of operetta fame, he was joint editor of a popular Anglican hymnal of his day.

232

The tune for this hymn, "Munich," is named after the German city. It was adapted from a melody found in an old German hymnal of 1693. It was later used by the nineteenth century German composer, Felix Mendelssohn, for a choral, "Cast Thy Burden on the Lord," from his oratorio *Elijah*, first heard in England on August 26, 1846.

"O Word of God Incarnate" appeared in the 1867 supplement to *Psalms and Hymns*, edited by T. B. Morrell and W. W. How. Although Bishop How and John Ellerton (No. 79) were known as the two leading churchmen in the broad, liberal faction of the Anglican Church, it is interesting to observe, that in the first verse of this hymn, How clearly establishes the Bible as the revealed Word of God. In verse two he develops the thought that the Church is the agency by which the Bible has been and still is transmitted to mankind. In verse three he uses a number of metaphors that describe the Scriptures in their relationship to daily living–banner, lighthouse, chart and compass. Verse four concludes with a prayer that the Church may ever be the faithful custodian and administrator of this treasure in guiding men to their eternal destiny.

Great men throughout history have been impressed with the uniqueness of the Bible. They have observed how its teachings have altered societies, changed the destiny of nations, and transformed individual lives. The following statement by Abraham Lincoln is representative of this attitude:

Read this book for what on reason you can accept and take the rest on faith, and you will live and die a better man.

*　　*　　*

"For feelings come and feelings go,
　And feelings are deceiving;
My warrant is the Word of God,
　Naught else is worth believing.

"Though all my heart should feel condemned
　For want of some sweet token,
There is One greater than my heart
　Whose Word cannot be broken.

"I'll trust in God's unchanging Word
　Till soul and body sever:
For, though all things shall pass away,
　His Word shall stand forever."

233

Martin Luther, 1483–1546

"Within this ample volume lies
　The mystery of mysteries.
Happiest they of human race
　To whom their God has given grace
To read, to fear, to hope, to pray,
　To lift the latch, to force the way;
But better had they ne'er been born
　That read to doubt or read to scorn."

Sir Walter Scott, 1771–1832

"Study it carefully, think of it prayerfully,
　Till in thy heart its precepts dwell.
Slight not its history, ponder its mystery;
　None can e'er prize it too fondly or well."

Author Unknown

O Worship the King

LYONS

ROBERT GRANT, 1779-1838   Arr. from J. MICHAEL HAYDN, 1737-1806

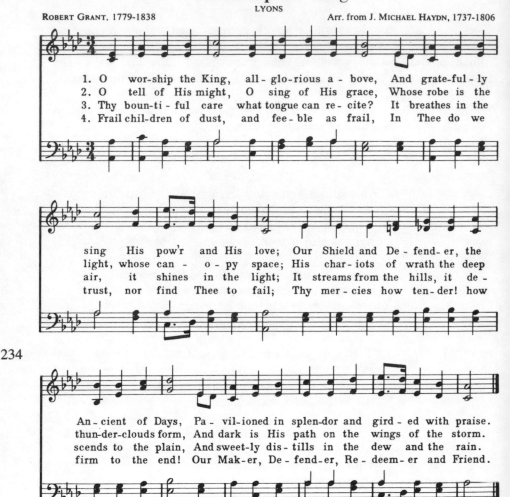

1. O wor-ship the King, all - glo-rious a - bove, And grate-ful - ly
2. O tell of His might, O sing of His grace, Whose robe is the
3. Thy boun-ti - ful care what tongue can re - cite? It breathes in the
4. Frail chil-dren of dust, and fee - ble as frail, In Thee do we

sing His pow'r and His love; Our Shield and De - fend- er, the
light, whose can - o - py space; His char- iots of wrath the deep
air, it shines in the light; It streams from the hills, it de-
trust, nor find Thee to fail; Thy mer - cies how ten-der! how

234

An - cient of Days, Pa - vil-ioned in splen-dor and gird - ed with praise.
thun-der-clouds form, And dark is His path on the wings of the storm.
scends to the plain, And sweet-ly dis- tills in the dew and the rain.
firm to the end! Our Mak- er, De - fend-er, Re - deem- er and Friend.

Author-Robert Grant, 1779–1838
Composer-Arranged from J. Michael Haydn, 1737–1806
Tune Name-"Lyons"
Meter-10 10. 11 11
Scripture Reference-Psalm 104

Bless the Lord, O my soul! O Lord my God, Thou art very great.   Psalm 104:1

Man is basically a religious though unregenerate being. In all human
life there is a consciousness of a supreme power. Even the most primitive

savage is a religious being as he attempts to fulfill his duties to the invisible powers he senses about him. Since the beginning of recorded time, music has always had a unique association with man's worship experiences.

The word "worship" is a contraction of an old expression in the English language, "woerth-scipe," denoting the ascription of reverence to an object of superlative worth. A more theological definition of worship is given as follows: "An act by a redeemed man, the creature, toward God, his Creator, whereby his will, intellect and emotions gratefully respond to the revelation of God's person expressed in the redemptive work of Jesus Christ, as the Holy Spirit illuminates the written Word to his heart."

This hymn, written and published in 1833 in a hymnal entitled *Christian Psalmody,* is one of the finest from the early nineteenth century Romantic Era. It has often been called a model hymn for worship. It has few equals in expressive lyrics in the exaltation of the Almighty. Each of the epithets applied to God–King, Shield, Defender, Ancient of Days, Maker, Redeemer, Friend–as well as the vivid imagery–such as, "His chariots of wrath the deep thunderclouds form" and the references to His attributes–power, might, grace, bountiful care, love–all combine to describe with literary eloquence and spiritual warmth the majesty and praise-worthiness of our God.

235

Sir Robert Grant was born into a setting of high political life in Bengal, India, in 1779. His father, Charles, was a respected ranking leader in India and a director of the East India Company. Later he became a member of the British Parliament from Scotland. He was also a zealous leader in the evangelical wing of the Anglican Church. Robert, too, became active in business and politics and eventually was appointed Governor of Bombay in 1834. Like his father, Robert was a devout and deeply spiritual lay evangelical Christian all of his life. Though involved in secular and political pursuits, Robert Grant maintained a strong interest in the missionary outreach of the church throughout his lifetime. He was greatly loved by the people of India, who established a lasting memorial there in the form of a medical college bearing his name.

In 1839, a year after his death in India, his brother, Charles, had twelve of Robert's poems published in a little volume entitled *Sacred Poems.* Although several of these poem hymns received some acceptance, only this text is still in common usage in most hymnals today.

The tune for this hymn, "Lyons," first appeared in the second volume of William Gardiner's *Sacred Melodies,* London, 1815, where it was attributed to Haydn. However, there is an uncertainty, since in other works by these two Austrian brother musicians, Franz Joseph and the younger Johann Michael, there are several songs that begin with this same

SINGING WITH UNDERSTANDING

melody but none which compares exactly with Gardiner's adaptation. The first use of this tune in the United States was in 1818 in a collection entitled *Sacred Melodies* by Oliver Shaw.

Haydn is also the composer of the hymn, "The Day of Resurrection" (No. 89).

Also from William Gardiner's collection is the hymn, "Jesus, Thy Blood and Righteousness" (No. 50).

*   *   *

"Worship renews the spirit as sleep renews the body."
Richard Clarke Cabot

236 "Worship is transcendent wonder."

Thomas Carlyle

"It is only when men begin to worship that they begin to grow."
Calvin Coolidge

"Worship is the act of rising to a personal, experimental consciousness of the real presence of God which floods the soul with joy and bathes the whole inward spirit with refreshing streams of life."
Rufus Matthew Jones

"If Socrates would enter the room we should rise and do him honor. But if Jesus Christ came into the room we should fall down on our knees and worship Him."

Napoleon Bonaparte

73 Onward, Christian Soldiers

ST. GERTRUDE

Sabine Baring-Gould, 1834-1924

Arthur S. Sullivan, 1842-1900

1. On-ward, Chris-tian sol - diers, March-ing as to war, With the cross of
2. At the sign of tri - umph Sa - tan's host doth flee; On, then, Chris-tian
3. Like a might-y ar - my Moves the Church of God; Broth-ers, we are
4. On-ward, then, ye peo - ple, Join our hap-py throng; Blend with ours your

Je - sus Go - ing on be - fore! Christ, the roy - al Mas - ter, Leads a -
sol - diers, On to vic-to - ry! Hell's foun-da-tions quiv - er At the
tread - ing Where the saints have trod. We are not di - vid - ed, All one
voic - es In the tri - umph song. Glo - ry, laud and hon - or Un - to

gainst the foe; For-ward in - to bat - tle See His ban-ner go!
shout of praise; Broth-ers, lift your voic - es, Loud your an-thems raise!
bod - y we - One in hope and doc - trine, One in char - i - ty.
Christ the King - This thru count-less a - ges Men and an-gels sing.

REFRAIN

On-ward, Chris-tian sol - diers, March-ing as to war,

With the cross of Je - sus Go - ing on be - fore!

237

Onward, Christian Soldiers

Author–Sabine Baring-Gould, 1834–1924
Composer–Arthur S. Sullivan, 1842–1900
Tune Name–"St. Gertrude"
Meter–65.65 Doubled with Refrain

Thou therefore endure hardness, as a good soldier of Jesus Christ. 2 Timothy 2:3

Baring-Gould was one of the truly gifted preacher-literary men of the nineteenth century. In addition to being ordained to the Anglican ministry in 1864, he was a noted writer throughout his life. His publications include eighty-five books on such varied subjects as religion, travel, folk-lore, mythology, history, fiction, biography, sermons and popular theology. All are notable works. It is said that the British Museum shows more titles by him than by any other writer of this time. Yet, amazingly enough, the work for which Sabine Baring-Gould is best noted and re-membered today is a simple children's hymn written in 1865.

The author has left the following account regarding the writing of this hymn:

238

It was written in a very simple fashion, without thought of publication. Whitmonday is a great day for school festivals in Yorkshire, and one Whitmonday it was arranged that our school should join forces with that of a neighboring village. I wanted the children to sing when march-ing from one village to the other, but couldn't think of anything quite suitable, so I sat up at night resolved to write something myself. "On-ward, Christian Soldiers" was the result. It was written in great haste.

Commenting on this hymn some thirty years later, Baring-Gould re-marked:

It was written in great haste, and I am afraid that some of the rhymes are faulty. I am certain that nothing has surprised me more than its popularity.

One of the interesting verses not found in most hymnals shows the author's confidence for the endurance of the Church, based on such Scriptural promises as Matthew 16:18 and Matthew 28:18–20:

Crowns and throne may perish, kingdoms rise and wane,
But the Church of Jesus constant will remain;
Gates of hell can never 'gainst that Church prevail;
We have Christ's own promise, and that cannot fail.

Another omitted verse indicates something of the author's personal convictions:

> What the saints established that I hold for true
> What the saints believed that believe I too.
> Long as earth endureth men that faith will hold–
> Kingdoms, nations empires, in destruction rolled.

A great hymn text must always be wedded to a fine tune in order to have universal appeal. Baring-Gould's hymn was first sung to the slow movement of Haydn's Symphony in D, No. 15, but that union has long since been forgotten. The present tune, "St. Gertrude," written by Sir Arthur S. Sullivan, was composed six years after the writing of the text. Sullivan, born in Bolwell Terrace, Lambeth, England, on May 13, 1842, was a noted English organist and composer. This tune was written in the home of a Mrs. Gertrude Clay-Ker-Seymer in Dorsetshire, England, while Sullivan was a guest there. He dedicated the music to his hostess and the tune is known as "St. Gertrude" to this day. Sullivan is also the composer of the well-known secular classic, "The Lost Chord," as well as a number of operettas such as "Pinafore," "The Mikado," etc., done in collaboration with W. S. Gilbert, the libbretist. These popular works have gained international fame.

239

The present version of this hymn was first published in America in John R. Sweney's *Gems of Praise,* by the Methodist Episcopal Book Room in Philadelphia, 1873.

Sabine Baring-Gould is also the author as well as composer of another very lovely children's hymn, "Now the Day is Over" (No. 63).

Despite his unceasing labors as a writer and preacher, Sabine Baring-Gould lived to the ripe old age of ninety years. He died in 1924, but his hurriedly written "Onward, Christian Soldiers" is still marching on from the lips of young and old alike.

Peace, Perfect Peace

PAX TECUM

EDWARD H. BICKERSTETH, 1825-1906

GEORGE T. CALDBECK, 1852-1918
Arr. by Don Peterman, 1925-

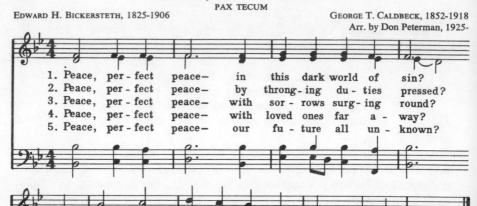

1. Peace, per - fect peace— in this dark world of sin?
2. Peace, per - fect peace— by throng - ing du - ties pressed?
3. Peace, per - fect peace— with sor - rows surg - ing round?
4. Peace, per - fect peace— with loved ones far a - way?
5. Peace, per - fect peace— our fu - ture all un - known?

The blood of Je - sus whis - pers peace with - in.
To do the will of Je - sus, this is rest.
On Je - sus' bos - om naught but calm is found.
In Je - sus' keep - ing we are safe, and they.
Je - sus we know, and He is on the throne.

Author-Edward H. Bickersteth, 1825–1906
Composer-George T. Caldbeck, 1852–1918
Tune Name-"Pax Tecum"
Meter-10 10.
Scripture Reference-Isaiah 26:3

> These things I have spoken unto you, that in me ye might have peace. In the world ye shall have tribulation: but be of good cheer; I have overcome the world. John 16:33

Is it really possible to experience a life of ultimate calm and tranquility in the midst of "this dark world of sin?" or when "pressed by thronging duties?" or when surrounded by "sorrows surging round?" or when "loved ones are far away?" or when "our future is all unknown?" These five questions form the basis for this very meaningful hymn. Yet for each of these imposing questions the author, Edward Bickersteth, provides a helpful and spiritual answer. Since most of us can relate easily to one or more of these difficult life situations, this hymn continues to provide comfort to God's people through the years as few other hymns are capable of doing.

Edward H. Bickersteth was born on January 26, 1825 in London, England, of a prominent clerical family. His father, also named Edward Bickersteth, was a clergyman in the Anglican Church. He had been at one time a missionary to West Africa and later the first secretary to the Church Missionary Society. He was also a poet and the editor of *Christian Psalmody*, the finest evangelical hymnal of its time. Four of his sons also became well-known clergymen in their day. Edward, Jr., was educated at Trinity College, Cambridge, where his poetic gifts obtained for him high honors. In 1848 he was ordained to the ministry of the Anglican Church. He rose in positions of leadership until he eventually was appointed Bishop of Exeter from 1885–1900. Throughout his ministry he was always known as a strong and influential evangelical leader within the Church. Edward, Jr., was also known for his voluminous writings, which included twelve books of sermons, hymns and poetry. Like his father he maintained a vital interest in hymnology and in 1870 was appointed editor of *The Hymnal Companion to the Book of Common Prayer*, a hymnal which soon superseded all other evangelical hymnals in Great Britain.

One Sunday in August, 1875, while vacationing in the town of Harrogate, England, Bickersteth listened to a sermon delivered by another minister, the Vicar of Harrogate, Canon Gibbon, on the text Isaiah 26:3. Bickersteth was deeply moved and impressed by his colleague's explanation that the original Hebrew version of this text reads, "Thou wilt keep him in *peace peace* whose mind is stayed on Thee. . . ." The point of the sermon was that in repetition the Hebrew conveyed the idea of absolute perfection. That afternoon Bickersteth paid a call upon an aged, dying relative, Arch Deacon Hill, of Liverpool. He found the man in a deeply depressed and disturbed emotional state of mind. Desiring to be of spiritual help, Bickersteth took his Bible and began reading and discussing the portion of the Scriptures still fresh in his mind from the morning's sermon. Then, taking a sheet of paper from a nearby desk, he quickly composed the comforting lines of his new poem and read them to the dying man. It is said that these helpful lines have remained exactly as they were originally written. From the Hebrew version of "peace peace" came the initial expression for each stanza, "Peace, Perfect Peace." The lines of this poem were no doubt a source of great comfort to the dying relative as he slipped into eternity, even as they have been to troubled hearts to the present time.

The tune, "Pax Tecum," Latin for "Peace be with You," was written especially for this text by a young missionary student, George T. Caldbeck, in 1877. The simply written music with its two note melodic range in the first line and its rising and falling melody in the second line is well-suited for these words. It should be noted that the first line of each verse is in the form of a question while the second line provides the answer. This can make for an interesting antiphonal possibility when using the hymn with a congregation. For example, a leader can have one group ask the question while another group responds with the second line's affirmative answer.

241

75 Praise Ye the Lord, the Almighty

LOBE DEN HERREN

JOACHIM NEANDER, 1650-1680
Trans. by Catherine Winkworth, 1827-1878

From *Stralsund Gesangbuch*, 1665
Arr. in Crüger's *Praxis Pietatas Melica*, 1668

1. Praise ye the Lord, the Al - might - y, the King of cre -
2. Praise ye the Lord, who o'er all things so won - drous - ly
3. Praise ye the Lord, who with mar - vel - ous wis - dom hath
4. Praise ye the Lord! O let all that is in me a -

a - - tion! O my soul, praise Him, for He is thy
reign - - eth, Shel - ters thee un - der His wings, yea, so
made thee, Decked thee with health, and with lov - ing hand
dore Him! All that hath life and breath, come now with

health and sal - va - tion! All ye who hear, Now to His
gen - tly sus - tain - eth! Hast thou not seen How thy de -
guid - ed and stayed thee; How oft in grief Hath not He
prais - es be - fore Him! Let the A - men Sound from His

tem - ple draw near; Join me in glad ad - o - ra - - tion!
sires e'er have been Grant - ed in what He or - dain - - eth?
brought thee re - lief, Spread - ing His wings for to shade thee!
peo - ple a - gain: Glad - ly for aye we a - dore Him.

Praise Ye the Lord, the Almighty

Author-Joachim Neander, 1650–1680
English Translation-Catherine Winkworth, 1827–1878
Music-From *Stralsund Gesangbuch,* 1665
Tune Name-"Lobe Den Herren"
Meter-14 14. 4 7 8
Scripture Reference-Psalm 103:1–6; Psalm 150

Let the people praise Thee, O God; let all the people praise Thee.   Psalm 67:3

Joachim Neander, called the greatest of all German-Calvinist Reformed hymn writers, was born in Bremen, Germany on May 31, 1650. He wrote approximately sixty hymns and composed many tunes. Nearly all of his hymns are triumphant expressions of praise. Neander, though only thirty years of age when he died, was a noted scholar in theology, literature and music, as well as pastor of the Reformed Church in Dusseldorf, Germany,. *The Julian Dictionary of Hymnology* calls this hymn "a magnificent hymn of praise, perhaps the finest production of its author and of the first rank in its class."

Catherine Winkworth was born in London, England, on September 13, 1827. She was a pioneer in the higher education of women. Miss Winkworth was regarded as one of the finest translators of the German language while expressing the text in English. Her translations helped to make German hymns popular in England during the nineteenth century. Prior to her work, very little of the German hymnody had been translated after the work of John Wesley in the eighteenth century. Miss Winkworth translated several books of German verse which became widely known. One of these books, *The Chorale Book for England,* 1863, contained the translation of this hymn. She also translated the well-known German chorale, "Now Thank We All Our God" (No. 62).

The tune, "Lobe Den Herren" ("Praise To the Lord"), first appeared in the *Stralsund Gesanbuch, 2nd edition,* in 1665. It is said that Joachim Neander personally chose this tune for his text, and his words have never been used with any other melody. The tune first appeared in England in the 1904 edition of *Hymns Ancient and Modern.*

243

76

Rescue the Perishing

Fanny J. Crosby, 1820-1915

William H. Doane, 1832-1915

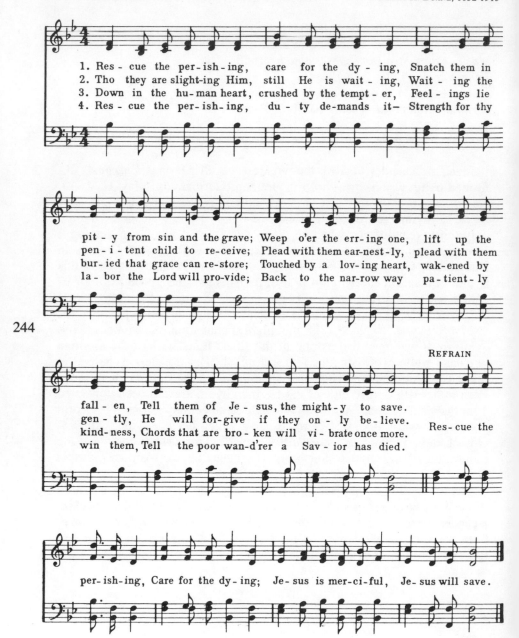

1. Res - cue the per - ish - ing, care for the dy - ing, Snatch them in
2. Tho they are slight-ing Him, still He is wait - ing, Wait - ing the
3. Down in the hu - man heart, crushed by the tempt - er, Feel - ings lie
4. Res - cue the per - ish - ing, du - ty de-mands it— Strength for thy

pit - y from sin and the grave; Weep o'er the err - ing one, lift up the
pen - i - tent child to re - ceive; Plead with them ear-nest - ly, plead with them
bur - ied that grace can re-store; Touched by a lov - ing heart, wak-ened by
la - bor the Lord will pro-vide; Back to the nar-row way pa - tient - ly

REFRAIN

fall - en, Tell them of Je - sus, the might - y to save.
gen - tly, He will for - give if they on - ly be - lieve. Res - cue the
kind - ness, Chords that are bro - ken will vi - brate once more.
win them, Tell the poor wan-d'rer a Sav - ior has died.

per - ish-ing, Care for the dy - ing; Je - sus is mer-ci-ful, Je - sus will save.

244

Rescue the Perishing

Author-Fanny J. Crosby, 1820–1915
Composer-William H. Doane, 1832–1915
Meter-11 10. 11 10 with Refrain
Scripture Reference-Luke 14:23

> The Spirit of the Lord God is upon me; because the Lord hath anointed me to preach good tidings unto the meek; He hath sent me to bind up the brokenhearted, to proclaim liberty to the captives, and the opening of the prison to them that are bound; to proclaim the acceptable year of the Lord, and the day of vengeance of our God; to comfort all that mourn.
> Isaiah 61:1,2

Fanny Crosby, the blind American poetess, has often been called the queen of gospel song writers. Although she did not begin writing gospel songs until she was forty-four years of age, from her radiant heart and prolific pen flowed more than 8,000 gospel hymns before her home-going at the age of ninety-five, on February 12, 1915.

The authoress has left the following account of the writing of this hymn:

> It was written in the year 1869. Many of my hymns were written after experiences in New York mission work. This one was thus written. I was addressing a large company of working men one hot summer evening, when the thought kept forcing itself on my mind that some mother's boy must be rescued that night or not at all. So I made a pressing plea that if there was a boy present who had wandered from his mother's home and teaching, he should come to me at the end of the service. A young man of eighteen came forward and said, "Did you mean me? I promised my mother to meet her in heaven, but as I am now living that will be impossible." We prayed for him and he finally arose with a new light in his eyes and exclaimed in triumph, "Now I can meet my mother in heaven, for I have found God."
>
> A few days before, Mr. Doane had sent me a theme for a new song, "Rescue the Perishing," based on Luke 14:23. While I sat in the mission that evening, the line came to me "Rescue the perishing, care for the dying." I could think of nothing else that night. When I arrived home, I went to work on the hymn at once, and before I retired it was ready for the melody. The song was first published in 1870 in Doane's *Songs of Devotion*.

This hymn, like so many of Fanny Crosby's soul-stirring songs, has been greatly used of God to bring conviction of repentance to many. Ira Sankey, who used this hymn continually in his evangelistic campaigns with D. L. Moody, tells this story in his book *My Life and the Story of the Gospel Hymn:*

245

On a stormy night a middle-aged man staggered into the Bowery Mission. He was intoxicated, his face unwashed and unshaved, with clothes soiled and torn. He sank into a seat, and, gazing around, seemed to wonder what kind of place he had come to. "Rescue the Perishing" and other familiar gospel hymns were sung and seemed to interest him and to recall some memories of his youth long forgotten. As the leader of the meeting told the simple story of the Gospel and how the Lord had come to seek and to save sinners, the man listened eagerly. The leader in his younger days had been a soldier and had seen hard and active service. In the course of his remarks he mentioned several incidents which had occurred in his experience during the war, and he gave the name of the company in which he had served. At the close of the meeting the man staggered up to the leader and in a broken voice said: "When were you in that company you spoke of?"

"Why all through the war," said the leader.

"Do you remember the battle of ————?"

"Perfectly."

"Do you remember the name of the captain of your company at that time?"

"Yes, his name was ————."

246 "You are right! I am that man. I was your captain. Look at me today, and see what a wreck I am. Can you save your old captain? I have lost everything I had in the world through drink and don't know where to turn."

He was converted that evening and was helped by his friend to a life of usefulness and respectability. The captain often retold the story of how God used his former soldier in a mission service to rescue his perishing soul.

Other hymns by Fanny J. Crosby include "All the Way My Savior Leads Me" (No. 5), "Blessed Assurance" (No. 11) and "My Savior First of All" (No. 60).

William H. Doane was born in Preston, Connecticut, on February 3, 1832. He was a prosperous factory president who was interested in music only as an avocation. Yet he was known as one of the leading gospel musicians of that era. He wrote and published more than 2,000 gospel songs and tunes, approximately forty hymnals as well as a number of cantatas. Doane was a close personal friend of Fanny Crosby and collaborated with her on many of her hymn texts. Throughout his life Mr. Doane was an active Baptist layman in the Mount Auburn Baptist Church of Cincinnati, Ohio, where he served as Sunday School superintendent and choir director for a number of years.

77

Ring the Bells of Heaven!

WILLIAM O. CUSHING, 1823-1902   GEORGE F. ROOT, 1820-1895

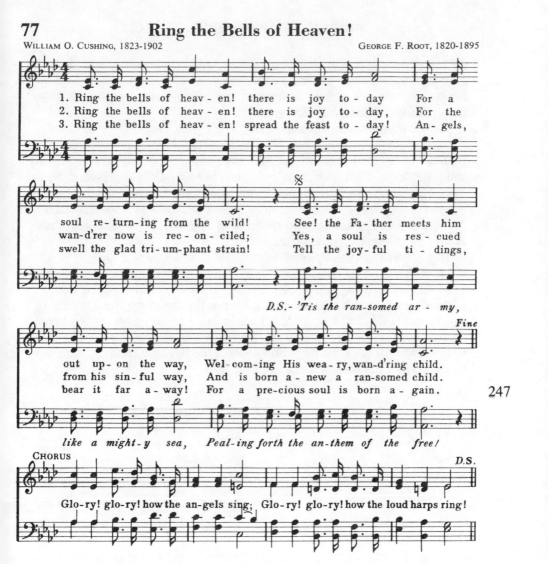

1. Ring the bells of heav-en! there is joy to-day For a soul re-turn-ing from the wild! See! the Fa-ther meets him out up-on the way, Wel-com-ing His wea-ry, wan-d'ring child.
2. Ring the bells of heav-en! there is joy to-day, For the wan-d'rer now is rec-on-ciled; Yes, a soul is res-cued from his sin-ful way, And is born a-new a ran-somed child.
3. Ring the bells of heav-en! spread the feast to-day! An-gels, swell the glad tri-um-phant strain! Tell the joy-ful ti-dings, bear it far a-way! For a pre-cious soul is born a-gain.

D.S.-'Tis the ran-somed ar-my, like a might-y sea, Peal-ing forth the an-them of the free!

CHORUS
Glo-ry! glo-ry! how the an-gels sing; Glo-ry! glo-ry! how the loud harps ring!

247

Author-William O. Cushing, 1823-1902
Composer-George F. Root, 1820-1895
Meter-11 9. 11 9 with Chorus

Likewise, I say unto you, there is joy in the presence of the angels of God over one sinner that repenteth.   Luke 15:10

William Orcott Cushing was born in Hingham, Massachusetts, in 1823. After many successful years in the pastorate, he lost his power of speech. In this time of despair, he prayed, "Lord, give me something to do for Thee.'' His prayer was answered, and it seemed as though God gave him the unusual gift for writing the catchy, Sunday School type of songs. He worked closely with such gospel musicians as Ira Sankey, Robert Lowry, George F. Root and others.

Mr. Cushing is also the author of "Hiding In Thee" (No. 29).

George Frederick Root was born in Sheffield, Massachusetts, on August 30, 1820. He studied music for a time under the noted Lowell Mason and later became a well-known music teacher himself. He moved to New York City and for a time taught at the New York Institute for the Blind, where Fanny Crosby was one of his pupils. Later George Root entered the music publishing business and established the successful Root and Cady Publishing Company in Chicago.

This particular melody was written by Dr. Root for a secular song. Later, when Cushing heard the melody, he wrote, "The melody ran in my head all day long, chiming and flowing in its sweet musical cadence. I wished greatly that I might secure this tune for use in the Sunday School and for other Christian purposes. Later when I heard of some sinner that had returned, it seemed like such a glad day with the very bells of heaven ringing in my soul. Then the words, "Ring the Bells Of Heaven," at once flowed down into this waiting melody.''

248

78

Rock of Ages

TOPLADY

Augustus M. Toplady, 1740-1778

Thomas Hastings, 1784-1872

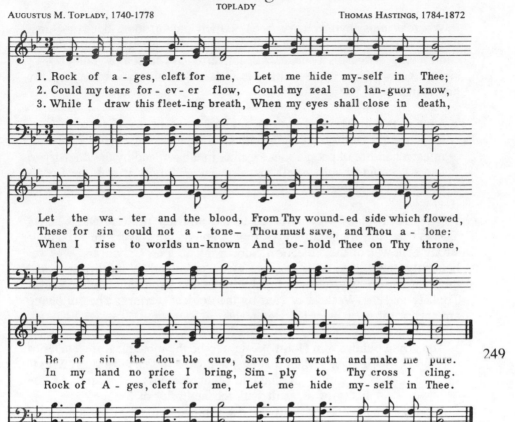

1. Rock of a - ges, cleft for me, Let me hide my-self in Thee;
2. Could my tears for - ev - er flow, Could my zeal no lan-guor know,
3. While I draw this fleet-ing breath, When my eyes shall close in death,

Let the wa - ter and the blood, From Thy wound-ed side which flowed,
These for sin could not a - tone— Thou must save, and Thou a - lone:
When I rise to worlds un-known And be-hold Thee on Thy throne,

Be of sin the dou - ble cure, Save from wrath and make me pure.
In my hand no price I bring, Sim - ply to Thy cross I cling.
Rock of A - ges, cleft for me, Let me hide my-self in Thee.

249

Author–Augustus M. Toplady, 1740–1778
Composer–Thomas Hastings, 1784–1872
Tune Name–"Toplady"
Meter–77.77.77

> Moreover, brethren, I would not that ye should be ignorant, how that all our fathers
> ... did all drink the same spiritual drink; for they drank of that spiritual Rock that
> followed them: And that Rock was Christ. I Corinthians 10:1, 4

This hymn has traditionally been ranked as one of the most popular
hymns ever written. It is certainly one of the best-known in the English
language. It has been described as a "hymn that meets the spiritual needs
of all sorts and conditions of men from the derelict snatched from the
gutter by the Salvation Army to Prime Minister Gladstone, at whose
funeral it echoed through the dim spaces of Westminster Abbey."

Whereas most hymns have been written out of some deep personal need or experience, this hymn evidently was born in a spirit of passionate controversy. Augustus Toplady was converted to Christ as a young boy of sixteen years of age while visiting in Ireland. Of his conversion Toplady has written,

> Strange that I, who had so long sat under the means of grace in England, should be brought right with God in an obscure part of Ireland, midst a handful of people met together in a barn, and by the ministry of one who could hardly spell his own name. Surely it was the Lord's doing and is marvellous.

For a time Toplady was attracted to the ministry of John and Charles Wesley and the Methodists. As time went on, however, he became a strong follower of the "election" doctrines of John Calvin and was vehemently opposed to the Arminian views promoted by the Wesleys and their supporters. By means of public debates, pamphlets and sermons, Toplady and the Wesleys carried on theological warfare. The following are several of their recorded statements:

250

Toplady–I believe him (John Wesley) to be the most rancorous hater of the gospel system that ever appeared in this Island. . . . Wesley is guilty of Satanic shamelessness . . . of uniting the sophistry of a Jesuit with the authority of a pope.

Wesley– I dare not speak of the deep things of God in the spirit of a prize fighter or a stage player, and I do not fight with chimney sweeps.

In 1776 Toplady published this hymn text in *The Gospel Magazine* as a climax to an article attempting to prove his argument that even as England could never pay her national debt, so man through his own efforts could never satisfy the eternal justice of a holy God. He entitled the hymn "A Living and Dying Prayer for the Holiest Believer in the World."

Some of the expressions in Toplady's hymn text are quite obviously satirical swipes at such Wesleyan teachings as the need for contrite and remorseful repentance and the Arminian concept of sanctification–the belief that it is possible for any believer to live without consciously sinning and thereby to find the promised "rest," the state of moral perfection as described in Hebrews 4:9. Note Toplady's rebuttal in the second stanza:

> Could my tears forever flow, could my zeal no languor know,
> these for sin could not atone–Thou must save, and Thou alone.

Dr. Louis J. Benson, a noted hymnologist, in *Studies of Familiar Hymns,* calls attention to the fact that Toplady actually plagiarized his text from a hymn Charles Wesley had written thirty years earlier in a collection, *Hymns on the Lord's Supper.* A paragraph of the preface from this collection reads as follows:

O Rock of Israel, Rock of Salvation, Rock struck for me, let those two streams of Blood and Water which once gushed out of Thy side, bring down Pardon and Holiness into my soul. And let me thirst after them now, as if I stood upon the Mountain whence sprang this Water; and near the Cleft of that Rock, the Wounds of my Lord, whence gushed this Sacred Blood.

Augustus Montague Toplady was born at Farnham, England, of November 4, 1740, the son of a Major Richard Toplady, who died in the service while his son was in infancy. Later young Toplady was graduated from Trinity College in Dublin, Ireland, and was ordained in 1762 to the ministry of the Anglican Church. His various pastorates included the French Calvinist Chapel at Leicester Fields, London, where he was known as a powerful and zealous evangelical preacher. Because of his frail constitution he died of overwork and tuberculosis at the early age of thirty-eight. Though known as a controversial preacher in his crusade against Arminian theology, Toplady was highly respected as a deeply spiritual, evangelical leader. His final statements just before his death are noteworthy:

251

My heart beats every day stronger and stronger for glory. Sickness is no affliction, pain no cause, death itself no dissolution. . . . My prayers are now all converted into praise.

The tune for Toplady's text was composed in 1830 by a well-known American church musician, Thomas Hastings. Hastings was the first musician of sacred music to dedicate his life to the task of elevating and improving the music of the churches in this country. He once wrote, "The homage that we owe Almighty God calls for the noblest and most reverential tribute that music can render."

Thomas Hastings was born on October 15, 1784, at Washington, Connecticut. Though his formal musical training was meager, and as an albino he was afflicted with eye problems throughout his life, yet he wrote no less than fifty volumes of church music, including 1000 hymn tunes and more than 600 original hymn texts as well as editing more than fifty music collections. In 1858 the University of the City of New York conferred the degree of Doctor of Music upon him in recognition of his accomplishments. Along with Lowell Mason, Thomas Hastings is generally credited with being the person most instrumental in shaping the development of church music in the United States.

Other hymns by Thomas Hastings include "From Every Stormy Wind That Blows" (No. 24) and "Majestic Sweetness Sits Enthroned" (No. 56).

It is encouraging to realize that, despite the original belligerent intent behind this text, God in His providence has chosen to preserve this hymn for the past two hundred years so that congregations of believers of both Calvinistic and Arminian theological persuasion can sing this hymn with spiritual profit and blessing.

252

Augustus Montague Toplady

79

Savior, Again to Thy Dear Name

ELLERS

JOHN ELLERTON, 1826-1893

EDWARD J. HOPKINS, 1818-1901
Arr. by Eldon Burkwall, 1928-

1. Sav - ior, a - gain to Thy dear name we raise With one ac -
2. Grant us Thy peace up - on our home-ward way: With Thee be -
3. Grant us Thy peace, Lord, thru the com - ing night, Turn Thou for
4. Grant us Thy peace thru - out our earth - ly life, Our balm in

cord our part-ing hymn of praise; Once more we bless Thee ere our
gan, with Thee shall end the day; Guard Thou the lips from sin, the
us its dark-ness in - to light; From harm and dan - ger keep Thy
sor - row and our stay in strife; Then, when Thy voice shall bid our

wor - ship cease, Then, low-ly kneel-ing, wait Thy word of peace.
hearts from shame, That in this house have called up-on Thy name.
chil - dren free, For dark and light are both a - like to Thee.
con - flict cease, Call us, O Lord, to Thine e - ter - nal peace.

253

Author-John Ellerton, 1826-1893
Composer-Edward J. Hopkins, 1818-1901
Tune Name-"Ellers"
Meter-10 10. 10 10.

The Lord will give strength unto His people; the Lord will bless His people with peace.   Psalm 29:11

Singing a parting hymn to close a service of worship has been one of the important practices of the Christian Church since the time of our

Lord's meeting with the disciples just before His crucifixion: "And when they had sung a hymn, they went out. . . ."

This hymn text, written in 1866 for a choral festival in Cheshire, England, by one of England's leading hymnists of that day, is generally considered one of the finest of all closing hymns. It was included in the important Anglican Church hymnal, *Hymns Ancient and Modern,* in 1868.

John Ellerton was born in London, England, of a strongly evangelical family. Following his graduation from Cambridge University, he became associated with the more broad or liberal faction of the Anglican Church with a vital concern for the social problems of his day. Ellerton along with William How (No. 71) were recognized as the leaders of the Anglican Church liberals. Yet it was said of Ellerton that he maintained warm and sympathetic relations with evangelicals as well, and that he could appreciate the best in everyone.

Ellerton spent his entire life ministering in poor and obscure parishes throughout England. Despite his humble pastorates he was known and respected as a minister. He was said to be a man of wide culture and noble character, and he was always greatly loved by his people. He was also highly regarded as a scholar and authority of hymnody. No hymnal was ever published at that time without his advice. Matthew Arnold, noted theologian of that era, called John Ellerton the greatest of the living hymn writers.

Ellerton personally composed approximately eighty-four hymns, including ten Latin translations. Many of these hymns are still in use today. It was Ellerton's practice never to copyright any of his hymns. He declared that if "his hymns were counted worthy to contribute to Christ's praise in the congregation, one ought to feel very thankful and humble."

Edward John Hopkins was born in London, on June 30, 1818. He was considered to be one of England's finest musicians of his time. He composed this tune for Ellerton's text in 1869. It was originally used as a unison setting with an accompaniment of variations for each stanza. It is interesting to observe the almost perfect melodic line, rising steadily until the exact center of the hymn, then falling quietly to the close.

80

Silent Night! Holy Night!

STILLE NACHT

JOSEPH MOHR, 1792-1848
Trans. by John F. Young, 1820-1885

FRANZ GRÜBER, 1787-1863

1. Si - lent night! ho - ly night! All is calm, all is bright
2. Si - lent night! ho - ly night! Shep-herds quake at the sight;
3. Si - lent night! ho - ly night! Son of God, love's pure light

Round yon vir - gin moth-er and Child, Ho - ly In-fant, so ten-der and mild —
Glo - ries stream from heav-en a - far, Heav'n-ly hosts sing al - le - lu - ia —
Ra - diant beams from Thy ho-ly face With the dawn of re - deem-ing grace —

Sleep in heav-en-ly peace, Sleep in heav-en-ly peace.
Christ the Sav-ior is born! Christ the Sav-ior is born!
Je - sus, Lord at Thy birth, Je - sus, Lord at Thy birth.

255

Author–Joseph Mohr, 1792–1848
English Translation–John F. Young, 1820–1885
Composer–Franz Grüber, 1787–1863
Tune Name–"Stille Nacht"
Meter–Irregular

For unto you is born this day in the city of David a Savior, which is Christ the
Lord.   Luke 2:11

Joseph Mohr was born in the lovely city of Salzburg, Austria, in 1792.
As a boy he was an active chorister in the Cathedral of Salzburg. In 1815
Mohr was ordained to the priesthood of the Roman Catholic Church.
Following his ordination, he served various parishes in the Salzburg area.
It was while serving as an assistant priest in 1818, at the newly erected
Church of St. Nicholas in Obernorf in the region of Tyrol, high in the
beautiful Alps, that Mohr wrote the text for this favorite of all Christmas
carols.

Father Mohr and Franz Grüber, the village schoolmaster and church organist, had often talked about the fact that the perfect Christmas hymn had never been written. With this goal in mind, and after he had received word that his own church organ would not function, Father Mohr decided that he must write his own Christmas hymn, immediately, in order to have music for the special Christmas Eve Mass and to avoid disappointing his faithful congregation. Upon completing the text, he took his words to Franz Grüber, who exclaimed when he saw them, "Friend Mohr, you have found it—the right song—God be praised!"

Soon Grüber completed his task of writing the right tune for the new text. His simple but beautiful music blended perfectly with the spirit of Father Mohr's words. The hymn was completed in time for the Christmas Eve Mass, and Father Mohr and Franz Grüber sang their hymn to the accompaniment of Grüber's guitar. The hymn made a deep impact upon the parishioners, even as it has on succeeding generations. The passing of time seems only to add to its appeal.

Neither Mohr nor Grüber intended that their hymn would be used outside of their little mountain village area. However, it is reported that within a few days after the Christmas Eve Mass, the organ repairman, Karl Maurachen of Zillerthal, a well-known organ builder of that area, came to the church and obtained a copy of the new hymn. Through his influence the carol spread throughout the entire Tyrol region, where it became popular as a Tyrolean Folk Song. Soon various performing groups such as the well-known Strasser Children's Quartet began using the hymn in concert throughout Austria and Germany. In 1838 it first appeared in a German hymnal, where it was titled a "hymn of unknown origin." It was first heard in the United States in 1839 when a family of Tyrolean Singers, the Rainers, used the music during their concert tour. Soon it was translated into English as well as into other languages. At least eight different English translations are known today. The carol is presently sung in all of the major languages of the world and is a universal favorite wherever songs of the Christmas message are sung.

The translation by John F. Young is the version most widely used in this country. Young was born at Pittston, Kennebec County, Maryland, on October 30, 1820. He was ordained to the Episcopal Church and served a number of years as a bishop in the State of Florida. Throughout his church ministry he had a keen interest in sacred music. This translation of Mohr's German text first appeared in 1863 in Clark Hollister's *Service and Tune Book*. In addition to this translation of this text, Young is also known as the editor of two published hymnals, *Hymns and Music for the Young*, 1861, and *Great Hymns of the Church*, published posthumously by John Henry Hopkins, 1887.

256

81 Sing Praise to God Who Reigns Above

MIT FREUDEN ZART

JOHANN J. SCHÜTZ, 1640-1690
Trans. by Frances E. Cox, 1812-1897

From the Bohemian Brethren's
Kirchengesänge, 1566

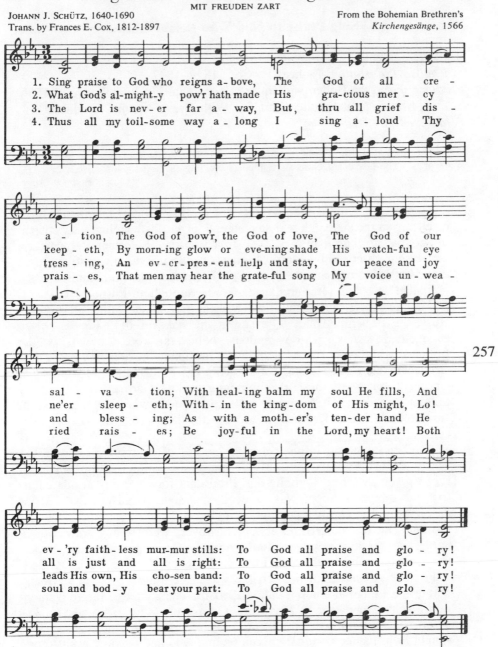

1. Sing praise to God who reigns a-bove, The God of all cre-
2. What God's al-might-y pow'r hath made His gra-cious mer-cy
3. The Lord is nev-er far a-way, But, thru all grief dis-
4. Thus all my toil-some way a-long I sing a-loud Thy

a-tion, The God of pow'r, the God of love, The God of our
keep-eth, By morn-ing glow or eve-ning shade His watch-ful eye
tress-ing, An ev-er-pres-ent help and stay, Our peace and joy
prais-es, That men may hear the grate-ful song My voice un-wea-

sal-va-tion; With heal-ing balm my soul He fills, And
ne'er sleep-eth; With-in the king-dom of His might, Lo!
and bless-ing; As with a moth-er's ten-der hand He
ried rais-es; Be joy-ful in the Lord, my heart! Both

ev-'ry faith-less mur-mur stills: To God all praise and glo-ry!
all is just and all is right: To God all praise and glo-ry!
leads His own, His cho-sen band: To God all praise and glo-ry!
soul and bod-y bear your part: To God all praise and glo-ry!

257

Sing Praise to God Who Reigns Above

Author–Johann J. Schütz, 1640–1690
English Translation–Frances E. Cox, 1812–1897
Music–From the Bohemian Brethren's Hymnal *Kirchengesänge* of 1566
Tune Name–"Mit Freuden Zart" ("With Great Personal Gladness")
Meter–87.87.887

> The Lord reigneth; let the earth rejoice; let the multitude of isles be glad there-
> of. . . . The heavens declare his righteousness, and all the people see His glory.
>
> Psalm 97:1,6

This stately hymn is the product of several significant historical events occurring in the sixteenth and seventeenth centuries which greatly shaped the course of church history. The first was the Protestant Reformation Movement climaxed by Martin Luther's posting of the ninety-five theses at the Cathedral of Wittenberg in 1517. From this time Lutheranism was a dominant religious force in Germany and throughout Europe.

Another factor during this time was the role of the followers of John Huss, the Bohemian martyr burned at the stake in 1415 for his strong evangelical views. These zealous believers were known as the Bohemian-Moravian Brethren and were located in the area of what is now Czechoslovakia and Hungary. Following the Reformation Movement in Germany, many of these Brethren migrated to Germany in search of religious freedom. These people were known everywhere for their vibrant singing and Christian witness as well as for their strong missionary concern.

Another important influence in the course of church history was the Thirty-Years' War (1618–1648). Germany, the battleground of this conflict between warring Catholic and Protestant forces from various countries throughout Europe, was reduced to a state of misery that baffles description. The German population dwindled from sixteen million to six million. Out of this terrible epoch, however, were wrung some of the noblest expressions of praise in all hymnody. As is often the case, it took the great tragedies of the time to again focus men's attention upon God.

From the tragedies of this terrible war arose a movement in Germany within the Lutheran Church called Pietism. The leader of the movement was a Lutheran pastor in Frankfort, Germany, Philip J. Spener (1635–1705). Mainly through small cell prayer and Bible study groups, he sought to influence nominal church people who had become accustomed to the dead orthodoxy that had overtaken the church. Spener taught them the meaning of inner personal faith in Christ and the demands that such faith make upon the believer for holy Christian living.

From these important influences–the German Reformation; the

dynamic beliefs and practices of the Bohemian-Moravian Brethren; the terrible tragedies of the Thirty-Years' War, causing many to realize as never before a personal dependence upon a sovereign God and not mere reliance upon a church; the rise of the Pietist Movement with its emphasis upon individual faith and holy living–there developed a great wealth of excellent German hymns. These influences produced hymns that had greater subjectivity and were more passionate in character than were the earlier Lutheran hymns.

One of the important characteristics of the seventeenth century Pietistic Movement was the involvement of laymen in the church. One finds that many of the hymn writers and important voices were the lay people from all walks of life. Such was the case with Johann J. Schütz, an authority in civil and canon law, living in Frankfort, Germany. He was closely allied with Philip Spener and the practices of the pietists in establishing small cell groups. These groups were known as collegia pietatis, which gave rise to the name Pietists. Schütz wrote a number of religious publications as well as five hymns. Of the hymns only this one, however, is still in use.

The Pietist Movement gave birth to a great revival in hymnody in Germany, both in Lutheran and Reformed circles. It took considerable time for the English-speaking world, however, to discover this great wealth of hymnody. Finally, in the eighteenth and nineteenth centuries, English translations were made of many of these fine hymns. Among the important English translators of the nineteenth century was Frances E. Cox, a member of the Anglican Church and a native of Oxford, England. She was one of the first to rediscover and translate German hymns. Her collection of translations was first published in 1841.

The music for this fine hymn was taken from a Bohemian Brethren hymnal, *Kirchengesänge,* published in Eibenschutz, Moravia, in 1566.

259

So Send I You

E. Margaret Clarkson, 1915-

John W. Peterson, 1921-

260

1. So send I you to la-bor un-re-ward-ed, To serve un-
2. So send I you to bind the bruised and bro-ken, O'er wan-d'ring
3. So send I you to lone-li-ness and long-ing, With heart a-
4. So send I you to leave your life's am-bi-tion, To die to
5. So send I you to hearts made hard by ha-tred, To eyes made

paid, un-loved, un-sought, un-known, To bear re-buke, to suf-fer
souls to work, to weep, to wake, To bear the bur-dens of a
hung-'ring for the loved and known, For-sak-ing home and kin-dred,
dear de-sire, self-will re-sign, To la-bor long and love where
blind be-cause they will not see, To spend— tho it be blood— to

scorn and scoff-ing— So send I you to toil for Me a-lone.
world a-wea-ry— So send I you to suf-fer for My sake.
friend and dear one— So send I you to know My love a-lone.
men re-vile you— So send I you to lose your life in Mine.
spend and spare not— So send I you to taste of Cal-va-

ry. "As the Fa-ther hath sent Me, So send I you."

So Send I You

Author–E. Margaret Clarkson, 1915–
Composer–John W. Peterson, 1921–
Meter–11 10. 11 10 with closing refrain
Scripture Reference–John 20:21

> I heard the voice of the Lord, saying, "Whom shall I send, and who will go for us?"
> Then said I, "Here am I; send me." Isaiah 6:8

This hymn has been labeled by many evangelical leaders as the finest missionary hymn of the twentieth century. It was first published in 1954 after having been written sixteen years earlier by a Canadian school teacher, Margaret Clarkson.

Margaret Clarkson was born in Saskatchewan, Canada, in the year 1915 and has spent most of her life in the area of Toronto, Ontario, Canada. She is a member of the Knox Presbyterian Church of that city. Miss Clarkson has been involved in the Toronto Public School System in various capacities for a number of years. For nearly fifty years she has been known for her many articles, books and poems appearing in Christian and educational periodicals, and she has written for various publishers. Some of her published books are *Let's Listen to Music, The Creative Classroom, Susie's Babies,* and *The Wondrous Cross.* Miss Clarkson has written the following statement regarding the writing of this well-known hymn:

261

> In 1935 teaching jobs were so scarce that I had to take my first job as a teacher in a lumber camp some 1400 miles from home, out in the Rainy River District of northwestern Ontario. From there I moved to the gold mining camp of Kirkland Lake, 450 miles north of Toronto. In all, I spent seven years in the north. I experienced loneliness of every kind–mental, cultural, but particularly spiritual, for in all of those seven years I never found real Christian fellowship–churches were modern and born-again Christians almost non-existent.
>
> I was studying the Word one night and meditating on the loneliness of my situation and came in my reading to John 20, and the words "so send I you." Because of a physical disability I knew that I could never go to the mission field, but God seemed to tell me that night that this was my mission field, and this was where He had sent me. I was then twenty-three, in my third year of teaching. I had written and published verse all of my life, so it was natural for me to put my thoughts into verse.

Interestingly enough, Miss Clarkson became dissatisfied with her own text in later years. She has given this account regarding the change in her thinking:

A few years ago I began to realize that this poem was really very one-sided; it told only the sorrows and privations of the missionary call and none of its triumphs. I wrote another song in the same rhythm so that verses could be used interchangeably, setting forth the glory and the hope of the missionary calling.

Several verses from this newer setting by Miss Clarkson, published in 1963, read as follows:

1. So send I you–by grace made strong to triumph
   O'er hosts of hell, o'er darkness, death and sin,
   My name to bear, and in that name to conquer–
   So send I you, My victory to win.

2. So send I you–to bear my cross with patience,
   And then one day with joy to lay it down,
   To hear my voice, "Well done, My faithful servant-
   Come, share my throne, my kingdom and my crown."

262

The music for "So Send I You" was composed especially for Margaret Clarkson's hymn by John W. Peterson, often called the dean of contemporary gospel song writers. The impact and contributions to church music of John Peterson's fruitful ministry since World War II are generally well-known to most evangelical Christians. He has composed more than 1200 gospel songs, hymns and choruses as well as supplying church choirs with more than twenty cantatas and musicals, which have thrilled and inspired Christian audiences with various themes from the gospel message.

John W. Peterson was born in Lindsborg, Kansas, on November 1, 1921, and spent his early days in Salina, Kansas. In 1939 he began a radio evangelistic work with his two brothers and at that time began writing his first gospel songs. In 1942 Mr. Peterson entered military service and served as a pilot in the Chinese-Burma theater. Commenting about this period of his life, he says, "I had many precious spiritual experiences during those days, and many of my songs now in print had their beginnings somewhere in India or Burma or high above the Himalayan Mountains."

After his military service Mr. Peterson matriculated and was graduated from the Moody Bible Institute, later continuing his musical training at the American Conservatory of Music, completing a major in music theory in 1950. John Peterson has since been awarded an honorary Doctor's degree from Western Conservative Baptist Seminary and also from Brown University in recognition of his musical contributions to the gospel ministry. The Peterson family presently resides in a small community near Phoenix, Arizona, where John continues to write new sacred compositions. He also travels around the country conducting choral workshops.

In his book, *The Miracle Goes On,* Mr. Peterson often mentions his conviction about the power of a gospel song to change a person's life. He cites the following example:

"So Send I You," a song I wrote in collaboration with Margaret Clarkson, was used by God in the life of an actress who had come to know Christ and who faced an agonizing decision: Should she maintain her professional contacts or give up her career and dedicate her life completely to the Lord for service, wherever He might lead? In the midst of her dilemma she sat listening to a recording of this song, and its challenge came through with stunning impact. The actress fell to her knees and made a total commitment of her life to God, and in due time He resolved the question of her vocation.

263

John W. Peterson

83 Softly and Tenderly

WILL L. THOMPSON, 1847-1909

WILL L. THOMPSON, 1847-1909

264

1. Soft-ly and ten-der-ly Je-sus is call-ing, Call-ing for
2. Why should we tar-ry when Je-sus is plead-ing, Plead-ing for
3. Time is now fleet-ing, the mo-ments are pass-ing, Pass-ing from
4. O for the won-der-ful love He has prom-ised, Prom-ised for

you and for me; See, on the por-tals He's wait-ing and watch-ing,
you and for me? Why should we lin-ger and heed not His mer-cies,
you and from me; Shad-ows are gath-er-ing, death-beds are com-ing,
you and for me; Tho we have sinned He has mer-cy and par-don,

CHORUS

Watch-ing for you and for me.
Mer-cies for you and for me? Come home, come home,
Com-ing for you and for me. Come home, come home,
Par-don for you and for me.

Ye who are wea-ry, come home; Ear-nest-ly,

ten-der-ly, Je-sus is call-ing— Call-ing, "O sin-ner, come home!"

Softly and Tenderly

Author-Will L. Thompson, 1847-1909
Composer-Will L. Thompson, 1847-1909
Meter-11 7. 11 7 with Chorus

For what shall it profit a man, if he shall gain the whole world, and lose his own soul:
Or what shall a man give in exchange for his soul?   Mark 8:36,37

Will L. Thompson was born at East Liverpool, Ohio, on November 7, 1847. His father, Josiah Thompson, was a member of the Ohio State Legislature for two terms. Young Thompson attended the Boston Music School from 1870-73. Later he did additional musical study in Germany. His chief ambition always was to write music for the people; in this he became eminent. After a very successful career of writing secular music, Thompson turned his talents to writing gospel hymns. Later he started his own publishing and music store business in East Liverpool and Chicago, Illinois. His business earned him a sizable income in his lifetime, yet he was always known as a kind, quiet and unassuming Christian gentleman, greatly loved and admired by his associates. Thompson was also known for his travels by horse and buggy from one small community to another throughout Ohio singing his songs to people everywhere.

265

Will Thompson was a personal friend of evangelist D. L. Moody. This particular hymn was one of Moody's favorites. It is said that on his deathbed while being visited by Mr. Thompson, Moody feebly whispered, "Will, I would rather have written 'Softly and Tenderly' than anything I have been able to do in my whole life." This hymn was widely used as an invitation hymn in the great evangelistic meetings conducted by Moody and Sankey throughout Great Britain and this country.

*   *   *

"We can learn nothing of the gospel except by feeling its truths. There are some sciences that may be learned by the head, but the science of Christ crucified can only be learned by the heart."

Charles Haddon Spurgeon

84   Spirit of God, Descend upon My Heart

MORECAMBE

GEORGE CROLY, 1780-1860   FREDERICK C. ATKINSON, 1841-1897

1. Spir - it of God, de - scend up - on my heart: Wean it from earth, through all its puls - es move. Stoop to my weak - ness, might - y as Thou art, And make me love Thee as I ought to love.

2. Hast Thou not bid us love Thee, God and King? All, all Thine own— soul, heart and strength and mind. I see Thy cross— there teach my heart to cling; O let me seek Thee, and O let me find.

3. Teach me to feel that Thou art al - ways nigh; Teach me the strug - gles of the soul to bear— To check the ris - ing doubt, the reb - el sigh; Teach me the pa - tience of un - an - swered prayer.

4. Teach me to love Thee as Thine an - gels love, One ho - ly pas - sion fill - ing all my frame; The bap - tism of the heav'n - de - scend - ed Dove— My heart an al - tar and Thy love the flame.

266

Author-George Croly, 1780-1860
Composer-Frederick C. Atkinson, 1841-1897
Tune Name-"Morecambe"
Meter-10 10. 10 10

> Let no corrupt communication proceed out of your mouth, but that which is good to the use of edifying, that it may minister grace unto the hearers. And grieve not the Holy Spirit of God, whereby ye are sealed unto the day of redemption. Ephesians 4:29,30

Following the celebration of Easter, there are two other important Church calendar days which many evangelical Christians often neglect to recognize. The first is Ascension Day-forty days following Easter (see No. 55). The second important day is Pentecost Sunday-ten days after Christ's ascension. It is thrilling at Christmas to recall the events of our

Savior's birth, or at Easter his triumph over death. Yet if He had never ascended to make intercession for us or had never sent the Holy Spirit to dwell within and to guide us, our relationship with God would be most incomplete.

One of the finest of all hymns for Pentecost is this hymn, "Spirit of God, Descend Upon My Heart." It was written by the Rev. George Croly, a minister in the Anglican Church. Croly was born in Dublin, Ireland, and was graduated from Trinity College. He came to London, England, around 1810, where he served a small parish church. He was also active during this time as a literary writer of poems and novels as well as biographical, historical and scriptural material. Later, in 1835, he was asked by the church's leadership to re-open a church in the worst slum area of London, St. Stephen's Church, which had been closed for more than a century. His forceful, magnetic preaching soon attracted large crowds. Croly was characterized by his associates as a "fundamentalist in theology, a fierce conservative in politics, and intensely opposed to all forms of liberalism."

In 1854, when he was seventy-four years of age, he desired a new hymnal for his congregation and eventually prepared and published his own *Psalms and Hymns for Public Worship*. This text is from that collection and was originally entitled "Holiness Desired." It is Croly's only surviving hymn from that collection.

267

The four stanzas, though strongly personal, have a moving, universal appeal for each of us today:

Stanza One–A desire to change the focus of one's life from things temporal to things spiritual–"to love Thee as I ought to love."

Stanza Two–The total dedication of one's self to God–"soul, heart, strength and mind."

Stanza Three–A prayerful concern for knowing fully the Spirit's abiding presence as an antidote for the soul's impatience when confronted with struggle, doubt, rebellion, or a delayed answer to prayer–"teach me the patience of unanswered prayer."

Stanza Four–The last phrase of this verse is considered by many students of hymnody to be one of the most beautiful metaphors found in any hymn–"my heart an altar, and Thy love the flame."

The tune, "Morecambe," was written by Frederick C. Atkinson, an English church organist, in 1870. It was originally intended for Henry Lyte's hymn, "Abide with Me" (No. 2). It is thought that the tune was named after an English town in the Midland district where music festivals were held periodically.

Sun of My Soul

JOHN KEBLE, 1792-1866

From *Katholisches Gesangbuch*,
Vienna, c. 1774

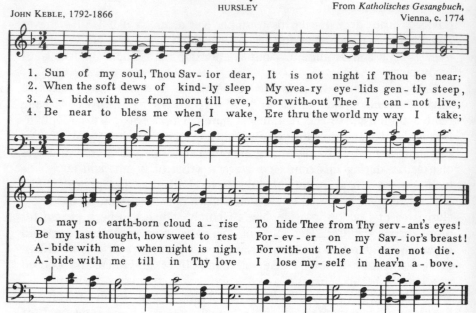

1. Sun of my soul, Thou Sav-ior dear, It is not night if Thou be near;
2. When the soft dews of kind-ly sleep My wea-ry eye-lids gen-tly steep,
3. A-bide with me from morn till eve, For with-out Thee I can-not live;
4. Be near to bless me when I wake, Ere thru the world my way I take;

O may no earth-born cloud a-rise To hide Thee from Thy serv-ant's eyes!
Be my last thought, how sweet to rest For-ev-er on my Sav-ior's breast!
A-bide with me when night is nigh, For with-out Thee I dare not die.
A-bide with me till in Thy love I lose my-self in heav'n a-bove.

268
Author-John Keble, 1792-1866
Music-From the *Katholisches Gesangbuch*, Vienna, c. 1774
Tune Name-"Hursley"
Meter-LM (88.88)
Scripture Reference-Luke 24:29

> For the Lord God is a sun and shield: The Lord will give grace and glory: no good thing
> will He withhold from them that walk uprightly.   Psalm 84:11

John Keble, the son of an Anglican country preacher, was born at Fairford, Gloucestershire, England, on April 25, 1792. Following his training at Oxford University, he served as a professor of poetry at that school for ten years. From 1835 until his death in 1866 he served the humble parish church in the village of Hursley, England, a population of 1,500 people.

In 1827 Keble published a volume of poems entitled *The Christian Year,* with all of the poems following the church calendar year. "Sun of My Soul" was one of the poems from that collection. It was never intended, however, to be used as a hymn. It was Keble's intention that his book of poetry be a devotional companion to the Anglican Book of Common Prayer. Being an extremely modest man, Keble had his book of poems published anonymously. The book proved extremely successful, going through 109 editions before Keble's death in 1866. He used the proceeds from the book to maintain the ministry of his small church at Hursley.

In 1833 Keble preached at Oxford his famous sermon on "National Apostasy" which is credited with originating the nineteenth century Oxford Movement. The leaders of this movement sought to bring about a spiritual awakening in the Church of England without resorting to the more aggressive practices of the evangelical leaders of this time, the Wesleys and Whitefield followers. The Oxford Leaders were of the conviction that they had to increase the ritualistic and liturgical practices of the church in order to deepen this spiritual awakening. Several of these prominent leaders such as John Henry Newman "Lead, Kindly Light" (No. 53), "Faith of Our Fathers" (No. 22), and Edward Caswall "May Jesus Christ be Praised" (No. 57), eventually left the Anglican Church and became leaders in the Roman Catholic Church. John Keble, however, did remain a humble yet high church Anglican minister until his death. In 1869 Keble College was founded at Oxford University as a tribute to him. Throughout his ministry he was recognized as an outstanding preacher and a thorough Bible scholar. He wrote a total of 765 hymns as well as a companion book of tunes, which he composed or collected to be used with his texts.

The tune, "Hursley," is adapted from a melody which first appeared in the hymnal, *Katholisches Gesangbuch,* Vienna, Austria, about 1774. This tune was Keble's personal choice for his text when it appeared in the *Metrical Psalter* in 1855. The tune was named in honor of the little church which Keble had served faithfully for many years.

269

John Keble

86   Stand Up for Jesus

GEORGE DUFFIELD, 1818-1888   GEIBEL   ADAM GEIBEL, 1885-1933
Arr. by Harold DeCou, 1932-

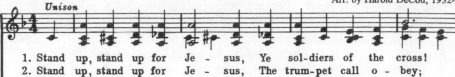

1. Stand up, stand up for Je - sus, Ye sol-diers of the cross!
2. Stand up, stand up for Je - sus, The trum-pet call o - bey;
3. Stand up, stand up for Je - sus, The strife will not be long;

Lift high His roy - al ban - ner— It must not suf - fer loss.
Forth to the might - y con - flict In this His glo - rious day:
This day the noise of bat - tle— The next, the vic - tor's song.

270

From vic - t'ry un - to vic - t'ry His ar - my shall He lead,
Ye that are men now serve Him A - gainst un-num-bered foes;
To Him that o - ver - com - eth A crown of life shall be:

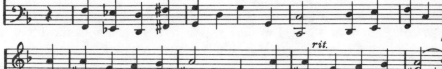

rit.

Till ev - 'ry foe is van - quished And Christ is Lord in - deed.
Let cour - age rise with dan - ger And strength to strength op - pose.
He with the King of glo - ry Shall reign e - ter - nal - ly.

CHORUS
Parts

Stand up   for Je - sus, Ye sol-diers of the cross! Lift
    stand up

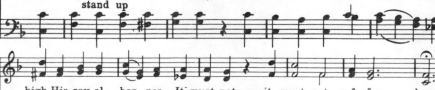

high His roy-al ban - ner— It must not, it must not suf - fer loss!

Stand Up for Jesus

Author–George Duffield, 1818–1888
Composers–George J. Webb, 1803–1887
             Adam Geibel, 1885–1933
Tune Names–"Webb" and "Geibel"
Meter–76.76 Doubled
Scripture Reference–Ephesians 6:14

... be strong in the Lord, and in the power of His might.   Ephesians 6:10

In the year 1858 a great city-wide revival swept across the city of Philadelphia. It was called The Work of God in Philadelphia. Of the participating ministers none was more powerful than the twenty-nine year old Episcopalian, Dudley Tyng. He was known as a bold, fearless and uncompromising preacher with great influence on the other spiritual leaders around him. His father, the Rev. Stephen H. Tyng, was for many years the pastor of the large Episcopalian Church of the Epiphany in Philadelphia. After serving a short time as his father's assistant, Dudley succeeded his father in this pulpit. However, some of the more fashionable members soon became upset with their young preacher because of his straight-forward doctrinal preaching and his strong stand against slavery. He resigned this pulpit and with a group of faithful followers organized The Church of the Covenant.

271

In addition to his duties as pastor of the new and growing congregation, Tyng began holding noon-day services at the downtown YMCA. Great crowds were attracted to hear this dynamic young preacher. On Tuesday, March 30, 1858, over 5,000 men gathered for a noon mass meeting to hear young Tyng preach from Exodus 10:11–"Go now ye that are men and serve the Lord." Over 1,000 of these men responded by committing their hearts and lives to Christ and His service; the sermon was often termed one of the most successful of the times.

During the sermon the young preacher remarked, "I must tell my Master's errand, and I would rather that this right arm were amputated at the trunk than that I should come short of my duty to you in delivering God's message." The next week, while visiting in the country and watching the operation of a corn thrasher in a barn, he accidentally caught his loose sleeve between the cogs; the arm was lacerated severely, the main artery was severed and the median nerve was injured. Four days later infection developed. As a result of shock and a great loss of blood, Dudley Tyng died on April 19, 1858. At his death bed, when asked by a group of sorrowful friends and ministers for a final statement, he whispered, "Let us all stand up for Jesus."

The next Sunday Tyng's close friend and fellow worker, the Rev.

George Duffield, pastor of the Temple Presbyterian Church in Philadelphia, preached his morning sermon as a tribute to his departed friend, choosing as his text Ephesians 6:14: "Stand, therefore, having your loins girt about with truth, and having on the breastplate of righteousness." He closed his sermon by reading a poem of six stanzas that he had written, inspired, as he told his people, by the dying words of his esteemed friend. Rev. Duffield's Sunday School superintendent was so impressed by the verses that he had them printed for distribution throughout the Sunday School. The editor of a Baptist periodical happened to receive one of these pamphlets and promptly gave it a wider circulation. From there it eventually found its way into the hymnals and hearts of God's people across the world.

George Duffield was born in Carlisle, Pennsylvania, on September 12, 1818. He studied at Yale University and Union Theological Seminary. He received a D.D. Degree from Knox College in recognition of his many accomplishments. For seven years he served as a member of the Board of Regents of the University of Michigan.

The most familiar tune, "Webb," was borrowed by an editor of a hymnal from a secular song written by George J. Webb, a song entitled "Tis Dawn, the Lark is Singing," which had been used for a musical show on board a ship crossing the Atlantic. Webb was born in Salisbury, England, on June 24, 1803, and came to the United States in 1830. He settled in Boston and became active in the musical affairs of that city, serving as organist of the Old South Church for forty years.

The stirring but less familiar "Geibel" tune was composed by Adam Geibel especially for Duffield's text in 1901. Adam Geibel was born in Germany, on September 15, 1885. Upon settling in this country, he became an organist and music teacher. He founded the Adam Geibel Music Company, which later became the Hall-Mack Company and eventually merged with the Rodeheaver Hall-Mack Company. Geibel was totally blind, the result of an eye infection at the age of eight. Yet despite this affliction, he was a skillful organist, conductor and a prolific composer, both of sacred and secular songs. His most popular secular songs were "Kentucky Babe" and "Sleep, Sleep, Sleep." He was especially known for his ability to write and arrange for male voices.

Truly God moves in mysterious ways His wonders to perform. A dynamic young Episcopalian preacher, a corn-threshing machine, a tragic fatal accident, a Presbyterian minister's hymn text tribute, two tunes–one secular and another by a blind composer–and the revival of 1858, the Work of God in Philadelphia, still have their influence on us today each time we open our hymnals to this hymn.

272

Take My Life and Let It Be

HENDON

FRANCES R. HAVERGAL, 1836-1879   H. A. CÉSAR MALAN, 1787-1864

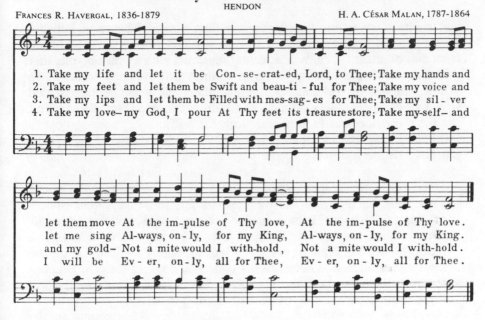

1. Take my life and let it be Con-se-crat-ed, Lord, to Thee; Take my hands and
2. Take my feet and let them be Swift and beau-ti-ful for Thee; Take my voice and
3. Take my lips and let them be Filled with mes-sag-es for Thee; Take my sil-ver
4. Take my love— my God, I pour At Thy feet its treasure store; Take my-self— and

let them move At the im-pulse of Thy love, At the im-pulse of Thy love.
let me sing Al-ways, on-ly, for my King, Al-ways, on-ly, for my King.
and my gold— Not a mite would I with-hold, Not a mite would I with-hold.
I will be Ev-er, on-ly, all for Thee, Ev-er, on-ly, all for Thee.

Author-Frances R. Havergal, 1836–1879
Composer-H. A. Cesar Malan, 1787–1864
Tune Name-"Hendon"
Meter-77.77

Whether therefore ye eat, or drink, or whatsoever ye do, do all to the glory of God.
1 Corinthians 10:31

Frances Ridley Havergal, born on December 14, 1836, at Astley, Worcestershire, England, is often referred to as "the consecration poet." It has been said that the beauty of a consecrated life has never been more perfectly revealed than in her daily living. Wherever she saw spiritual and physical needs, Frances Havergal was there with genuine concern.

At the age of four she began reading and memorizing the Bible. At the age of seven she was already writing her thoughts in verse. She was greatly encouraged by her father, William Havergal, an influential Anglican clergyman, who for many years was involved in improving and composing English hymnody. Throughout her brief life Miss Havergal was frail and delicate in health, yet she was an avid student, writer and composer. She learned several modern languages as well as Greek and Hebrew.

In her childhood years Frances lived in morbid fear that she would not be counted among God's elect. However, during early adolescence she had a vital conversion experience and later wrote, "There and then I committed my soul to the Savior–and earth and heaven seemed bright from that moment." She was a natural musician with a voice so pleasing that she was sought after as a concert soloist. She was also known as a brilliant pianist of the classics. Despite these musical talents, coupled with a vibrant personality offering possibilities for much worldly acclaim, her life's mission was to sing and work for Jesus.

"Take My Life and Let It Be" was written by Miss Havergal in 1874. She has left the following account:

> I went for a little visit of five days. There were ten persons in the house; some were unconverted and long prayed for, some converted but not rejoicing Christians. He gave me the prayer, "Lord, give me all in this house." And He just did. Before I left the house, everyone had got a blessing. The last night of my visit I was too happy to sleep and passed most of the night in renewal of my consecration, and these little couplets formed themselves and chimed in my heart one after another till they finished with "ever only, ALL FOR THEE!"

Her prayer, "Take my silver and my gold; not a mite would I withhold," 274 was not lightly stated. In August, 1878, Miss Havergal wrote to a friend,

> The Lord has shown me another little step, and, of course, I have taken it with extreme delight. "Take my silver and my gold" now means shipping off all my ornaments to the church Missionary House, including a jewel cabinet that is really fit for a countess, where all will be accepted and disposed of for me.... Nearly fifty articles are being packed up. I don't think I ever packed a box with such pleasure.

While Frances Havergal was writing her many fine hymns in England, Fanny Crosby, America's blind poetess, was also enriching lives with her numerous favorites. Although these two women never met, each was an ardent admirer of the other.

At the age of forty-two, when told by her physician that her physical condition was serious and that she did not have long to live, Miss Havergal replied, "If I am really going, it is too good to be true." At the bottom of her bed she had her favorite text placed where she could readily see it: "The blood of Jesus Christ His Son cleanseth us from all sin."

Frances R. Havergal is also the author of the hymn, "I Gave My Life for Thee" (No. 34).

Cesar Malan, composer of this tune in 1823, was an ordained pastor of the State Reformed Church in Switzerland. Later he was dismissed from this church for his strong preaching against its formalism and spiritual apathy, and he became a fervent leader in his country for the evangelical faith. He was also a noted evangelist who made preaching tours of France, Belgium and Great Britain. Although he wrote over 1000 hymn texts and tunes, he is remembered chiefly for this particular tune, "Hendon," thought to be named after a high hill located a few miles northeast of St. Paul's Cathedral in London, England. The tune first appeared in an American hymnal published by Lowell Mason in 1841.

275

Frances Ridley Havergal

88 The Church's One Foundation

AURELIA

SAMUEL J. STONE, 1839-1900

SAMUEL S. WESLEY, 1810-1876

1. The Church's one foun-da-tion Is Je-sus Christ her Lord;
2. E - lect from ev-'ry na-tion, Yet one o'er all the earth,
3. 'Mid toil and trib-u-la-tion And tu-mult of her war,
4. Yet she on earth hath un-ion With God the Three in One,

She is His new cre-a-tion By wa-ter and the Word:
Her char-ter of sal-va-tion One Lord, one faith, one birth;
She waits the con-sum-ma-tion Of peace for-ev-er-more;
And mys-tic sweet com-mun-ion With those whose rest is won:

From heav'n He came and sought her To be His ho-ly bride;
One ho-ly name she bless-es, Par-takes one ho-ly food,
Till with the vi-sion glo-rious Her long-ing eyes are blest,
O hap-py ones and ho-ly! Lord, give us grace that we,

With His own blood He bought her, And for her life He died.
And to one hope she press-es, With ev-'ry grace en-dued.
And the great Church vic-to-rious Shall be the Church at rest.
Like them, the meek and low-ly, On high may dwell with Thee.

The Church's One Foundation

Author-Samuel J. Stone
Composer-Samuel S. Wesley, 1810–1876
Tune Name-"Aurelia"
Meter-76.76 Doubled

... Christ is the head of the Church: And He is the Savior of the body.
Ephesians 5:23

One cannot study church history without becoming aware of the continuous harassment and persecution suffered by the Christian Church from its inception to the present time. As Protestants we are especially mindful of one of the important climaxes in this struggle, that historic date, October 31, 1517, when Martin Luther nailed to the door of the Cathedral of Wittenberg his ninety-five theses for consideration by the medieval church, condemning many of its practices and teachings. But prior to that date as well as since that time, it has been necessary for other committed men of God to defend the Church from those who would defile and destroy it with heretical doctrines and practices.

Such was the occasion for the writing of this hymn. It was written by a Church of England pastor, Samuel J. Stone, in 1866. It was during this period that there existed much turmoil within the Anglican Church over a book written three years earlier by one of the influential Anglican Bishops, John William Colenso, in which this liberal bishop attacked the historic accuracy of the Pentateuch. The book, *The Pentateuch and the Book of Joshua, Critically Examined,* was vehemently opposed by another Anglican leader, Bishop Gray. Soon the theological dispute between these two leaders became a widespread controversy throughout the entire Anglican Church.

277

Samuel Stone was deeply stirred by this matter and in 1866 wrote a collection of hymns, *Lyra Fidelium* ("Lyra of the Faithful"), containing twelve creedal hymns based on the Apostles' Creed to combat the attacks of modern scholarship and liberalism which he felt would soon divide and destroy the church. This particular hymn was based on the Ninth Article of the Creed, which reads, "The Holy Catholic (Universal) Church; the Communion of Saints: He is the Head of this Body." It was Stone's conviction that the unity of the Church must rest solely with a recognition of the Lordship of Christ as its head and not on the views and interpretations of men.

The hymn soon became highly popular throughout Great Britain. It was also translated into a number of different languages, including Latin. Two years later all of the Anglican bishops assembled in London for a great theological conclave known as the Lambeth Conference. Stone's hymn was chosen as the processional and thematic hymn for that historic meeting. He became widely known and respected as a prolific writer of hymns with several of his hymnal publications running into many editions. Stone wrote a total of seven books of verse and served on the committee which prepared the 1909 edition of the well-known Anglican hymnal, *Hymns Ancient and Modern*. Today, however, this hymn is his only hymn which is still in general use.

Samuel John Stone was born in Whitmore, Staffordshire, England, in 1839. Following his graduation from Oxford, he spent most of his remaining ministry in just two parishes in London, where he was affectionately known as the poor man's pastor. Here his time was spent in ministering to the poor and underprivileged populace in the East End of London, where it was said "he created a beautiful place of worship for the humble folk, and made it a center of light in the dark places." Stone was known as a man of spotless character; he was chivalrous toward the weak and needy, yet he was a violent fighter for the conservative faith that was being so sternly attacked in his day. He refused to compromise one iota before Higher Criticism and the evolutionary philosophies that were becoming increasingly popular. A personal faith in the inspired Scriptures was enough for him. All of his writings have been described as "strongly outspoken utterances of a manly faith, where dogma, prayer and praise are interwoven with much skill."

278

Stone's text originally contained seven stanzas. However, most hymnals today use just his first, second and fifth verses; our last stanza is actually a compilation of the first four lines of both his sixth and seventh verses. His original third stanza, omitted in today's hymnals, is also interesting:

> The Church shall never perish! Her dear Lord to defend,
> To guide, sustain and cherish, is with her to the end;
> Though there be those that hate her, and false sons in her pale
> Against the foe or traitor she ever shall prevail.

The composer of this music, Samuel S. Wesley, was born in London, England, on August 14, 1810. He was the grandson of Charles Wesley and was recognized as one of the leading church musicians of his day. He received his Doctorate in Music from Oxford University when only twenty-nine years of age. He composed a great deal of church service music as well as a number of original hymn tunes. This tune, known as "Aurelia," taken from the word "Aureus," the Latin word for "golden," was originally composed for the hymn text "Jerusalem the Golden." It was first matched with Stone's text in 1868 for use at the Bishops' Lambeth Conference.

89 **The Day of Resurrection**

JOHN OF DAMASCUS, early 8th century
Trans. by John M. Neale, 1818-1866

GREENLAND

Arr. from J. MICHAEL HAYDN, 1737-1806

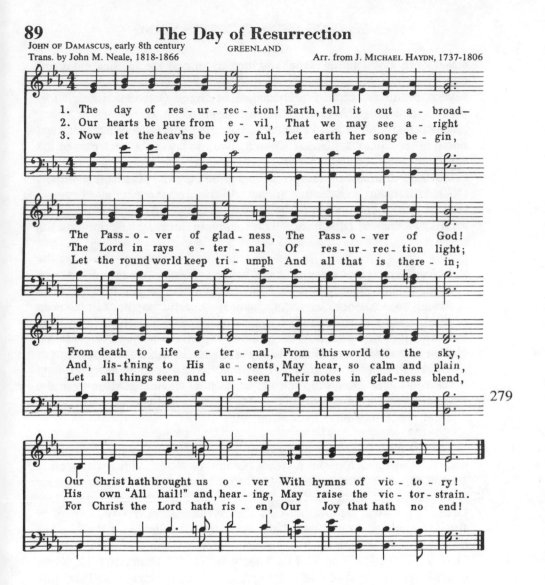

1. The day of res - ur - rec - tion! Earth, tell it out a - broad—
2. Our hearts be pure from e - vil, That we may see a - right
3. Now let the heav'ns be joy - ful, Let earth her song be - gin,

The Pass - o - ver of glad - ness, The Pass - o - ver of God!
The Lord in rays e - ter - nal Of res - ur - rec - tion light;
Let the round world keep tri - umph And all that is there - in;

From death to life e - ter - nal, From this world to the sky,
And, lis - t'ning to His ac - cents, May hear, so calm and plain,
Let all things seen and un - seen Their notes in glad - ness blend,

279

Our Christ hath brought us o - ver With hymns of vic - to - ry!
His own "All hail!" and, hear - ing, May raise the vic - tor - strain.
For Christ the Lord hath ris - en, Our Joy that hath no end!

Author–John of Damascus, early 8th century
English Translation–John M. Neale, 1818–1866
Music–Arranged from J. Michael Haydn, 1737–1806
Tune Name–"Greenland"
Meter–76.76 Doubled

Now thanks be unto God, which always causeth us to triumph in Christ.
2 Corinthians 2:14

This hymn from the early eighth century is one of the oldest expressions found in most hymnals. Its origin is rooted in the liturgy of the

Greek Orthodox Church. It was written by one of the famous monks of that Church, John of Damascus, c. 676-c. 780. This writing occurred several centuries before the Byzantine or Greek Orthodox Church formally split with the Western Roman Church in 1044.

The celebration of Easter has always been a spectacle of ecclesiastical pomp in the Greek Orthodox Church. Even today, as a vital part of the ceremony, the worshipers bury a cross under the high altar on Good Friday and dramatically resurrect it with shouts of "Christos egerthe" ("Christ is risen") on Easter Sunday. With this announcement begins a time of joyous celebration. Torches are lit, bells and trumpets peel, and salvos of cannons fill the air. The following account describes such a scene:

> Everywhere men clasped each other's hands, congratulated one another, and embraced with countenances beaming with delight, as though to each one separately some wonderful happiness had been proclaimed–and so in truth it was; and all the while rising above the mingling of many sounds, each one of which was a sound of gladness, the aged priests were distinctly heard chanting forth a glorious hymn of victory in tones so loud and clear, that they seemed to have regained the youth and strength to tell the world how "Christ is risen from the dead, having trampled death beneath His feet, and henceforth they that are in the tombs have everlasting life."

280

During the Oxford Movement of the nineteenth century, Anglican Church leaders such as John Neale became obsessed with rediscovering ancient Greek hymns from the Orthodox liturgy as well as Latin texts from the Roman Medieval Church. One of the important sources of these Greek hymns was an Orthodox Monastery located in the Wilderness of Judea known as Mar Saba. This monastery, begun in 484 A.D., has produced some of the most important leaders for the Orthodox Church. One of the greatest sons of Mar Saba was John of Damascus. He wrote extensively in the fields of theology, philosophy, science and the fine arts. His chief accomplishments, however, were the encouragements he gave to Greek hymnody and music. He did much to perfect the "Canon"–artistic, liturgical chants–as well as to adapt choral music to church use. His most famous canon is one for Easter–a song of triumph and thanksgiving. It is known as the Golden Canon or the Queen of Canons–said to be the grandest example of Greek sacred poetry. "The Day of Resurrection" hymn text is adapted from that work.

John Mason Neale is generally regarded as one of the leading translators of ancient hymns. Following his graduation from Cambridge University, where he was the leading scholar of his class, Neale was ordained to the ministry of the Church of England. Like many of the gifted church scholars of the mid-nineteenth century, Neale was strongly influenced by the prevailing Oxford Movement. Unlike many of the Church's leaders of this time, however, Neale remained with the Anglican Church instead of seceding to the Roman Catholic fold. He was recognized as one of the most learned hymnologists of his day with a knowledge of twenty languages. Neale, along with Edward Caswall (No. 57), did more to supply the Christian Church with a knowledge of ancient and medieval hymnody than all other authors combined.

John M. Neale is also the translator of the Latin advent hymn, "O Come, O Come, Emmanuel" (No. 64).

The free translation of this Greek text by John Neale first appeared in his *Hymns of the Eastern Church,* published in 1862. The tune, "Greenland," is from J. Michael Haydn's Collection, *Services for Country Churches.* The tune was originally used for Reginald Heber's "From Greenland's Icy Mountains" (No. 25), for which it was named. Haydn is also said to be the composer of the "Lyon" tune used for the hymn text, "O Worship the King" (No. 72).

* * *

281

Art thou weary, art thou languid, art thou sore distrest?
"Come to Me," saith One, "and, coming, be at rest."

Hath He marks to lead me to Him, if He be my guide?
"In His feet and hands are wound-prints, and His side."

Is there diadem, as Monarch, that His brow adorns?
"Yea, a crown, in very surety, but of thorns."

If I still hold closely to Him, what hath He at last?
"Sorrow vanquished, labor ended, Jordan passed."

If I ask Him to receive me, will He say me nay?
"Not till earth and not till heaven pass away."

Finding, foll'wing, keeping, struggling, is He sure to bless?
Saints, apostles, prophets, martyrs answer, "Yes."

Another Greek 8th century hymn translated by John M. Neale

90 The God of Abraham Praise

LEONI

THOMAS OLIVERS, 1725-1799
Based on the revised *Yigdal*
of Daniel ben Judah, 14th century

From a Hebrew melody
Arr. by Meyer Lyon (Leoni), 1751-1797

1. The God of A-braham praise, Who reigns en-throned a - bove,
2. The God of A-braham praise, At whose su - preme com - mand
3. He by Him-self hath sworn— I on His oath de - pend;
4. The whole tri - um-phant host Give thanks to God on high;

An - cient of ev - er - last-ing days, And God of love.
From earth I rise and seek the joys At His right hand.
I shall, on ea - gles' wings up-borne, To heav'n as _ cend.
"Hail, Fa - ther, Son and Ho - ly Ghost!" They ev - er cry.

282

Je - ho - vah, great I AM, By earth and heav'n con - fessed,
I all on earth for-sake, Its wis - dom, fame and pow'r,
I shall be-hold His face, I shall His pow'r a - dore,
Hail, A-braham's God and mine! I join the heav'n - ly lays;

I bow and bless the sa - cred Name For - ev - er blest.
And Him my on - ly por - tion make, My shield and tow'r.
And sing the won - ders of His grace For - ev - er - more.
All might and maj - es - ty are Thine, And end - less praise.

The God of Abraham Praise

Author-Thomas Olivers, 1725-1799. Based on the revised *Yigdal* of
 Daniel ben Judah, 14th century
Music-From a Hebrew melody. Arranged by Meyer Lyon, 1751-1797
Tune Name-"Leoni"
Meter-66.84 Doubled
Scripture Reference-Exodus 15:1-19

> Ye that fear the Lord, praise Him; all ye the seed of Jacob, glorify Him; and fear Him,
> all ye the seed of Israel.   Psalm 22:23

During the eighteenth century Wesleyan revivals, many "down and
outs" were converted to Christ through the evangelistic preaching of the
gospel and in turn became great ministers for God. Such is the testimony
of Thomas Olivers.

Thomas Olivers was born in Tregonan, England, in 1725. His parents
died when he was only four years of age. At an early age he became an
apprentice to a shoemaker and began leading a dissolute life. Young
Olivers was known in his community as the worst boy around. One day
while in Bristol, England, he heard George Whitefield preach on the text,
"Is not this a brand plucked out of the fire?" Thomas Olivers was
converted and his life miraculously changed. Later John Wesley, recognizing unusual latent talents in young Olivers, persuaded him to become
one of his evangelists. He traveled extensively throughout England and
Ireland, fearlessly preaching the gospel but often encountering violent
opposition.

Thomas Olivers wrote a number of hymn texts but this is the only one
still in use. Many students of hymnology have judged this hymn to be one
of the finest of all English hymns. Olivers states that he wrote this hymn
after listening to the preaching of a Jewish rabbi at the Duke's Place
Synagogue, Oldgate, London. There he also heard Meyer Lyon (Leoni),
a well-known Jewish cantor, sing the Doxology of Yigdal from the Hebrew liturgy. The Yigdal was composed around 1400 by Daniel ben
Judah and was based upon the thirteen articles of Jewish faith. The
service and especially the music so impressed Olivers that soon he began
writing this text to fit the meter of the tune he had heard. The tune name,
"Leoni," was named in honor of Cantor Meyer Lyon.

283

91

The Ninety and Nine

ELIZABETH C. CLEPHANE, 1830–1869   IRA D. SANKEY, 1840–1908

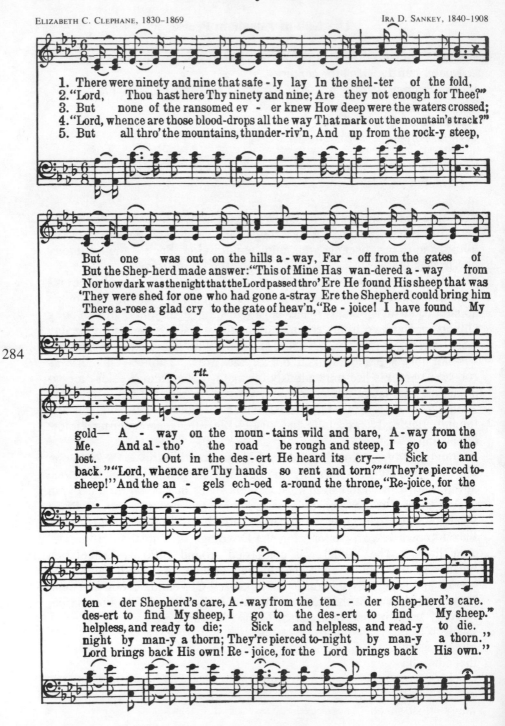

1. There were ninety and nine that safe - ly lay In the shel-ter of the fold,
2. "Lord, Thou hast here Thy ninety and nine; Are they not enough for Thee?"
3. But none of the ransomed ev - er knew How deep were the waters crossed;
4. "Lord, whence are those blood-drops all the way That mark out the mountain's track?"
5. But all thro' the mountains, thunder-riv'n, And up from the rock-y steep,

But one was out on the hills a - way, Far - off from the gates of
But the Shep-herd made answer: "This of Mine Has wan-dered a - way from
Nor how dark was the night that the Lord passed thro' Ere He found His sheep that was
'They were shed for one who had gone a-stray Ere the Shepherd could bring him
There a-rose a glad cry to the gate of heav'n, "Re - joice! I have found My

284

rit.

gold— A - way on the moun - tains wild and bare, A - way from the
Me, And al - tho' the road be rough and steep, I go to the
lost. Out in the des - ert He heard its cry— Sick and
back." "Lord, whence are Thy hands so rent and torn?" "They're pierced to-
sheep!" And the an - gels ech-oed a-round the throne, "Re-joice, for the

ten - der Shepherd's care, A - way from the ten - der Shep-herd's care.
des-ert to find My sheep, I go to the des-ert to find My sheep."
helpless, and ready to die; Sick and helpless, and read-y to die.
night by man-y a thorn; They're pierced to-night by man-y a thorn."
Lord brings back His own! Re - joice, for the Lord brings back His own."

The Ninety and Nine

Author-Elizabeth C. Clephane, 1830–1869
Composer-Ira D. Sankey, 1840–1908
Meter-Irregular
Scripture Reference-Luke 15:3–7

> I say unto you, that likewise joy shall be in heaven over one sinner that repenteth, more than over ninety and nine just persons, which need no repentance.   Luke 15:7

Elizabeth C. Clephane was born in Edinburgh, Scotland, but grew up in Melrose, in the lovely area of Abbotsford. Throughout her brief lifetime she was plagued with illness and a frail body. Despite her physical afflictions she was affectionately known to the townspeople as the Sunbeam. Elizabeth enjoyed writing poetry and had several of her poems published in a Scottish Presbyterian magazine entitled *The Family Treasury*. However, the majority of her writings appeared anonymously in this magazine in 1872, three years after her early death in 1869.

Miss Clephane wrote the text for "The Ninety and Nine" especially for children a short time before her death. It was published in a magazine called *The Children's Hour*. Five years later the American evangelists, D. L. Moody and Ira Sankey, were in Great Britain for one of their noted revival campaigns. The story is told of Moody and Sankey riding a train one morning from Glasgow to Edinburgh to conduct a service in the Free Assembly Hall of Edinburgh. Sankey stopped to purchase a newspaper in the train depot, hoping to get news from America. As he idly turned over the pages of the paper during the ride, he discovered Elizabeth Clephane's poem. He tried to interest Moody in its contents, but the evangelist was too busy preparing his sermon. Finally, Sankey simply cut out the poem and placed it in his pocket.

At the meeting that afternoon in Edinburgh, the subject of Moody's message was "The Good Shepherd," based on Luke 15:3–7. Finishing his address, Moody turned to Sankey and asked him to sing some fitting solo. Sankey could think of nothing that was appropriate. Then suddenly he recalled the little poem he had put into his vest pocket. Placing his newspaper clipping on the folding organ before him and breathing a prayer for divine help, he struck the chord of A flat and began to sing. Note by note the tune was given, and that same tune has remained unchanged to the present time. Sankey declared that it was one of the most intense moments of his life. He said that he could sense immediately that the song had reached the hearts of the Scottish audience. "When I reached the end of the song," reported Sankey, "Mr. Moody was in tears and so was I." When Moody arose to give the invitation for salvation, many "lost sheep" responded to the call of Christ.

285

During their campaign in Great Britain, Moody and Sankey visited Melrose, Scotland. Elizabeth Clephane's two sisters were in the audience. One may imagine their delight and surprise when they heard their departed sister's poem set to Sankey's music and learned of the spiritual impact this hymn had in the furtherance of the gospel, even as it has had to the present time.

Elizabeth C. Clephane is also the author of the hymn, "Beneath the Cross of Jesus" (No. 10).

Ira D. Sankey was born of Scotch-Irish ancestry on August 28, 1840. In 1857 his family moved to Newcastle, Pennsylvania, where he attended high school and joined the Methodist Episcopal Church. Here he began his first choir work. His strong baritone voice soon began to attract attention and crowds came to hear him sing.

In 1860 Sankey enlisted in the Twelfth Pennsylvania Regiment. While in the army he frequently led the singing for religious services. However, the idea of devoting his life to the music ministry did not seem feasible to him. Upon his return from the military, he became a clerk in the Internal Revenue Service.

Sankey was sent as a delegate to the Y.M.C.A. convention at Indianapolis, Indiana, in 1870. Here he first met the noted evangelist, D. L. Moody. The singing for the convention's services had been extremely poor. Finally the suggestion was made that Sankey should lead. Immediately there was a new spirit and enthusiasm injected into the gatherings. At the close of the convention Sankey was introduced personally to Moody. Sankey has left the following account of this initial meeting with the evangelist:

> As I drew near Mr. Moody, he stepped forward, took me by the hand, and looked at me with that keen, piercing fashion of his, as if reading my very soul. Then he said abruptly, "Where are you from?"
> "Pennsylvania," I replied.
> "Are you married?"
> "I am."
> "How many children do you have?"
> "Two."
> "What is your business?"
> "I am a government officer."
> "Well," said Mr. Moody, "you'll have to give it up."
> I was too much astonished to make any reply, and he went on speaking as if the matter had already been decided. "I have been looking for you for the last eight years," he said. "You have to come to Chicago and help me in my work."

After several months of indecision, Sankey resigned his government position and moved to Chicago with his family to begin his fruitful evangelistic endeavors with Moody as well as to be used of God in the promotion of gospel music.

Today the famed organ on which Ira D. Sankey composed his spontaneous melody to Elizabeth Clephane's text sits in the chapel at the Billy Graham Evangelistic Association headquarters in Minneapolis, Minnesota.

Ira D. Sankey is also the composer of the hymn, ''Hiding in Thee'' (No. 29).

D. L. Moody

287

Ira D. Sankey

92

The Old Rugged Cross

George Bennard, 1873-1958

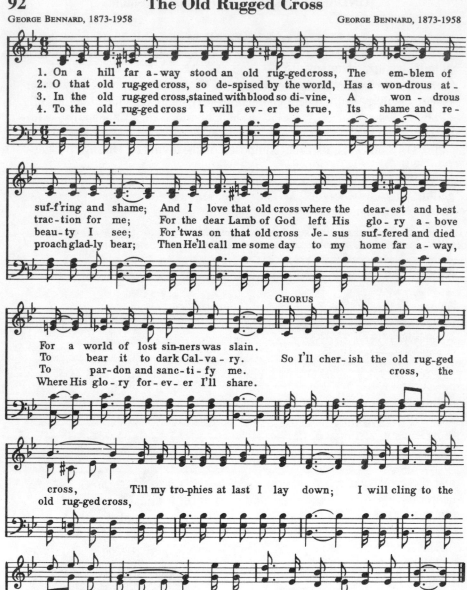

288

1. On a hill far a-way stood an old rug-ged cross, The em-blem of
2. O that old rug-ged cross, so de-spised by the world, Has a won-drous at-
3. In the old rug-ged cross, stained with blood so di-vine, A won-drous
4. To the old rug-ged cross I will ev-er be true, Its shame and re-

suf-f'ring and shame; And I love that old cross where the dear-est and best
trac-tion for me; For the dear Lamb of God left His glo-ry a-bove
beau-ty I see; For 'twas on that old cross Je-sus suf-fered and died
proach glad-ly bear; Then He'll call me some day to my home far a-way,

CHORUS

For a world of lost sin-ners was slain.
To bear it to dark Cal-va-ry. So I'll cher-ish the old rug-ged
To par-don and sanc-ti-fy me. cross, the
Where His glo-ry for-ev-er I'll share.

cross, Till my tro-phies at last I lay down; I will cling to the
old rug-ged cross,

old rug-ged cross, And ex-change it some day for a crown.
cross, the old rug-ged cross,

The Old Rugged Cross

Author–George Bennard, 1873–1958
Composer–George Bennard, 1873–1958
Meter–Irregular with Chorus

> Who His own self bare our sins in His own body on the tree, that we, being dead to
> sins, should live unto righteousness: By whose stripes ye were healed. I Peter 2:24

Seldom can a song leader suggest a time for favorites from any congregation without receiving at least one request for "The Old Rugged Cross." This gospel hymn, a sentimental favorite of Christians and unsaved alike, was written by George Bennard in 1913. It is generally conceded to be the most popular of all twentieth century hymns.

George Bennard was born in Youngstown, Ohio, but his parents soon moved to Albia, Iowa, and later to the town of Lucas in the same state. It was here that young George made his personal acceptance of Christ as his Savior. Following the death of his father before George was sixteen years of age, he entered the ranks of the Salvation Army. Bennard and his first wife served for a period of time as officers in this organization.

Consequently, Bennard was ordained by the Methodist Episcopal Church, where his devoted ministry was highly esteemed. For some time he was busily involved in conducting revival services, especially throughout the states of Michigan and New York. One time, after returning to Michigan, he passed through a trying experience which caused him to reflect seriously about the significance of the cross and what the Apostle Paul meant when he spoke of entering into the fellowship of Christ's suffering. As Bennard contemplated these truths, he became convinced that the cross was more than just a religious symbol but rather the very heart of the gospel. George Bennard has left the following account regarding the writing of this hymn:

> The inspiration came to me one day in 1913, when I was staying in Albion, Michigan. I began to write "The Old Rugged Cross." I composed the melody first. The words that I first wrote were imperfect. The words of the finished hymn were put into my heart in answer to my own need. Shortly thereafter it was introduced at special meetings in Pokagon, Michigan on June 7, 1913. The first occasion where it was heard outside of the church at Pokagon was at the Chicago Evangelistic Institute. There it was introduced before a large convention and soon it became extremely popular throughout the country.

Shortly after writing this hymn, George Bennard sent a manuscript copy to Charles Gabriel, one of the leading gospel hymn composers of that era. Gabriel's prophecy, "You will certainly hear from this song," was soon realized as "The Old Rugged Cross" became one of the most widely published songs, either sacred or secular, in this country.

Bennard continued his evangelistic ministries for forty additional years following the writing of this hymn. He wrote other favorite gospel hymns, but none ever achieved the response of "The Old Rugged Cross." On October 9, 1958, at the age of eighty-five, Bennard exchanged his "cross for a crown." He spent the last years of his life by the "side of the road," a few miles north of Reed City, Michigan. Near this home there still stands a twelve foot high cross with the words, " 'The Old Rugged Cross'-Home of George Bennard, composer of this beloved hymn."

Although it has often been stated that we do not worship the cross as such but rather the Christ of the cross, one cannot ponder the truths of Christ's atonement without a keen awareness of the centrality of the cross in God's plan of redemption for lost mankind.

93 The Sands of Time Are Sinking

RUTHERFORD

ANNE ROSS COUSIN, 1824-1906

CHRÉTIEN URHAN, 1790-1845
Arr. by Edward F. Rimbault, 1816-1876

1. The sands of time are sink-ing, The dawn of heav-en breaks;
2. O Christ, He is the foun-tain, The deep, sweet well of love!
3. O I am my Be-lov-ed's, And my Be-lov-ed's mine!
4. The Bride eyes not her gar-ment But her dear Bride-groom's face;

The sum-mer morn I've sighed for— The fair, sweet morn a-wakes:
The streams on earth I've tast-ed More deep I'll drink a-bove:
He brings a poor vile sin-ner In-to His "house of wine."
I will not gaze at glo-ry But on my King of grace.

291

Dark, dark hath been the mid-night, But day-spring is at hand,
There to an o-cean ful-ness His mer-cy doth ex-pand,
I stand up-on His mer-it— I know no oth-er stand,
Not at the crown He giv-eth But on His pierc-ed hand:

And glo-ry, glo-ry dwell-eth In Im-man-uel's land.
And glo-ry, glo-ry dwell-eth In Im-man-uel's land.
Not e'en where glo-ry dwell-eth In Im-man-uel's land.
The Lamb is all the glo-ry Of Im-man-uel's land.

The Star-Spangled Banner

FRANCIS SCOTT KEY, 1779-1843

Attributed to
John Stafford Smith, 1750-1836

294

The Star-Spangled Banner

Author–Francis Scott Key, 1779–1843
Composer–Attributed to John Stafford Smith, 1750–1836
Meter–Irregular

> Submit yourselves to every ordinance of man for the Lord's sake: whether it be to the king, as supreme; or unto governors, as unto them that are sent by him for the punishment of evildoers, and for the praise of them that do well.   I Peter 2:13,14

Francis Scott Key, author of our national anthem, was born on August 1, 1779 in Frederick, Maryland. He was the son of a distinguished Revolutionary War Officer. Throughout his life Francis was known as a fine spiritual gentleman and an active lay leader in the Protestant Episcopal Church. He was trained in law and later served as the District Attorney at Georgetown, District of Columbia, for three terms.

During our War of 1812 with England, Francis Scott Key was authorized by President Madison to visit the British Fleet located near the mouth of the Potomac to negotiate the release of a physician friend, Dr. Beanes, who had been taken prisoner by the invaders. The British admiral finally granted the American's request, but because the British ships had planned an attack on Fort McHenry, which guarded the harbor of Baltimore, Key and his party were detained all night aboard the truce boat on which they had come.

That night, September 13, 1813, was a night of unforgettable anxiety for Key and his party. The fierce bombardment continued during the hours of darkness. As long as the shore fortification replied to the attack, Key and his friends were certain that all was still well. Toward morning the firing from the shore seemed to cease, causing the American delegation great dismay. While the other members rested briefly from their weariness, Key continued to pace the deck until the first rays of dawn revealed that the "flag was still there"–assurance that we were still free. Inspired by this experience, Scott began to write his poem hastily on the back of a letter. Later that evening upon being released, he completed his work in his home. Shortly afterward he had it printed in handbill form. The poem had an immediate response with the American people, still exhilarated by news of their victory. Approximately one month later Scott's poem was published in sheet music form by Joseph Carr. It was set to a tune known as "Anacron in Heaven." This tune, known as early as the 1790's in this country as an old hunting tune, had been used previously with other texts. Since its first use with Scott's poem, however, it has been the accepted tune for our national anthem. Although the wide twelve-note range of this melody is difficult for many to sing, it does provide an inspirational setting for this text. It is not known for certain who the composer might be, but it is generally attributed to a John Stafford Smith, born in Gloucester, England, 1750. Smith was a composer for the Covent Garden Theater and the conductor of the Academy of Ancient Music. He died on September 20, 1836.

The flag that waved during that night of September 13 had been made and given to the McHenry Fort by a fifteen year old girl, later identified as Mrs. Sanderson. The flag is still on display in the Sanderson family home in Baltimore, Maryland. The city of Baltimore has also erected an elaborate statue in honor of the author of our national anthem.

Despite the early enthusiastic acceptance of this patriotic hymn, it was not officially adopted and declared to be our National Anthem by Congress until March 3, 1931.

*　　*　　*

296

"Give me the making of the songs of a nation, and I care not who makes its laws."

Andrew Fletcher 1655–1716

95   There Is a Fountain

CLEANSING FOUNTAIN

WILLIAM COWPER, 1731-1800

American melody

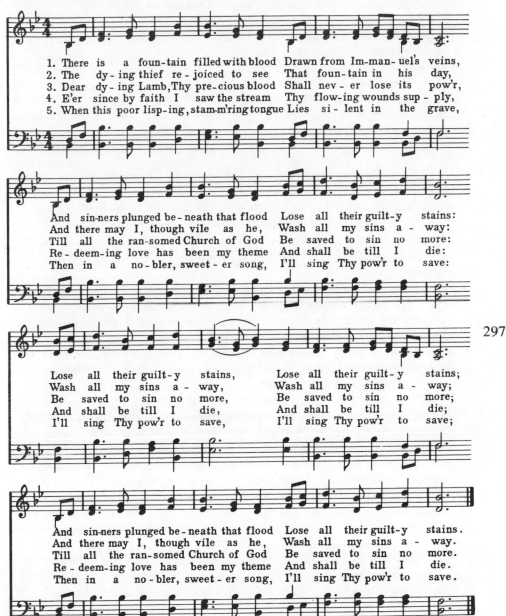

1. There is a foun-tain filled with blood Drawn from Im-man-uel's veins,
2. The dy-ing thief re-joiced to see That foun-tain in his day,
3. Dear dy-ing Lamb, Thy pre-cious blood Shall nev-er lose its pow'r,
4. E'er since by faith I saw the stream Thy flow-ing wounds sup-ply,
5. When this poor lisp-ing, stam-m'ring tongue Lies si-lent in the grave,

And sin-ners plunged be-neath that flood Lose all their guilt-y stains:
And there may I, though vile as he, Wash all my sins a-way:
Till all the ran-somed Church of God Be saved to sin no more:
Re-deem-ing love has been my theme And shall be till I die:
Then in a no-bler, sweet-er song, I'll sing Thy pow'r to save:

Lose all their guilt-y stains, Lose all their guilt-y stains;
Wash all my sins a-way, Wash all my sins a-way;
Be saved to sin no more, Be saved to sin no more;
And shall be till I die, And shall be till I die;
I'll sing Thy pow'r to save, I'll sing Thy pow'r to save;

And sin-ners plunged be-neath that flood Lose all their guilt-y stains.
And there may I, though vile as he, Wash all my sins a-way.
Till all the ran-somed Church of God Be saved to sin no more.
Re-deem-ing love has been my theme And shall be till I die.
Then in a no-bler, sweet-er song, I'll sing Thy pow'r to save.

There Is a Fountain

Author – William Cowper, 1731–1800
Music – American Melody
Tune Name – "Cleansing Fountain"
Meter – 86.86.66.86
Scripture Reference – Zechariah 13:1

> But now in Christ Jesus ye who sometimes were far off are made nigh by the blood of Christ.
> Ephesians 2:13

William Cowper (pronounced "Kooper") is a name highly respected in English classic literary circles. He is the most honored poet between Pope and Shelley and is viewed by some as one of the finest of all English writers. Several of his best known secular works include a translation of Homer, a widely acclaimed volume of poems entitled *The Task,* along with his most famous literary poem, "John Gilpin," a happy and mirthful narrative.

Cowper was born in Great Berkhamstead, England, on November 15, 1731. His father was an English clergyman while his mother was from a well-known family of royalty. Throughout his childhood Cowper was physically frail and emotionally sensitive. Contributing to his instability was the death of his mother when he was only six years old. Near the end of his life he once remarked that there had never been a day when he had not mourned his mother's death.

At an early age he was directed by his father to study law. Upon completion of his studies, however, the prospect of appearing for his final examination before the bar so frightened him that it caused a mental breakdown and even an attempted suicide. Later he was placed in an insane asylum for a period of eighteen months. During this detention, he one day read from the Scriptures the passage in Romans 3:25 that Jesus Christ is "set forth to be a propitiation through faith in His blood, to declare his righteousness for the remission of sins that are past, through the forbearance of God." Through his reading of the Bible, Cowper soon realized a personal relationship with Christ and a sense of forgiveness of sin. This was in 1764 when he was thirty-three years old.

After his conversion and mental recovery, Cowper made friends with the family of the Reverend Morley Unwin, who were a great help to him. Mrs. Unwin remained his devoted friend and guardian till the end of her days.

After Rev. Unwin's death in 1767, John Newton, the converted slave ship captain (author of "Amazing Grace" [No. 6]), persuaded Mrs. Unwin and her family along with William Cowper to move to Olney, England, where Newton pastored the parish Anglican Church. It was here

298

for nearly two decades that Newton and Cowper had a close personal friendship, and eventually in 1799 their combined talents produced the famous *Olney Hymns* hymnal, one of the most important single contributions made to the field of evangelical hymnody. In this ambitious collection of 349 hymns, sixty-seven were written by Cowper with the remainder by Newton.

"There Is a Fountain" was originally entitled "Peace for the Fountain Opened." It is undoubtedly one of Cowper's best loved hymns. Only eternity will reveal the hosts who, through the singing of this hymn, have been made aware of the efficacy of Christ's complete atonement. The text, with its vivid imagery, is based on the Old Testament text, Zechariah 13:1, "In that day there shall be a fountain opened to the house of David and to the inhabitants of Jerusalem for sin and uncleanness." The tune for this text is borrowed from an American folk melody, probably one of the typical tunes used in the camp meetings of the early nineteenth century.

Throughout his life Cowper continued to be plagued by periodic melancholia. Often during these periods he even sought to end his life. It is interesting that some of his most meaningful hymns were written after these times. Till the end of his days Cowper could never completely shake off the belief that God would not turn His back upon him. On his death bed, however, it is said that his face lit up as he uttered these last words, "I am not shut out of heaven after all." Despite William Cowper's physical and emotional frailties, God endued him with extraordinary literary talents to enrich the lives of Christian people for more than two centuries.

299

William Cowper

96 There Is a Green Hill Far Away

GREEN HILL

CECIL F. ALEXANDER, 1818-1895

GEORGE C. STEBBINS, 1846-1945

1. There is a green hill far a-way, With-out a cit-y wall,
2. We may not know, we can-not tell What pains He had to bear;
3. He died that we might be for-giv'n, He died to make us good,
4. There was no oth-er good e-nough To pay the price of sin;

Where the dear Lord was cru-ci-fied, Who died to save us all.
But we be-lieve it was for us He hung and suf-fered there.
That we might go at last to heav'n, Saved by His pre-cious blood.
He on-ly could un-lock the gate Of heav'n and let us in.

300

CHORUS

O dear-ly, dear-ly has He loved! And we must love Him too,

And trust in His re-deem-ing blood, And try His works to do.

There Is a Green Hill Far Away

Author–Mrs. Cecil F. Alexander, 1818–1895
Composer–George C. Stebbins, 1846–1945
Tune Name–"Green Hill"
Meter–CM (86.86 with Chorus)

> Then delivered he Him therefore unto them to be crucified. And they took Jesus, and led Him away.   John 19:16

A mark of greatness is the ability to make profound truths understandable to children. Such was the gift of Mrs. Cecil Frances Alexander, generally regarded as one of the finest of English women hymn writers.

Mrs. Alexander was born in Tyrone, Ireland. Before her marriage in 1850 to the Rev. William Alexander, who later became archbishop and Primate of the Anglican Church for all of Ireland, she was active and successful in the Sunday School movement just beginning in Great Britain. Mrs. Alexander never lost her love for children and the desire to teach them sound spiritual truths, which she maintained could best be done through the use of suitable hymns.

In 1848 she published a volume of children's hymns that has never been excelled. It covered a wide range of doctrinal subjects such as Baptism, the Apostles' Creed, the Ten Commandments, and the Lord's Prayer. Practically all of the 400 poems and hymns written by Mrs. Alexander throughout her life were intended for children, and for this reason the language is direct and easily understood, as in this hymn. A child has no difficulty in comprehending it, yet this lovely hymn expounds in a most touching and meaningful way the story of Christ's atonement.

This hymn text was written especially by Mrs. Alexander for the purpose of teaching her own Sunday School class the meaning of the phrase from the Apostles' Creed, "suffered under Pontius Pilate, was crucified, dead and buried." The text, though intended for children, has been greatly used by adult congregations for more than a century. Like most of her writings, this text is said to have a simplicity that an adult Christian person need never outgrow.

After her marriage Mrs. Alexander maintained a keen interest in her husband's parish duties, and her life continued to be filled with deeds of helpfulness and charity. Her husband once wrote this tribute of her, "From one poor home to another she went. Christ was ever with her, and in her, and all felt her influence." Those who knew her intimately claimed that her life was even more beautiful than her hymns and poetry. She was a very humble woman who disdained praise for her accomplishments. However, the account is given that on one occasion when

301

someone wrote to tell her of the change in heart and life which had come to a worldly man through the influence of one of her hymns as it was sung, Mrs. Alexander sprang to her feet, joyfully exclaiming, "Thank God, I do like to hear that."

George C. Stebbins, composer of the music, is well-known in the field of American gospel music. He was born on February 26, 1846 in Orleans County, about fifty miles northeast of Niagara Falls, Ontario, Canada. At the age of twenty-three he moved to Chicago to be associated with the Lyon and Healy Music Company. In 1874 he moved to Boston and became music director of the Clarendon Street Baptist Church. It was here that he met D. L. Moody and Ira Sankey and began a close association with them. He also worked with such leading evangelists as George F. Pentecost, Major D. W. Whittle, and others. After the untimely death of Philip P. Bliss in 1876, Stebbins and James McGranahan assisted Ira Sankey in editing and compiling the third, fourth, fifth and sixth editions of the *Gospel Hymns* series.

Stebbins composed this tune for Mrs. Alexander's text in 1878, and it first appeared that same year in *Gospel Hymns No. 3*. The hymn became one of the widely used songs in the great evangelistic campaigns of Moody and Sankey and other leading teams conducting similar gospel meetings during that era.

302

97 This Is My Father's World

TERRA BEATA

MALTBIE D. BABCOCK, 1858-1901

FRANKLIN L. SHEPPARD, 1852-1930
Arr. by Norman Johnson, 1928-

1. This is my Fa-ther's world, And to my list-'ning ears
2. This is my Fa-ther's world— The birds their car-ols raise;
3. This is my Fa-ther's world— O let me ne'er for-get

All na-ture sings, and round me rings The mu-sic of the spheres.
The morn-ing light, the lil-y white, De-clare their Mak-er's praise.
That tho the wrong seems oft so strong God is the Rul-er yet.

This is my Fa-ther's world! I rest me in the thought Of
This is my Fa-ther's world! He shines in all that's fair; In the
This is my Fa-ther's world! The bat-tle is not done; Je-

rocks and trees, of skies and seas— His hand the won-ders wrought.
rus-tling grass I hear Him pass— He speaks to me ev-'ry-where.
sus who died shall be sat-is-fied, And earth and heav'n be one.

303

This is My Father's World

Author–Maltbie D. Babcock, 1858–1901
Composer–Franklin L. Sheppard, 1852–1930
Tune Name–"Terra Beata"
Meter–SM (66.86 Doubled)

> He loveth righteousness and judgment: The earth is full of the goodness of the Lord.   Psalm 33:5

This hymn is taken from a sixteen-verse poem written by the Rev. Maltbie D. Babcock and published posthumously in 1901. The first line of each of the sixteen stanzas begins with "This is my Father's world."

Maltbie D. Babcock was born in Syracuse, New York, on August 3, 1858 of a socially prominent family. Later he became recognized as one of the outstanding Presbyterian ministers of his generation. It has been said that a manlier man never stood in a Christian pulpit. He was tall and broad-shouldered with muscles of iron, a superb specimen of physical manhood. He was a champion baseball pitcher and swimmer. The young men of his church fairly idolized and yet respected their pastor for his strong convictions and principles. He was as full of fun and mischief as the next man, but some things he would not tolerate. One day when an older fellow was trying to bully one younger than himself and was indulging in some unsavory language, Babcock quietly seized him by the nape of his neck and the seat of the trousers and with a word of forceful warning pitched him over the fence. Something of the virile character of Babcock, both as a man and preacher, is reflected in one of his well-known poems, "Be Strong:"

> We are not here to play, to dream, to drift,
> We have hard work to do, and loads to lift,
> Shun not the struggle; face it;
> 'Tis God's gift.

Rev. Mr. Babcock was also known as a skilled musician, performing on the organ, piano and violin. He was a great admirer of nature, as reflected in this text. While a pastor in Lockport, New York, Dr. Babcock was in the habit of taking morning walks to the top of a hill north of town where he had a full view of Lake Ontario and the surrounding country. He was characterized by his frequent expression, "I'm going out to see my Father's world." However, as one writer has noted, "This hymn is more than a mere outburst of song about nature, but rather a seasoned appreciation, beautifully worded, of unfailing trust in the ways and judgments of

304

God. In the hymn Babcock portrays the message of God's Presence, God's Personality, God's Power, God's Purpose.''

The tune for this text was arranged from an old English melody by one of Babcock's close friends, F. L. Sheppard, an accomplished musician. It was first published in his book, *Alleluia,* a Presbyterian Sunday School book published in 1915. The tune name, ''Terra Beata,'' is Latin for ''blessed earth.''

*　*　*

''All things bright and beautiful,
　All creatures great and small,
All things wise and wonderful,
　The Lord God made them all.

''Each little flower that opens,
　Each little bird that sings,
He made their glowing colors,
　He made their tiny wings.

''The purple-headed mountain,
　The river running by,
The sunset, and the morning
　That brightens up the sky.

''The cold wind in the winter,
　The pleasant summer sun,
The ripe fruits in the garden,
　He made them every one.

''The tall trees in the greenwood,
　The meadows where we play,
The rushes by the water,
　We gather every day.

''He gave us eyes to see them,
　And lips that we might tell
How great is God Almighty,
　Who has made all things well.''

Cecil Frances Alexander, 1818–1895

305

98

Thou Didst Leave Thy Throne

MARGARET

EMILY E. S. ELLIOTT, 1836-1897

TIMOTHY R. MATTHEWS, 1826-1910

1. Thou didst leave Thy throne And Thy king-ly crown When Thou
2. Heav-en's arch - es rang When the an - gels sang, Pro -
3. The fox - es found rest, And the birds their nest In the
4. Thou cam - est, O Lord, With the liv - ing word That should
5. When the heav - ens shall ring And the an - gels sing At Thy

cam - est to earth for me; But in Beth - le - hem's home
claim - ing Thy roy - al de - gree; But of low - ly birth
shade of the for - est tree; But Thy couch was the sod,
set Thy peo - ple free; But with mock - ing scorn
com - ing to vic - to - ry, Let Thy voice call me home,

Was there found no room For Thy ho - ly na-tiv - i - ty.
Didst Thou come to earth, And in great hu - mil - i - ty.
O Thou Son of God, In the des - erts of Gal - i - lee.
And with crown of thorn They bore Thee to Cal - va - ry.
Say - ing, "Yet there is room— There is room at My side for thee."

REFRAIN

1.-4. O come to my heart, Lord Je - sus—There is room in my heart for Thee!
5. My heart shall re-joice, Lord Je - sus, When Thou com-est and call-est for me!

306

Thou Didst Leave Thy Throne

Author–Emily E.S. Elliott, 1836–1897
Composer–Timothy R. Matthews, 1826–1910
Tune Name–"Margaret"
Meter–Irregular
Scripture Reference–Luke 2:7

> I am come that they might have life, and that they might have it more abundantly.
> John 10:10b

Emily Elliott was born at Brighton, England, on July 22, 1836. Throughout her life she was associated with the evangelical faction of the Anglican Church. She gave of herself tirelessly in working with the rescue missions and Sunday Schools in her area. Emily was a niece of Charlotte Elliott, author of the hymn "Just As I Am" (No. 52). For six years she edited a magazine called the *Church Missionary Juvenile Instructor.* Forty-eight of her hymns were published in a book entitled *Under the Pillow,* a book of verse for the special use of people who are ill in hospitals, infirmaries or at home.

This particular text was printed by Miss Elliott privately for the choir and for the school children of her father's church, St. Mark's, at Brighton, England. It was written for the purpose of teaching children the truths of the Advent and Nativity season. The text for the hymn was based on the haunting phrase taken from Luke 2:7, "but there was no room for them in the inn."

It is interesting to note the vivid contrast that Miss Elliott achieved in the first four verses of this hymn with the contrasting phrase of each verse beginning with the word "but":

307

Stanza One... Heaven's throne and crown–*but* no room in Bethlehem.
Stanza Two... Heaven's royal degree–*but* earth's great humiliation.
Stanza Three... Earth's creatures have their homes–*but* for Him the desert.
Stanza Four... He came bringing redemption–*but* men gave Him Calvary.
Stanza Five... Here the contrast is reversed: Death is changed into victory, and Heaven's arches of stanza two will ring again when He comes for His second advent.
The refrain is the personalizing of the truth expressed in each stanza.

The tune, "Margaret," was composed especially for this text by Timothy Richard Matthews. Matthews was born at Bedford, England, on

November 4, 1826, and was recognized in Great Britain as one of the leading organists of his day. He was also a clergyman and the composer of more than 100 hymn tunes.

Expectation has and always will be a necessary part of a believer's life. In the Old Testament there was the anxious expectancy of a coming Messiah. Our expectancy is the sound of the trumpet, meeting the Lord, and the prospect of an eternal home with our Savior.

* * *

"Hark! the glad sound! the Savior comes,
  The Savior promised long:
Let every heart prepare a throne,
  And every voice a song.

"He comes, the prisoners to release
  In Satan's bondage held;
The gates of brass before Him burst,
  The iron fetters yield.

"He comes, from the thick films of vice
  To clear the mental ray,
And on the eyeballs of the blind
  To pour celestial day.

"He comes, the broken heart to bind,
  The bleeding soul to cure,
And, with the treasures of His grace,
  To enrich the humble poor.

"Our glad hosannas, Prince of Peace,
  Thy welcome shall proclaim,
And Heaven's eternal arches ring
  With Thy beloved name."

Philip Doddridge, 1702–1751

99

What a Friend We Have in Jesus

CONVERSE

JOSEPH SCRIVEN, 1819-1886

CHARLES C. CONVERSE, 1832-1918

1. What a Friend we have in Je - sus, All our sins and griefs to bear!
2. Have we tri - als and temp-ta - tions? Is there trou-ble an - y - where?
3. Are we weak and heav-y - la - den, Cum-bered with a load of care?

What a priv - i - lege to car - ry Ev - 'ry-thing to God in prayer!
We should nev-er be dis - cour-aged— Take it to the Lord in prayer.
Pre - cious Sav-ior, still our ref - uge— Take it to the Lord in prayer.

O what peace we oft - en for - feit, O what need-less pain we bear,
Can we find a friend so faith-ful Who will all our sor-rows share?
Do thy friends de-spise, for - sake thee? Take it to the Lord in prayer;

309

All be - cause we do not car - ry Ev - 'ry-thing to God in prayer!
Je - sus knows our ev -'ry weak-ness— Take it to the Lord in prayer.
In His arms He'll take and shield thee— Thou wilt find a sol - ace there.

Author–Joseph Scriven, 1819–1886
Composer–Charles C. Converse, 1832–1918
Tune Name–"Converse"
Meter–87.87 Doubled

A man that hath friends must show himself friendly: And there is a friend that sticketh
closer than a brother.   Proverbs 18:24

Someone has well penned this statement, "A Christian's practical
theology is often his hymnology." Many of us could attest to this truth as

we recall some deeply moving experience–perhaps the loss of a dear loved one–and a simple hymn which has been used by the Holy Spirit to minister to our spiritual need.

Such a hymn is "What a Friend We Have in Jesus." Though it is not considered to be an example of great literary writing, its simply stated truths have brought solace and comfort to countless numbers of God's people since it was first written in 1857. So relevant to the basic spiritual needs of people are these words that many missionaries state that it is one of the first hymns taught to new converts. The very simplicity of the text and music has been its appeal and strength.

Joseph Scriven was born in 1819 of prosperous parents in Dublin, Ireland. He was a graduate of Trinity College, Dublin. At the age of twenty-five he decided to leave his native country and migrate to Canada. His reasons for leaving his family and country seem to be two-fold: the religious influence of the Plymouth Brethren upon his life estranging him from his family and the accidental drowning of his fiancee the night before their scheduled wedding.

From that time Scriven developed a totally different pattern of life. He took the Sermon on the Mount literally. It is said that he gave freely of his limited possessions, even sharing the clothing from his own body, if necessary, and never once refused to help anyone who needed it. Ira Sankey tells in his writings of the man who, seeing Scriven in the streets of Port Hope, Ontario, with his sawbuck and saw, asked, "Who is that man? I want him to work for me." The answer was, "You cannot get that man; he saws wood only for poor widows and sick people who cannot pay." Because of this manner of life Scriven was respected but was considered to be eccentric by those who knew him.

"What a Friend We Have in Jesus" was never intended by Scriven for publication. Upon learning of his mother's serious illness and unable to be with her in far-off Dublin, he wrote a letter of comfort enclosing the words of this text. Some time later when he himself was ill, a friend who came to call on him chanced to see the poem scribbled on scratch paper near the bed. The friend read it with keen interest and asked Scriven if he had written the words. Scriven, with typical modesty, replied, "The Lord and I did it between us." In 1869 a small collection of his poems was published. It was simply entitled *Hymns and Other Verses*.

After the death of Joseph Scriven, also by accidental drowning, the citizens of Port Hope, Ontario, erected a monument on the Port Hope-Peterborough Highway, which runs from Lake Ontario, with the text and these words inscribed:

Four miles north, in Pengally's Cemetery, lies the philanthropist and author of this great masterpiece, written at Port Hope, 1857.

310

The composer of the music, Charles C. Converse, was a well-educated versatile and successful Christian, whose talents ranged from law to professional music. Under the pen name of Karl Reden, he wrote numerous scholarly articles on many subjects. Though he was an excellent musician and composer with many of his works performed by the leading American orchestras and choirs of his day, his life is best remembered for this simple music so well suited to Scriven's text.

Ira D. Sankey discovered the hymn in 1875, just in time to include it in his well-known collection, *Sankey's Gospel Hymns Number One*. Later Sankey wrote, "The last hymn which went into the book became one of the first in favor."

311

The Grave of Joseph Scriven

100

When I Survey the Wondrous Cross

HAMBURG

ISAAC WATTS, 1674-1748

From a Gregorian Chant
Arr. by Lowell Mason, 1792-1872

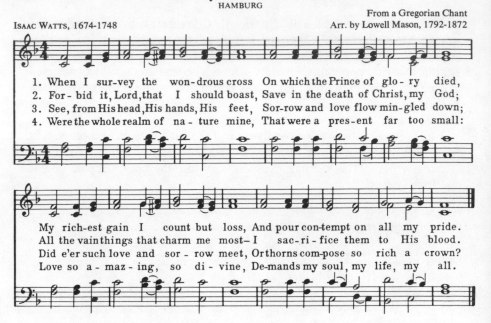

1. When I sur-vey the won-drous cross On which the Prince of glo-ry died,
2. For-bid it, Lord, that I should boast, Save in the death of Christ, my God;
3. See, from His head, His hands, His feet, Sor-row and love flow min-gled down;
4. Were the whole realm of na-ture mine, That were a pres-ent far too small:

My rich-est gain I count but loss, And pour con-tempt on all my pride.
All the vain things that charm me most— I sac-ri-fice them to His blood.
Did e'er such love and sor-row meet, Or thorns com-pose so rich a crown?
Love so a-maz-ing, so di-vine, De-mands my soul, my life, my all.

312

Author–Isaac Watts, 1674–1748
Music–From a Gregorian Chant
Arranged–Lowell Mason, 1792–1872
Meter–LM (88.88)
Scripture Reference–Galatians 6:14

> And He bearing His cross went forth into a place called the place of a skull, which is called in the Hebrew, Golgotha.   John 19:17

This hymn by Isaac Watts, labeled by the well-known theologian Matthew Arnold as the greatest hymn in the English language, was written in 1707 for use at a communion service conducted by Watts. It first appeared in print that same year in Watts's outstanding collection, *Hymns and Spiritual Songs*. Its original title was "Crucifixion to the World by the Cross of Christ."

Isaac Watts was born on July 17, 1674, in Southampton, England. The eldest of nine children, he was the son of an educated deacon in a dissenting Congregational church. At the time of Isaac's birth, his father was in prison for his non-conformist beliefs. Young Watts showed an unusual aptitude for study and learned Latin at the age of five, Greek at nine, French at eleven and Hebrew at thirteen. He began to write verses of good quality when he was very young.

Watts is frequently referred to as the father of English hymnody. One of his early concerns was the deplorable state to which congregational singing had degenerated in most English-speaking churches. The singing consisted of slow, ponderous Psalms in which each line was first read by an appointed deacon and was followed by the droning of the congregation. The texts of these Psalm-hymns were often crude and inelegant. Typical doggeral of the time is this:

> Ye monsters of the bubbling deep, your Master's praises spout;
> Up from the sands ye coddlings peep, and wag your tails about.

Watts once wrote, "The singing of God's praise is the part of worship most closely related to heaven; but its performance among us is the worst on earth." One Sunday after returning from a typically poor service, Watts continued to rail against the congregational singing. His father exclaimed, "Why don't you give us something better, young man!" Before the evening service began, young Isaac had written his first hymn, which was received with great enthusiasm by the people.

The youthful poet decided to write other hymn settings. For a period of two years Watts wrote a new hymn every Sunday. He went on to write new metrical versions of the Psalms with a desire to "Christianize the Psalms with the New Testament message and style." Several of his hymns that were based on these new Psalm settings are such favorites as "Jesus Shall Reign" (No. 48) and "O God, Our Help in Ages Past" (No. 66). Watts is also the author of a children's hymn, "I Sing the Mighty Power of God" (No. 38). Because of this bold departure from the traditional Psalms, Isaac Watts was often considered to be a radical churchman in his day.

Watts not only rewrote the Psalms in this way, but he also wrote a number of hymns based solely on personal feelings. These hymns were known as hymns of human composure. Such hymns were very controversial during his lifetime. "When I Survey the Wondrous Cross" is an example of this type of hymn written by Watts. In all Isaac Watts composed more than 600 hymns.

The tune for this text is known as the "Hamburg" tune. It was the work of Lowell Mason, who was often called the father of American public school and church music. Mason stated that he arranged this tune in 1824 from an ancient Gregorian chant, the earliest church music known. These church chants were inherited by the early Christians from the Hebrew Temple and Synagogue services. They represent some of the loveliest melodies known. Pope Gregory, who lived during the latter part of the sixth century, was one of the first church leaders to be concerned about church music. He did much to improve and organize these chants, hence the term "Gregorian Chants." These chants still form the basis of Roman Catholic church music today. The "Hamburg" tune first ap-

313

peared in the *Boston's Handel and Haydn Society Collection of Church Music* in 1825. It is interesting to note that the entire melody encompasses only a five note range.

Other hymns composed by Lowell Mason include "From Greenland's Icy Mountains" (No. 25) and "Nearer, My God, to Thee" (No. 61).

314

Isaac Watts

101

While Shepherds Watched Their Flocks

CHRISTMAS

NAHUM TATE, 1652-1715

Arr. from George F. Handel, 1685-1759
in Weyman's *Melodia Sacra*, 1815

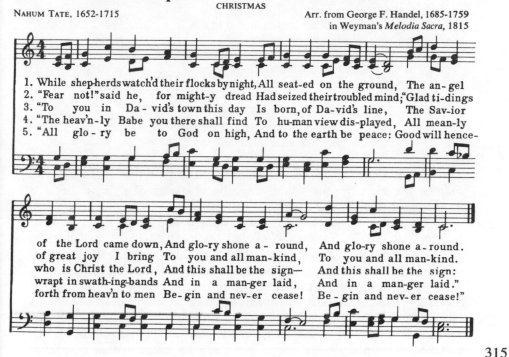

1. While shep-herds watch'd their flocks by night, All seat-ed on the ground, The an-gel
2. "Fear not!" said he, for might-y dread Had seized their troubled mind; "Glad ti-dings
3. "To you in Da-vid's town this day Is born, of Da-vid's line, The Sav-ior
4. "The heav'n-ly Babe you there shall find To hu-man view dis-played, All mean-ly
5. "All glo-ry be to God on high, And to the earth be peace: Good will hence-

of the Lord came down, And glo-ry shone a-round, And glo-ry shone a-round.
of great joy I bring To you and all man-kind, To you and all man-kind.
who is Christ the Lord, And this shall be the sign— And this shall be the sign:
wrapt in swath-ing-bands And in a man-ger laid, And in a man-ger laid."
forth from heav'n to men Be-gin and nev-er cease! Be-gin and nev-er cease!"

315

Author–Nahum Tate, 1652–1715
Composer–Arranged from George F. Handel, 1685–1759
Tune Name–"Christmas"
Meter–CM (86.86)
Scripture Reference–Luke 2:8–14

> And there were in the same country shepherds abiding in the field, keeping watch over
> their flocks by night.   Luke 2:8

The singing of hymns as we know it today was practically non-existent in England and the United States from the beginning of the sixteenth century Protestant Reformation until the dawn of the eighteenth century. During this time congregational singing consisted almost entirely of versified settings of the Psalms. The psalter used exclusively during this entire period was the *Sternhold-Hopkins Psalter,* published in 1562. This is a portion of Psalm One from that psalter:

> The man is blest that hath not lent
> To wicked men his ear,
> Nor led his life as sinners do,
> Nor sat in scorner's chair.

He shall be like a tree that is
Planted the rivers nigh,
Which in due season bringeth forth
Its fruit abundantly.

Whose leaf shall never fade nor fail,
But flourishing shall stand,
E'en so all things shall prosper well
That this man takes in hand.

Though the *Sternhold-Hopkins Psalter* was known for its faithfulness to the original Hebrew, the crude, unpoetic character of its texts became increasingly offensive to many congregations.

Finally, in 1696, during the reign of William and Mary, two Irishmen, Nahum Tate (1652–1715) and Nicholas Brady (1659–1726), collaborated in undertaking a new metrical version of the Psalms more in keeping with the literary tastes of the day. This new psalter, known as the *New Version,* was met with widespread popular resistance. Percy Dearmer, in his *Songs of Praise Discussed,* illustrates this typical prejudice against change by relating two incidents that occurred at the time. A pastor who asked a villager why he no longer participated in the singing in church received the reply, "Well, Sir, David speaks so plain that us cannot mistake 'un; but as for Mr. Tate and Brady, they have taken the Lord away." And Tate himself relates that when he was present at family prayers at the home of a friend, one of the maids explained her refusal to sing by saying, "If you must know the plain truth, Sir, as long as you sung Jesus Christ's Psalms, I sung along with ye; but now that you sing Psalms of your own invention, ye may sing by yourselves."

With the official endorsement by King William III, the *New Version* supplanted the old *Sternhold-Hopkins Psalter* throughout the Church of England. From England it came to America, where it was adopted by the American Episcopal Church in 1789. In 1700 Tate and Brady had already published a supplement to their *New Version.* The supplement contained sixteen hymns in addition to the metrical Psalms. One of these original hymns was Tate's Christmas carol description of the angels' appearance to the shepherds as described in Luke 2:8–14–"While Shepherds Watched Their Flocks." All of Tate's other hymns from this collection have since been forgotten.

Nahum Tate was born in Dublin in 1652, the son of an Irish clergyman. He was educated at Trinity College and in 1690 was proclaimed to be the Poet Laureate of England for the Court of William and Mary during their reign from 1689–1702. His intemperate living (as a drunkard and a spendthrift) eventually led to his downfall, and he died in 1715 at a debtor's refuge in Southwark, London. Nicholas Brady, another Irishman

316

and Tate's personal friend, was educated at both Oxford and Trinity Colleges and later served the Anglican Church at Cork, England.

"While Shepherds Watched Their Flocks" ranks as one of our most popular Christmas carols and is found in nearly every Protestant hymnal. Its purely narrative account about the shepherds is on a level that even children can visualize and understand easily. The music for this carol has been adapted from a work by master composer George Frederick Handel.

Handel was born in Halle, Germany, on February 23, 1685. After 1713 he made his home in England and became a naturalized English citizen in 1727. He is best known for his oratorio, *The Messiah,* composed in 1741 and completed in just twenty-four days. Though Handel wrote several tunes for specific hymn texts, his best-known hymn tunes, like this one, have been arranged from his major works.

317

Bailey, Albert E. *The Gospel in Hymns*. New York: Charles Scribner's Sons, 1950.

Barrows, Cliff, ed. *Crusade Hymn Stories*. Chicago: Hope Publishing Co., 1967.

Benson, Louis F. *The English Hymn*. New York: George H. Doran Co., 1915. (Reprint-John Knox Co., 1962).

Blanchard, Kathleen. *Stories of Favorite Hymns*. Grand Rapids, Michigan, Zondervan Publishing House, 1940.

Brown, Theron, and Butterworth, Hezekiah. *The Story of the Hymns and Tunes*. New York: George H. Doran Company, 1906.

Clark, W. Thorburn. *Stories of Fadeless Hymns*. Nashville: Broadman Press, 1949.

Davies, James P. *Sing with Understanding*. Chicago, Illinois: Covenant Press, 1966.

Douglas, Charles W. *Church Music in History and Practice*. New York: Charles Scribner's Sons, 1937. Revised 1962 by Leonard Ellinwood.

Emurian, Ernest K. *Living Stories of Famous Hymns*. Boston: W. A. Wilde Co., 1955.

Gabriel, C. H. *The Singers and Their Songs*. Winona Lake, Indiana. The Rodeheaver Co., 1915.

Hagedorn, Ivan H. *Stories of Great Hymn Writers*. Grand Rapids, Michigan: Zondervan Publishing House, 1948.

Hustad, Donald P. *Hymns for the Living Church*. Carol Stream, Illinois, Hope Publishing Co., 1978.

Julian, John. *A Dictionary of Hymnology*. New York: Charles Scribner's Sons, 1892. New York: Dover Publications, 1957 (reprint).

Kerr, Phil. *Music in Evangelism and Stories of Famous Christian Songs*. Glendale, California: Gospel Music Publishers, 1939.

Lillenas, Haldor. *Modern Gospel Song Stories*. Kansas City, Missouri: Lillenas Publishing Company, 1952.

McCutchan, Robert G. *Hymn Tune Names, Their Sources and Significance*. New York: Abingdon Press, 1957.

McCutchan, Robert G. *Our Hymnody: A Manual of the Methodist Hymnal*, 2nd ed. New York and Nashville: Abingdon-Cokesbury Press, 1942.

Reynolds, William Jensen. *Hymns of Our Faith, A Handbook for the Baptist Hymnal*. Nashville: 1964.

Reynolds, W. J. and Price, M. *A Joyful Sound*. New York: Holt, Rinehart and Winston, 1978.

Routley, Erik. Hymns Today and Tomorrow. New York: Abingdon Press, 1964.

Rudin, Cecilia Margaret. *Stories of Hymns We Love*. Chicago: John Rudin & Company, Inc., 1945.

319

Selected Bibliography

Ryden, Ernest Edwin. *The Story of Christian Hymnody*. Rock Island, Illinois: Augustana Press, 1959.

Sallee, James. *A History of Evangelistic Hymnody*. Grand Rapids Michigan, Baker Book House, 1978.

Sankey, Ira D. *My Life and the Story of the Gospel Hymns*. New York: Harper and Brothers Publishers, 1906.

Sanville, George W. *Forty Gospel Hymn Stories*. Winona Lake, Indiana: The Rodeheaver-Hall-Mack Company, 1943.

Smith, Oswald J. *Oswald J. Smith's Hymn Stories*. Winona Lake, Indiana: The Rodeheaver Company, 1963.

Stebbins, George C. *Reminiscences and Gospel Hymn Stories*. George H. Horan Company, 1924.

Sydnor, James R. *The Hymn and Congregational Singing*. Richmond: John Knox Press, 1960.

Thompson, Ronald W. *Who's Who of Hymn Writers*. London: Epworth Press, 1967.

Wake, Arthur N. *Companion to Hymnbook for Christian Worship*. St. Louis, Missouri: The Bethany Press, 1970.

INDEX OF AUTHORS, TRANSLATORS, COMPOSERS, TUNE NAMES

322

Index of Authors, Translators, Composers, Tune Names